An Annotated Bibliography of

Modern Anglo-Irish Drama

An Annotated Bibliography of

Modern Anglo-Irish Drama

by

E. H. Mikhail

The Whitston Publishing Company
Troy, New York
1981

Library of Congress Catalog Card Number 80-51874
ISBN 0-87875-201-3

Printed in the United States of America

Acknowledgements

It is a pleasant duty to record my appreciation to the staff of the University of Lethbridge Library; the National Library, Ottawa; the British Library, London; the Newspaper Library, Colindale; Trinity College Library, Dublin; the National Library of Ireland, Dublin; and the New York Public Library.

Thanks are also due to Miss Bea Ramtej for her usual patience and skill in typing and preparing the final typescript; and to Ms. Marianne Levander, Mrs. Nellie Jones, Miss Mary McCartin, Dr. Jacqueline Derksen, and Professor Peter Halter for rendering assistance and providing useful information.

Preface

The perfatory note to *A Bibliography of Modern Irish Drama 1899-1970* (1972) described it as "the first attempt toward a comprehensive general bibliography" of Irish drama. The present volume, although based on the earlier work, is not merely a second updated edition; it is an entirely new book. Some 1,775 entries have been included; annotations have been provided; and an index has been appended.

The scope of this Bibliography is general criticism on Anglo-Irish drama from 1899—with the foundation of the Irish Literary Theatre—to the end of 1977, although some later studies have been included. Reviews of individual plays are not listed, but "seasons" of theatrical productions are. All entries have been annotated unless the title is sufficiently self-explanatory. The annotations, however, are not evaluative, but descriptive and indicative of the content of the material they describe. Although this is a general bibliography, the researcher—with the help of these annotations and the index—should be able to find the material he needs on individual dramatists in books and periodical articles dealing with the Irish drama in general.[1] He should also be able to find criticism on such general topics as the Irish National Theatre Society, the Dublin Gate Theatre, drama in Ulster, or the Abbey Theatre's first American tour.

E. H. Mikhail

[1]Readers who are interested only in books or periodical articles devoted entirely to individual dramatists might like to consult the present author's work, *A Research Guide to Modern Irish Dramatists* (Troy, New York: Whitston, 1979).

Contents

I

Bibliographies and Library Holdings

Includes general bibliographies, check-lists, indexes, and catalogues

1 *Abstracts of English Studies* (Boulder, Colorado: National Council of Teachers of English), 1958 to the present

   Summaries of selected articles in periodicals.

2 Adelman, Irving, and Rita Dworkin. *Modern Drama; A Checklist of Critical Literature on 20th Century Plays* (Metuchen, New Jersey: The Scarecrow Press, 1967)

   Selected criticism in books and periodicals on individual dramatists.

3 *American Book Publishing Record [BPR]* (New York: Bowker), 1960 to the present

   A monthly listing of all books published in the U. S. A., organised by Dewey Decimal System.

4 *American Doctoral Dissertations.* Compiled for The Association of Research Libraries (Ann Arbor, Michigan: University Microfilms), 1963 to the present

   Continuation of *Doctoral Dissertations*, listed below.

5 *American Humanities Index* (Troy, New York: The Whitston

Publishing Company), 1975 to the present

Material mainly in little magazines not indexed elsewhere.

6 *Annotated Bibliography of New Publications in the Performing Arts* (New York: Drama Book Shop), 1973 to the present

A quarterly that catalogues books "as soon as they become generally available in the United States and England."

7 *Annual Bibliography of Enlgish Language and Literature* (London: Modern Humanities Research Association), 1920 to the present

Lists books and periodical articles.

8 *Annual Bibliography of Theatre Studies* (London: *Theatre Quarterly* Publications), 1975 to the present

A classified listing of all books in the English Language on theatre and related performing arts formerly published in quarterly instalments in *Theatrefacts*. Discontinued.

9 *Annual Magazine Subject-Index* (Boston: F. W. Faxon), 1907-1949. Reprinted as *Cumulated Magazine Subject-Index, 1907-1949* (Boston: G. K. Hall, 1964)

Lists articles in periodicals.

10 Baker, Blanch M. "Ireland," *Theatre and Allied Arts; A Guide to Books Dealing with the History, Criticism and Technic of the Drama and Theatre and Related Arts and Crafts* (New York: H. W. Wilson, 1952; Benjamin Blom, 1967), pp. 113-120

Selected annotated criticism on Irish drama and on some individual dramatists.

11   Bateson, F. W., and Harrison T. Meserole. *A Guide to English and American Literature*, 3rd ed. (London and New York: Longman, 1976)

Lists selected criticism for each author.

12   Batho, Edith Clara, and Bonamy Dobrée. *The Victorians and After, 1830-1914*. Introductions to English Literature, vol. IV, ed. Bonamy Dobrée (London: Cresset Press; New York: R. M. McBride, 1938)

A guide for the beginning student.

13   Bell, Inglis F., and Jennifer Gallup. *A Reference Guide to English, American, and Canadian Literature; An Annotated Checklist of Bibliographical and Other Reference Materials* (Vancouver, B. C.: University of British Columbia Press, 1971)

Includes a section on Drama.

14   Bell, Sam Hanna. "Appendixes," *The Theatre in Ulster: A Survey of the Dramatic Movement in Ulster from 1902 Until the Present Day* (Dublin: Gill and Macmillan; Totowa, New Jersey: Rowman and Littlefield, 1972), pp. 134-147

Includes: I. "First Productions of the Ulster Literary Theatre"; II. "First Productions of the Ulster Group Theatre (1941-60)"; III. "Lyric Players Theatre Productions (1951-71)."

15   Besterman, Theodore. "Drama and Stage," *A World Bibliography of Bibliographies*, 5 vols. Fourth Edition (Lausanne: Societas Bibliographica, 1965-66)

Annotated and arranged under general and specific subject matter.

16   —. *Literature: English & American; A Bibliography of*

Bibliographies (Totowa, New Jersey: Rowman and Littlefield, 1971)

Includes selected bibliographies of individual authors.

17   *Bibliographica Hibernica* (Dublin: Hodges Figgis)

A Bookseller's occasional catalogue providing a useful list of publications of Irish interest in the English language.

18   *Bibliographic Index; A Cumulative Bibliography of Bibliographies* (New York: H. W. Wilson), 1937 to the present

The standard serial bibliography of bibliographies.

19   Black, Donald Taylor. "Eire," *Theatrefacts: International Theatre Reference* (London), No. 4 (November-January 1975) to the present

Theatre diary.

20   Bond, Donald F. *A Reference Guide to English Studies*, Second Edition (Chicago and London: University of Chicago Press, 1971)

"Designed primarily for the use of the graduate student."

21   *Book Review Digest* (New York: H. W. Wilson), 1906 to the present

An index to reviews, in selected periodicals, of books published in the United States. Some excerpts are included.

22   *Book Review Index* (Detroit, Michigan: Gale Research Company), 1965 to the present

Lists reviews of books in periodicals.

23   *Books from Ireland* (Dublin: Irish Book Publishers' Association), 1969 to the present

Lists books published by members of the Association.

24 *Books Ireland; A Monthly Review* (Dublin), March 1976
    to the present

Lists new books of Irish interest.

25 Boyd, Ernest A. "Bibliography," *Ireland's Literary Ren-
    aissance* (Dublin: Talbot Press; New York: John Lane,
    1916, 2nd rev. ed. New York: Alfred A. Knopf,
    1922; rpt. Dublin: Allen Figgis, 1968), pp. 429-445

Primary books of dramatists and selected studies in books.

26 —. "Bibliographical Appendix," *The Contemporary Drama
    of Ireland* (Dublin: Talbot Press; London: T. Fisher
    Unwin, 1918; rpt. Boston: Little, Brown, 1928),
    pp. 201-211

Primary works of dramatists and selected studies in books.

27 Breed, Paul F., and Florence M. Sniderman, eds. *Dramatic
    Criticism Index; A Bibliography of Commentaries on
    Playwrights from Ibsen to the Avant-Garde* (Detroit,
    Michigan: Gale Research Company, 1972)

Selected criticism in books and periodicals.

28 The British Drama League. *The Players Library; The Cata-
    logue of the Library of the British Drama League*
    (London: Faber, 1950). *First Supplement*, 1951;
    Second Supplement, 1954; *Third Supplement*, 1956.

The bulk of each volume is taken up with a catalogue of plays
in the British Drama League Library, but in each there is also
a short list of books on the theatre, also indexed by author.

29 *British Humanities Index* (London: The Library Association),
    1962 to the present. Continuation of *Subject Index*

to Periodicals

Subject and author index to articles in periodicals.

30   *British Museum Subject Index* (London: The Trustees of
the British Museum), 1881 to the present

> Includes a section listing books on "Drama and Stage: Great
> Britain and Ireland."

31   *The British National Bibliography* (London: The Council of
the British National Bibliography), 1950 to the present

> "A Subject Catalogue of new books published in the British
> Isles . . . classified, with modifications, according to the Dewey
> Decimal Classification."

32   Brown, Stephen J., ed. *A Guide to Books on Ireland* (London: Longmans, Green; Dublin: Hodges, Figgis, 1912;
rpt. 1970), pp. 46-56

> A selection of books and articles on the theatre in Ireland.

33   Bushrui, Suheil Badi, ed. *Anglo-Irish Literature in Lebanon
and the Arab World; Triennial Report 1970-1973*,
presented to the IASAIL Conference in Cork, 1973

> Checklist of studies in Arabic.

34   *Canadian Periodical Index* (Ottawa: Canadian Library Association), 1938 to the present

> Lists articles in Canadian periodicals.

35   *Canadian Theses 1947-1960*, 2 vols. (Ottawa National
Library of Canada, 1973).

36   *Canadian Theses* (Ottawa: National Library of Canada),
1960/61 to the present.

37   Cant, Monica. "A Bibliography of English Drama from 1890 to 1920," *The Library Association Record*, XXIV (February 1922), 41-57

     Lists only published plays.

38   Carlson, Marvin. "Modern Drama: A Selected Bibliography of Bibliographies," *Modern Drama*, VIII, No. 1 (May 1965), 112-118

     Annotated list of bibliographies devoted in whole or part to critical works. Includes a section on "Irish Drama."

39   Carpenter, Charles A. "Modern Drama Studies: An Annual Bibliography," *Modern Drama*, XVII, No. 1 (March 1974) to the present

     Lists critical studies in books and periodicals on drama in general and on individual dramatists.

40   Cheshire, David. "Ireland," *Theatre: History, Criticism and Reference*. The Readers' Guide Series (London: Clive Bingley; Hamden, Connecticut: Archon Books, 1967), pp. 50-51

     Selected annotated criticism in books on Irish drama in general.

41   Chicorel, Marietta, ed. *Chicorel Theater Index to Plays in Collections, Anthologies, Periodicals and Discs*, 3 vols. (New York: Chicorel, 1970-72)

     Indexes plays, playwrights, editors, and play collections.

42   —, ed. *Chicorel Theater Index to Anthologies, Periodicals, Discs and Tapes: Plays on Discs and Tapes* (New York: Chicorel, 1972)

     Indexes plays and performers on recorded media.

43   —, ed. *Chicorel Theater Index to Plays in Anthologies and Collections, 1970-1976* (New York: Chicorel, 1976).

44   Clough, Peter H. "A Subject Index to *Drama Survey*, 1961-1968," *Theatre Documentation*, III, Nos. 1-2 (Fall 1970 and Spring 1971), 81-100

   A cumulative index arranged under twelve topic areas. Includes a section on "Ireland."

45   Coleman, Arthur, and Gary R. Tyler. *Drama Criticism, Volume One: A Checklist of Interpretation Since 1940 of English and American Plays* (Denver, Colorado: Alan Swallow, 1966)

   Selected criticism in books and periodicals on individual dramatists.

46   *Comprehensive Dissertation Index 1861-1972* (Ann Arbor, Michigan: Xerox University Microfilms), vol. 29, p. 708

   Lists some American dissertations on Irish drama.

47   Connor, John M. and Billie M. *Ottemiller's Index to Plays in Collections: An Author and Title Index to Plays Appearing in Collections Published Between 1900 and Early 1975*, 6th ed. rev. (Metuchen, New Jersey: Scarecrow Press, 1976).

48   Cornyn, Stan. *A Selective Index to Theatre Magazine* (New York and London: Scarecrow Press, 1964)

   A selective guide to the articles, authors, subjects, and dramatic works in *Theatre Magazine* from 1901 to 1931.

49   *Cumulative Book Index* (New York: H. W. Wilson) 1928 to the present

A world list of new books in the English language.

50 Cutler, B. D., and Villa Stiles. *Modern British Authors; Their First Editions* (Greenberg: G. Allen, 1930; Folcroft, Pennsylvania: Folcroft Press, 1969)

Includes primary bibliographies of Lord Dunsany, George Moore, Bernard Shaw, and W. B. Yeats.

51 Daiches, David. *The Present Age: After 1920.* Introductions to English Literature, vol. V, ed. Bonamy Dobrée (London: Cresset Press; Bloomington: Indiana University Press, 1958)

A guide for the beginning student.

52 *Dissertation Abstracts* (Ann Arbor, Michigan: University Microfilms), 1938 to the present

Indexes American dissertations.

53 *Doctoral Dissertations Accepted by American Universities,* ed. Arnold H. Trotier and Marian Harman (New York: H. W. Wilson, 1933-1955). Continued as *Index to American Doctoral Dissertations,* 1955 to the present.

54 Dolmen Press. *Books and Booklets Published by the Dolmen Press, Dublin, August 1951-April 1971: A Checklist* (Dublin: The Dolmen Press, 1971).

55 Eager, Alan R. "Drama," *A Guide to Irish Bibliographical Material; Being a Bibliography of Irish Bibliographies and Some Sources of Information* (London: The Library Association, 1964), pp. 208-209

A reference guide.

56 Edwards, Hilton. "Dublin Gate Productions 1928-1958," *The Mantle of Harlequin* (Dublin: Progress House,

1958), pp. ix-xii

Listed under author.

57   Ellis-Fermor, Una. "Appendix," *The Irish Dramatic Move-
      ment* (London: Methuen, 1939; 2nd ed., 1954; rpt.
      University Paperbacks, 1967), pp. 208-235

      Includes: 1. "Chronological Table of the Main Events in the
      First Years of the Movement"; 2. "Some Materials Bearing on
      the Early History of the Movement"; 3. "The Main Dates
      Connected with the Spread of Ibsen's Work and Thought";
      4. "A List of Plays Produced in London in the Last Decade of
      the Nineteenth Century"; 5. "A Subject Index of the Main
      Critical Opinions of W. B. Yeats and Lady Gregory"; 6. "A
      Note on Editions and General Works of Reference."

58   Enser, A. G. S. *Filmed Books and Plays; A List of Books and
      Plays from Which Films Have Been Made, 1928-1967*
      (Elmsford, New York: London House and Maxwell,
      1968; London: Andre Deutsch, 1971)

      Author and title indexes.

59   *Essay and General Literature Index* (New York: H. W. Wil-
      son), 1900 to the present

      Essays in books.

60   *Études Irlandaises: Bulletin de Liaison des Specialistes
      Franco-phones d'Histoire, Civilisation et Littérature
      de l'Irlande* (Lille-Cedex, France: C. E. R. I. U. L.),
      1972 to the present

      Surveys activities of Irish studies in France, and gives biblio-
      graphical information on publications and dissertations.

61   Faxon, F. W. *Dramatic Index, 1909-1949* (Boston: F. W.
      Faxon). Reprinted as *Cumulated Dramatic Index*

1909-1949, ed. F. W. Faxon, M. E. Bates, and A. C. Sutherland (Boston: G. K. Hall, 1965)

Lists articles and illustrations of theatrical subjects from both American and English periodicals.

62　Fay, Gerard. "Play List," *The Abbey Theatre, Cradle of Genius* (Dublin: Clonmore & Reynolds; London: Hollis & Carter, 1958), pp. 161-186

Play productions, 1899-1958.

63　Fay, W[illiam] G[eorge], and Catherine Carswell. "A List of First Productions, with Casts," *The Fays of the Abbey Theatre; An Autobiographical Record* (London: Rich & Cowan; New York: Harcourt, Brace, 1935), pp. 298-309.

64　Finneran, Richard J. *Anglo-Irish Literature; A Review of Research* (New York: Modern Language Association, 1976)

Includes chapters on George Moore, Bernard Shaw, W. B. Yeats, J. M. Synge, James Joyce, Lady Gregory, George Russell, Oliver St. John Gogarty, James Stephens, Sean O'Casey, and "The Modern Drama".

65　Ford, James J. "Current Books of Irish Interest," *American Committee for Irish Studies Newsletter*, (January 1969) to the present

Annual compilation.

66　Foshay, Florence E. "Twentieth Century Dramas, Part II: Irish Drama," *Bulletin of Bibliography*, VIII, No. 7 (July 1915), 221-222

Lists reviews and articles on Irish plays published between 1900 and 1915.

67 French, Frances-Jane. *The Abbey Theatre Series of Plays: A Bibliography* (Dublin: Dolmen Press; London: Oxford University Press, 1969)

> Deals with the original "Abbey Theatre Series" of fifteen volumes and the later "Abbey Theatre Series" of nine unnumbered volumes.

68 Gilder, Rosamond. "Ireland," *A Theatre Library; A Bibliography of One Hundred Books Relating to the Theatre* (New York: Theatre Arts, Inc. for National Theatre Conference, 1932), pp. 22-23. For additions see *Booklist*, XXXIII (1937). Continued by Roy Stallings and Paul Myers as *A Guide to Theatre Reading* (New York: Theatre Arts, 1949)

> This last *Guide* adds biographies, dramatic criticism and technical books not considered by Gilder.

69 —, and George Freedley. "Great Britain and Ireland," *Theatre Collections in Libraries and Museums; An International Handbook* (New York: Theatre Arts; London: B. F. Stevens and Brown, 1936; New York: Johnson Reprint, 1970), pp. 98-113.

70 Glandon, Virginia E. "Index of Irish Newspapers, 1900-1922," *Eire-Ireland* (St. Paul, Minnesota), XI, No. 4 (Winter 1976), 84-121; XII, No. 1 (Spring 1977), 86-115

> Gives place of publication, year established, frequency, publisher, editorial policy, and circulation.

71 Gregory, Lady. "Plays Produced by the Abbey Theatre Co. and Its Predecessors, with Dates of First Performances," *Our Irish Theatre* (New York and London: G. P. Putnam, 1914; rpt. New York: Capricorn Books, 1965; new enl. ed. with foreword by Roger McHugh, New York: Oxford University Press, 1973)

> List of productions from 1899 to 1913.

72 *Guide to Reference Books* (Chicago: American Library Association), 1902 to the present

> Includes a section on "English Drama".

73 *Guide to the Performing Arts* (New York: The Scarecrow Press), 1957 to the present

> Lists selected articles in periodicals.

74 Harmon, Maurice. *Modern Irish Literature, 1800-1967; A Reader's Guide* (Dublin: The Dolmen Press, 1967)

> Lists primary books and selected criticism in books.

75 —. *Selected Bibliography for the Study of Anglo-Irish Literature and Its Backgrounds* (Portmarnock, Dublin: Wolfhound Press, 1976)

> Includes a section on drama and checklists of individual playwrights.

76 Haskell, John D., Jr., and Robert G. Shedd. "Modern Drama: A Selective Bibliography of Works Published in English," *Modern Drama*, X, No. 2 (September 1967), 202-215; XI, No. 2 (September 1968), 195-213

> Lists critical studies in books and periodicals on drama in general and on individual dramatists.

77 Hayman, Ronald. "Britain and Ireland," *One Hundred Years of Drama; A Selected List* (London: National Book League, 1972), pp. 6-12

> Primary works of selected dramatists.

78 Henderson, Gordon, comp. *An Index to 'The Journal of Irish Literature' Volumes 1-5 (January 1972-September 1976)* (Newark, Delaware: Proscenium Press, 1976).

79 Hogan, Robert. "Bibliography," *After the Irish Renaissance;*

A Critical History of the Irish Drama Since "The Plough and the Stars" (Minneapolis: University of Minnesota Press, 1967; London: Macmillan, 1968), pp. 259-271

Includes a checklist of general criticism and primary and secondary bibliographies of individual dramatists.

80 Holden, David F. *An Analytical Index to 'Modern Drama' Volumes I-XIII, May 1958-February 1971* (Toronto: Hakkert, 1972)

Consists of General Index, Contributors Index, and Book Review Index to articles in *Modern Drama.*

81 Holloway, Joseph, "Books about the Theatre in Ireland" and "Irish Plays," *A Guide to Books on Ireland, Part I: Prose Literature, Poetry, Music and Plays*, ed. Stephen J. Brown (Dublin: Hodges Figgis; London: Longmans Green, 1912; rpt. 1970), pp. 46-56 and 244-324

Annotated checklists of criticism and of first productions.

82 Holzapfel, Rudi. *An Index of Contributors to 'The Dublin Magazine'* (Dublin: Museum Bookshop, 1966)

Lists contributors and titles of articles appearing in *The Dublin Magazine*, 1923-1958.

83 —. *An Index of Contributors to 'The Bell'* (Blackrock, Co. Dublin: Carraig Books, 1970)

Lists contributors and titles of articles appearing in *The Bell*, 1940-1954.

84 Hornby, Richard, comp. "TDR Books and Theatre; A Bibliography," *Tulane Drama Review*, IX, No. 4 (Summer 1965), 179-207; X, No. 4 (Summer 1966), 239-264

Listings of new books published in the United States.

85 Horniman, A. E. F. A Collection of Newspaper Cuttings & c., Concerning the Abbey Theatre, Dublin, Compiled by Miss A. E. F. Horniman, in 10 vols., in the possession of the John Rylands Library, Manchester, England.

86 Howard, Diana, comp. *Directory of Theatre Research Resources in Greater London* (London: British Theatre Institute, 1974)

   A central catalogue of the collections of the theatre material in London.

87 Howard, Patsy C., ed. *Theses in English Literature 1894-1970* (Ann Arbor, Michigan: The Pierian Press, 1973)

   M. A. theses in American universities.

88 Howard-Hill, T. H. *Bibliography of British Literary Bibliographies* (Oxford: Clarendon Press, 1969); *Supplement* (Oxford: Clarendon Press, 1971)

   Includes lists of bibliographies of 20th century authors.

89 *Index to American Doctoral Dissertations* (New York: H. W. Wilson), 1955 to the present. Continuation of *Doctoral Dissertations Accepted by American Universities*, ed. Arnold H. Trotier and Marian Harman (New York: H. W. Wilson, 1933-1955)

   Cumulative index by general subject matter and author.

90 *An Index to Book Reviews in the Humanities* (Williamston, Michigan: Phillip Thomson), 1961 to the present

   Lists only reviews in English.

91   *Index to Little Magazines* (Denver, Colorado: Alan Swallow), 1943 to the present

   An author-subject of a selected list of American little magazines.

92   *An Index to One-Act Plays*, comp. Hannah Logasa and Winnifred Ver Nooy (Boston: F. W. Faxon, 1924); *Supplement* 1924-1931 (Boston: F. W. Faxon, 1932); *Second Supplement* 1932-1940 (Boston: F. W. Faxon, 1941); *Third Supplement* 1941-1948 (Boston: F. W. Faxon, 1950); *Fourth Supplement* 1948-1957 (Boston: F. W. Faxon, 1958)

   Contains titles of one-act plays published since 1900. Author, number of characters, background, and location of published play are given.

93   *Index to Theses Accepted for Higher Degrees in the Universities of Great Britain and Ireland* (London: ASLIB), 1950 to the present.

94   International Association for the Study of Anglo-Irish Literature. "Bibliography Bulletin," *Irish University Review; A Journal of Irish Studies* (Dublin), 1972 to the present

   Lists books and articles on Anglo-Irish literature.

95   International Federation of Library Associations (International Section for Performing Arts Libraries and Museums). *Bibliothèque et musées des arts du spectacle dans le monde* (Paris: Editions du Centre National de la Rechèrche Scientifique, 1960); *Performing Arts Libraries and Museums of the World* (New York: Theatre Arts, 1967)

   A fully revised and expanded edition of Rosamond Gilder's *Theatre Collections in Libraries and Museums.*

96 *International Index to Periodicals* (New York: H. W. Wilson). 1907 to the present. From vol. 19 (April 1965-March 1966) called *Social Sciences and Humanities Index*

Author and subject index to selected world periodicals.

97 Ireland, Norma Olin. *Index to Full Length Plays, 1944-1964* (Boston: F. W. Faxon, 1965)

A selective coverage of full length plays published in English.

98 *Irish Publishing Record*. Compiled by the School of Librarianship University College Dublin (Dublin: University College), 1967 to the present

Lists all publications in Ireland. Includes a section on literature.

99 Johnson, Albert E. "Doctoral Projects in Progress in Theatre Arts," *Educational Theatre Journal*, VIII, No. 2 (May 1956) to the present

Furnishes the following information: the researcher's name, title, institution, supervisor, and expected date of completion.

100 *Journal of Modern Literature* (Temple University), 1970 to the present

Contains an Annual Review Number including a section on "Criticism of Drama."

101 Junge, Ewald. "World Drama on Records," *Theatre Research*, VI, No. 1 (1964), 16-49

A list of complete plays in their original language, published on long-playing records.

102 Kahn, A. M. C., ed. *Library Resources in the Greater London area. No. 4: Theatre Collections; A Symposium*

(London: Library Association Reference and Special Libraries Section—South Eastern Group, 1953)

A directory of libraries and institutions, grouped under the headings of national, public, special, and private.

103   Keller, Dean H. *Index to Plays in Periodicals* (Metuchen, New Jersey: Scarecrow Press, 1971); *Supplement* (Metuchen, New Jersey: Scarecrow Press, 1973)

Author-title index.

104   Kersnowski, Frank L., C. W. Spinks, and Laird Loomis. *A Bibliography of Modern Irish and Anglo-Irish Literature* (San Antonio, Texas: Trinity University Press, 1976)

Deals with individual writers. Lists primary works and selected criticism in books.

105   Knower, Franklin H. "Graduate Theses in Theatre," *Educational Theatre Journal*, III, No. 2 (May 1951)—XV, No. 2 (May 1963)

Lists dissertations submitted to American universities, classified under categories of subject matter.

106   Lauterbach, Edward S., and W. Eugene Davis. *The Transitional Age: British Literature 1880-1920* (Troy, New York: The Whitston Publishing Company, 1973)

Lists primary books and selected secondary material in books and periodicals.

107   *Literature and Psychology*, 1951 to the present

Includes an annual "Bibliography" issued as a supplement in the fourth issue.

108 Litto, Frederic M. *American Dissertations on the Drama and the Theatre; A Bibliography* (Kent, Ohio: Kent State University Press, 1969)

> Contains Author Index, Key Word-in-Context Index, and Subject Index.

109 Loewenberg, Alfred. *The Theatre of the British Isles Excluding London; A Bibliography* (London: Printed for The Society for Theatre Research, 1950), pp. 19-27 "Dublin"; pp. 38-39 "Ireland"

> Bibliographical information about books which describe theatres and theatrical performances.

110 Longaker, Mark, and Edwin C. Bolles. "The Celtic Renaissance," *Contemporary English Literature* (New York: Appleton-Century-Crofts, 1953), pp. 34-66

> Lists primary books of, and selected criticism on, individual authors.

111 Lower, Henry Eastman, and George Heron Milne. *The Dramatic Books and Plays Published During 1912-1916* (Boston: The Boston Book Company, 1913-1917)

> Lists only works written in English.

112 "The Lyric Players, Belfast," *Threshold* (Belfast), III, No. 4 (Winter 1959), 76-78

> List of productions, 1951-1960.

113 McCoy, Ralph E. "Manuscript Collections in Morris Library," *I Carb S*, I, No. 2 (Spring-Summer 1974), 153-162

> Includes brief descriptions of collections relating to James Joyce, Lennox Robinson, and the Irish Renaissance.

114   MacNamara, Brinsley, ed. *Abbey Plays 1899-1948. Including the Productions of the Irish Literary Theatre* (Dublin: At the Sign of the Three Candles [1949])

> Also includes a Commentary by MacNamara and an Index of Playwrights.

115   McNamee, Lawrence F. *Dissertations in English and American Literature: Theses Accepted by American, British and German Universities, 1865-1964* (New York and London: R. R. Bowker, 1968); *Supplement One* (New York and London: R. R. Bowker, 1969); *Supplement Two* (New York and London: R. R. Bowker, 1974)

> Subject-author index.

116   McQuillan, Deirdre, comp. *The Abbey Theatre Dublin 1966-1976; A Commemorative Record* (Dublin: The Abbey Theatre, 1976)

> Includes a checklist of productions at the Abbey Theatre and at the Peacock Theatre.

117   Manchester Public Libraries. *Handlist of Plays* (Manchester: Manchester Libraries Committee, 1965)

> Sets available for loan from the Language and Literature Library. Author index.

118   Malone, Andrew E. "Appendices," *The Irish Drama* (London: Constable; New York: Scribner's, 1929; rpt. New York: Benjamin Blom, 1965), pp. 326-344

> Includes: I. "Number of First Productions Each Year, 1899-1928"; II. "Chronological List of First Productions, 1899-1928"; III. "Alphabetical List of Authors, with Plays and Dates."

119 Mellown, Elgin W. *A Descriptive Catalogue of the Bibliographies of 20th Century British Writers* (Troy, New York: The Whitston Publishing Company, 1972)

>   Lists primary and secondary bibliographies and checklists of British writers whose work appeared after 1890.

120 Melnitz, William W., ed. *Theatre Arts Publications in the United States, 1947-1952; A Five-Year Bibliography.* American Educational Theatre Association Monographs No. 1 (New York: American Educational Theatre Association, 1959)

>   Oriented toward production, but a section on dramatists is included.

121 Mersand, Joseph, ed. *Guide to Play Selection; A Selective Bibliography for Production and Study of Modern Plays*, 3rd ed. (Urbana, Illinois: National Council of Teachers of English; New York: R. R. Bowker, 1975)

>   Includes guides to several modern Irish plays.

122 Mikhail, E. H. *A Bibliography of Modern Irish Drama 1899-1970.* With an Introduction by William A. Armstrong (London: Macmillan; Seattle, Washington: University of Washington Press, 1972)

>   Lists bibliographies, books, periodical articles, and unpublished material devoted to modern Irish drama in general.

123 —. *Dissertations on Anglo-Irish Drama: A Bibliography of Studies 1870-1970* (London: Macmillan; Totowa, New Jersey: Rowman and Littlefield, 1973)

>   Indexed under general studies and individual dramatists.

124 —. *Contemporary British Drama 1950-1976; An Annotated Critical Bibliography* (London: Macmillan, 1976)

Lists bibliographies, reference works, books, and periodical articles devoted to contemporary British drama in general.

125   —. *English Drama 1900-1950; A Guide to Information Sources* (Detroit, Michigan: Gale Research Company, 1977)

Includes selected bibliographies of William Boyle, Paul Vincent Carroll, Padraic Colum, Daniel Corkery, Lord Dunsany, St. John Ervine, George Fitzmaurice, Lady Gregory, Douglas Hyde, Denis Johnston, Winifred Letts, Brinsley MacNamara, Edward Martyn, George Moore, T. C. Murray, Sean O'Casey, Seamus O'Kelly, Conal O'Riordan, Lennox Robinson, George Russell, Bernard Shaw, George Shiels, J. M. Synge, and W. B. Yeats.

126   —. *A Research Guide to Modern Irish Dramatists* (Troy, New York: Whitston Publishing Company, 1979)

A bibliography of bibliographies of some 95 Irish dramatists from 1899 to the present.

127   Miller, Anna Irene. "Bibliography: Ireland," *The Independent Theatre in Europe, 1887 to the Present* (New York: Ray Long and Richard R. Smith, 1931; rpt. New York: Benjamin Blom, 1966), pp. 396-400

Criticism in books and periodicals.

128   Miller, Liam, comp. *Dolmen XXV: An Illustrated Bibliography of the Dolmen Press 1951-1976* (Dublin: Dolmen Press, 1976)

The record of 25 years of publishing.

129   Millett, Fred B. *Contemporary British Literature; A Critical Survey and 232 Author-Bibliographies.* Third revised and enlarged edition, based on the second revised and enlarged edition by John M. Manly and Edith Rickert

(New York: Harcourt, Brace, 1935; rpt. New York: Johnson Reprint, 1969)

Lists primary books and selected criticism in books and periodicals.

130 *MLA Bibliography* (New York: The Modern Language Association of America), 1919 to the present

Lists books and periodical articles.

131 *Modern Drama, 1900-1938: A Select List of Plays Published Since 1900, and of Works on Dramatic Theory and Other Related Subjects* (London: Library Association, 1939). *Supplement, 1939-1945* (1946)

Lists selected plays from the period with certain works of theory and criticism.

132 New York Public Library. *Catalog of the Theatre and Drama Collections* (Boston: G. K. Hall, 1967)

Entries are made under author, subject, title, and other secondary headings.

133 —. Reference Department. *Theatre Subject Headings*. Second Edition. Enlarged (Boston: G. K. Hall, 1966)

The subject headings are intended for use in the catalogue of the Theatre Collection of the Reference Department of the New York Public Library.

134 *The New York Times Directory of the Theater* (New York: Arno Press, 1973)

Material in *The New York Times*, 1920-1970, arranged under subject headings.

135 *The New York Times Index*, 1913 to the present

Lists articles and reviews published in *The New York Times*, arranged under subject headings.

136 Nicoll, Allardyce. "Hand-List of Plays," appended to *English Drama 1900-1930; The Beginnings of the Modern Period* (Cambridge: Cambridge University Press, 1973)

Gives dates of first productions and publication information.

137 NicShiubhlaigh, Maire. "Theatre of Ireland Productions 1906-1912," appended to *The Splendid Years: Recollections of Maire Nic Shiubhlaigh, As Told to Edward Kenny* (Dublin: James Duffy, 1955), pp. 204-206

The only list in print.

138 *Nineteenth Century Readers' Guide to Periodical Literature 1890-1899. With Supplementary Indexing 1900-1922*, ed. Helen Grant Cushing and Adah V. Morris, 2 vols. (New York: H. W. Wilson, 1944)

Arranged under subject headings.

139 Norton, Elizabeth Towne, and Robert G. Shedd. "Modern Drama: A Selective Bibliography of Works Published in English in 1959," *Modern Drama*, III, No. 2 (September 1960), 143-161

Lists books and articles on drama in general and on individual dramatists.

140 O'Brien, Maurice N. *Irish Plays* (New York: National Service Bureau, 1938)

A selected bibliography, with synopses and production notes.

141 O'Donoghue, D. J. *The Poets of Ireland; A Biographical and Bibliographical Dictionary* (Dublin: Hodges, Figgis; London: Oxford University Press, 1912)

> "I confined myself to the Irish men and women who used the English language."

142 O'Hegarty, P. S. "Bibliographical Notes: The Abbey Theatre (Wolfhound) Series of Plays," *The Dublin Magazine*, XXII (April-June 1947), 41-42

> Sets down some points in connection with the Series.

143 O'Mahony, Mathew. *Guide to Anglo-Irish Plays* (Dublin: Progress House, 1960)

> "A survey of Anglo-Irish plays in suitable form for quick reference." An up-to-date elaboration of the author's *Play Guide for Irish Amateurs*, published in 1947.

144 O'Neill, James J. *A Bibliographical Account of Irish Theatrical Literature*. Bibliographical Society of Ireland Publications, Vol. I, No. 6 (Dublin: John Falconer, 1920)

> Contents: General Theatrical History, Players, and Theatrical Periodicals.

145 Orel, Harold. "Playbills of the Abbey Theatre, 1904-1941," *Books and Libraries at the University of Kansas*, No. 17 (February 1958), 11-15

> Describes the P. S. O'Hegarty Collection.

146 Ottemiller, John H. *Ottemiller's Index to Plays in Collections*. See Connor, John M., above.

147 Palmer, Helen, and Anne Jane Dyson. *European Drama Criticism* (Hamden, Connecticut: The Shoe String Press, 1968); *Supplement I* (Hamden, Connecticut: The Shoe String Press, 1970); *Supplement II* (Hamden, Connecticut: The Shoe String Press, 1974)

> Selected criticism of plays in books and periodicals.

148   Patterson, Charlotte A., comp. *Plays in Periodicals: An Index to English Language Scripts in Twentieth Century Journals* (Boston, Massachusetts: G. K. Hall, 1970)

Author-title index of plays published 1900-1968.

149   *Play-Index, 1949-1952*, ed. Dorothy Herbert West and Dorothy Margaret Peake (New York: H. W. Wilson, 1953); *Play Index, 1953-1960*, ed. Estelle A. Fidell and Dorothy Margaret Peake (New York: H. W. Wilson, 1963); *Play Index, 1961-1967*, ed. Estelle A. Fidell (New York: H. W. Wilson, 1968); *Play Index, 1968-1972*, ed. Estelle A. Fidell (New York: H. W. Wilson, 1973)

Entries are indexed under author, title, and subject.

150   Pohle, Helen Loudora. "The New Drama," *Bulletin of Bibliography*, XV, No. 5 (September-December 1934), 94-95; XV, No. 6 (January-April, 1935), 114-116

Annotated checklist of selected critical studies in books and periodicals.

151   Pownall, David E. *Articles on Twentieth Century Literature: An Annotated Bibliography 1954-1970* (Millwood, New York: Kraus-Thomson Organisation, 1973-   )

"An expanded cumulation of 'Current Bibliography' in the journal *Twentieth Century Literature*, Volume One to Volume Sixteen: 1955 to 1970."

152   Quinn, John. *Complete Catalogue of the Library of John Quinn*, 2 vols. (New York: The Anderson Galleries, 1924)

An auction sale catalogue of the important private collection comprising 12,096 items.

153   Raines, Lester. "Five Years of One-Act Plays 1925-1929,"

Bulletin of Bibliography, XIII, No. 10 (September-December 1929), 200-201; XIV, No. 3 (September-December 1930), 50-52; XIV, No. 4 (January-April 1931), 78-82

Lists plays published separately or in anthologies.

154 *Readers' Guide to Periodical Literature* (New York: H. W. Wilson), 1900 to the present

Author and subject index to selected world periodicals.

155 *Research in Progress in English and Historical Studies in the Universities of the British Isles*, 1971 to the present (London: St. James Press)

Starting 1975, also includes research in progress in Commonwealth universities.

156 *Revue d'Histoire du Théâtre* (Paris: Société des Historiens du Théâtre), 1948 to the present

Includes a "Bibliographie" of published material, indexed by subject.

157 Roach, Helen. *Spoken Records* (New York and London: Scarecrow Press, 1963); 2nd ed. (New York and London: Scarecrow Press, 1966), 3rd ed. (Metuchen, New Jersey: Scarecrow Press, 1970)

Annotated index.

158 —. "A Selective Discography of Irish Spoken Records," *Eire-Ireland*, II, No. 1 (Spring 1967), 97-100

Includes plays on records.

159 Roberts, Peter. *Theatre in Britain* (London: Pitman, 1973)

Includes a lisitng of major theatrical collections.

160   Robinson, Lennox. *Ireland's Abbey Theatre; A History 1899-1951* (London: Sidgwick & Jackson, 1951; rpt. Port Washington, New York: Kennikat Press, 1968)

Includes dates and casts of first productions.

161   Royal Irish Academy. The Committee for the Study of Anglo-Irish Language and Literature. *Handlist of Work in Progress* (Dublin), 1969 to the present

Arranged under subject headings and individual writers.

162   —. The Committee for the Study of Anglo-Irish Language and Literature. *Irish and Anglo-Irish Periodicals* (Dublin: Royal Irish Academy, 1970)

Lists and gives the locations in Ireland of all those periodicals published in Ireland, which are likely to be of interest to scholars of Anglo-Irish Literature. To be supplemented by International Association for the Study of Anglo-Irish Literature, "Irish Periodicals 1970, Devoted To, or Frequently Including Anglo-Irish Literature," *Irish University Review*, II, No. 1 (Spring 1972), 90-92.

163   —. The Committee for the Study of Anglo-Irish Language and Literature. *Handlist of Theses Completed but Not Published* (Dublin), 1973 to the present

Lists dissertations on Irish writers.

164   Ryan, Pat M., Jr. "Ireland," *History of the Modern Theatre: A Selective Bibliography* (Tuscon, Arizona: University of Arizona, Department of Drama, 1960), pp. 19-23

A reading list.

165   Saddlemyer, Ann. "The Irish School," *English Drama (excluding Shakespeare), Select Bibliographical Guides,* ed. Stanley Wells (London: Oxford University Press, 1975), pp. 248-267

    Provides a critical guide as well as a list giving bibliographical information about the writings mentioned in the text.

166   Sader, Marion, ed. *Comprehensive Index to English-Language Little Magazines, 1890-1970,* 8 vols. (Millwood, New York: Kraus-Thomson, 1976)

    Selected criticism in little magazines arranged under subject headings.

167   Salem, James M. *A Guide to Critical Reviews, Part III: British and Continental Drama from Ibsen to Pinter* (Metuchen, New Jersey: The Scarecrow Press, 1968)

    Selected criticism of plays in periodicals.

168   Samples, Gordon. *The Drama Scholars' Index to Plays and Filmscripts: A Guide to Plays and Filmscripts in Selected Anthologies, Series and Periodicals* (Metuchen, New Jersey: The Scarecrow Press, 1974)

    Lists plays and filmscripts in their original languages, or in translations.

169   Santaniello, A. E. "British Theatre: Nineteenth and Twentieth Century Drama," *Theatre Books in Print; An Annotated Guide to the Literature of the Theatre, Motion Pictures, Television and Radio*, Second Edition (New York: The Drama Book Shop, 1966), pp. 71-93

    Selected check-list.

170   Saul, George Brandon. "An Introductory Bibliography in Anglo-Irish Literature," *The New York Public Library Bulletin*, LVIII (September 1954), 429-435

A "purely selective bibliography"; includes books and period-ical articles.

171   Schlösser, Anselm. *Die Englische Literatur in Deutschland von 1895 bis 1934* (Jena: Walter Bledermann, 1937)

> Includes bibliographical survey of studies on Lord Dunsany, Lady Gregory, James Joyce, George Moore, Liam O'Flaherty, George Russell, Bernard Shaw, James Stephens, J. M. Synge, and W. B. Yeats.

172   Schoolcraft, Ralph Newman. *Performing Arts Books in Print: An Annotated Bibliography* (New York: Drama Book Specialists, 1973)

> Revised edition of *Theatre Books in Print*, originally published in 1963 and revised in 1966. Includes a section on "Ireland".

173   Shedd, Robert G. "Modern Drama: A Selective Bibliography of Works Published in English," *Modern Drama*, V, No. 2 (September 1962), 223-244; VI, No. 2 (September 1963), 204-217; VIII, No. 2 (September 1965), 204-226; IX, No. 2 (September 1966), 210-226

> Lists critical studies in books and periodicals on drama in general and on individual dramatists.

174   Simons, Eric N. "The Library as a Tool of the Theatre," *Aslib Proceedings* (London), I, No. 3 (November 1949), 271-278

> On sources of information regarding the theatre.

175   *Social Sciences and Humanities Index*, 1965 to the present. Continuation of *International Index to Periodicals*, above.

176   Stratman, Carl J., ed. *A Bibliography of British Dramatic Periodicals, 1720-1960* (New York: New York Public

Library, 1962)

A total of 670 titles are arranged chronologically with a note of location in libraries, both in the U. S. A. and Great Britain, for complete files.

Reprinted as *Britain's Theatrical Periodicals 1720-1967; A Bibliography* (New York: New York Public Library, 1972)

A major revision of the original edition; indexes 1,235 English periodicals; entries are descriptive. Includes Irish periodicals.

177 —. *Dramatic Play Lists, 1591-1963* (New York: New York Public Library, 1966)

Enumerates and evaluates those dramatic bibliographies concerned with actual play titles.

178 *Subject Index to Periodicals* (London: The Library Association), 1915-1961. Continued as *British Humanities Index*, 1962 to the present

Subject and author index to articles in periodicals.

179 Temple, Ruth Z., and Martin Tucker, eds. *Twentieth Century British Literature; A Reference Guide and Bibliography* (New York: Frederick Ungar, 1968)

Lists primary books and critical or bibliographical studies for each author.

180 *Theatrefacts; International Theatre Reference* (London), 1974 to the present

Includes Theatrediary in Ireland.

181 Thompson, Lawrence S. *Nineteenth and Twentieth Century Drama; A Selective Bibliography of English Language Works, Numbers 1-3029* (Boston: G. K. Hall, 1975)

A catalogue of books available in microreproduction from the General Microfilm Company, Cambridge, Massachusetts; other volumes to follow.

182   Thomson, Ruth G. *Index to Full-Length Plays: 1895-1925; 1926-1944* (Westwood, Massachusetts: Faxon, 1946, 1956)

Plays in English are listed, with cast requirement, type of play, and set and costume requirements.

183   *The Times Index* (London), 1790 to the present

Subject index to material published in *The Times.*

184   *The Times Literary Supplement Index*, (London), 1902 to the present

Subject index to material published in *The Times Literary Supplement.*

185   Trussler, Simon. "Current Bibliography," *Theatre Quarterly* (London), 1971-1973. Continued in *Theatrefacts; International Theatre Reference* (London), 1974-1975

A cumulative record of English-language books on theatre and related performing arts. Starting 1977 published separately as *Annual Bibliography of Theatre Studies.* Discontinued.

186   *Tulane Drama Review*, III (1959)—XI (1967)

Includes "Books and Theatre," selected lists of books on drama and the theatre arranged by general subject.

187   *Twentieth Century Literature*, 1955 to the present

Contains a regular quarterly annotated "Current Bibliography" of critical literature in periodicals listed alphabetically, according to author of article.

188 Underwood, Pierson. "The Little Theatre," *The Bookman* (N. Y.), LV (June 1922), 403-409

> Annotated bibliography, with a reading list. Includes "The Irish Players."

189 Veinstein, Andre, ed. *Performing Arts Libraries and Museums of the World*. Second Edition (Paris: Éditions du Centre National de la Rechèrche Scientifique, 1967)

> Originally published in 1960, this bilingual second edition, revised and enlarged by Cecile Giteau, is a census of all the known performing arts collections, libraries, and museums throughout the world.

190 Walford, A. J., ed. *Guide to Reference Material*, Vol. 3, 2nd ed. (London: The Library Association, 1975)

> Lists basic bibliographies.

191 Welker, David, ed. *'Educational Theatre Journal': A Ten-Year Index: 1949-1958* (East Lansing, Michigan: Michigan State University, n. d.)

> Classified index of material published in the first ten volumes of the *Educational Theatre Journal*.

192 Willison, I. R., ed. *The New Cambridge Bibliography of English Literature*, Vol. 4: 1900-1950 (Cambridge: Cambridge University Press, 1972)

> For most authors replaces *The Cambridge Bibliography of English Literature*.

193 Wilson, Sheila. "Ireland," *The Theatre of the 'Fifties* (London: Library Association, 1963), p. 45

> Selected reading list of criticism.

194 *World Premieres* (Paris: International Theatre Institute,

1940-64). Incorporated in *World Theatre*, 1965 to the present

Lists details of first productions of plays.

195   *Year's Work in English Studies* (London: The English Association), 1919 to the present

Annotated selective bibliography.

196   Young, William C. "Scholarly Works in Progress," *Educational Theatre Journal*, XXVI (October 1974) to the present

Yearly compilation.

II

Reference Works

Includes handbooks, guides, indexes, annuals, encyclopaedies, glossaries, and dictionnaries

197   Adams, W. D. *A Dictionary of the Drama; A Guide to the Plays, Playwrights, Players, and Playhouses of the United Kingdom and America from the Earliest Times to the Present.* Vol. 1: A-G (London: Chatto & Windus; Philadelphia: J. B. Lippincott, 1904; rpt. New York: Franklin, 1964)

As comprehensive as the sub-title suggests, but unfortunately never continued beyond the first volume.

198   Anderson, Michael, *et al. Crowell's Handbook of Contemporary Drama* (New York: Thomas Y. Crowell, 1971). British edition entitled *Handbook of Contemporary Drama* (London: Pitman, 1972)

An alphabetically arranged guide to written drama since World War II, with some critical appraisal of plays and playwrights as well as factual information.

199   Barnet, Sylvan, Morton Berman, and William Burto. *A Dictionary of Literary, Dramatic, and Cinematic Terms* (Boston: Little, Brown, 1971)

200   *The Best Plays of 1919-47,* ed. Burns Mantle, 27 vols. (New York: Dodd, Mead, 1920-47)

Includes an annual survey and details of first American productions.

201   *The Best Plays of 1947-52*, ed. John Chapman, 5 vols. (New York: Dodd, Mead, 1947-52).

202   *The Best Plays of 1952-61*, ed. Louis Kronenberger, 9 vols. (New York: Dodd, Mead, 1952-61).

203   *The Best Plays of 1961-64*, ed. Henry Hewes, 3 vols. (New York: Dodd, Mead, 1961-64).

204   *The Best Plays of 1964-   *, ed. Otis Guernsey, Jr. (New York: Dodd, Mead, 1964-   ).

205   Bowman, Walter Parker, and Robert Hamilton Ball. *Theatre Language: A Dictionary of Terms in English of the Drama and Stage from Medieval to Modern Times* (New York: Theatre Arts, 1961)

> Technical and standard non-technical terms, jargon, cant, and slang are defined and cross-referenced.

206   Browning, D. C., and John W. Cousin. *Everyman's Dictionary of Literary Biography; English & American* (London: J. M. Dent; New York: E. P. Dutton, 1965).

207   Buchanan-Brown, John, ed. *Cassell's Encyclopaedia of World Literature*, 3 vols. (London: Cassell; West Caldwell, New Jersey: Morrow, 1973).

208   Cartmell, Van H., ed. "Irish Plays," *Plot Outlines of 100 Famous Plays* (Garden City, New York: Doubleday, 1945; rpt. Dolphin Books, 1962)

> Synopses of famous plays.

209   Cleeve, Brian, comp. *Dictionary of Irish Writers*, 3 vols. (Cork: Mercier Press, 1967-71)

> Includes more than a thousand names in compilations on imaginative literature, non-fiction, and writers in Irish.

210   Crone, John S. *A Concise Dictionary of Irish Biography*. Revised and Enlarged Edition (Dublin, 1937; rpt. Nendeln/Liechtenstein: Kraus Reprint, 1970).

211   Daiches, David, ed. *The Penguin Companion to Literature: Britain and the Commonwealth* (Harmondsworth: Allen Lane; The Penguin Press, 1972).

212   Downs, Harold, ed. *Theatre and Stage; A Modern Guide to the Performance of All Classes of Amateur Dramatic, Operatic, and Theatrical Work*, 2 vols. (London: Pitman, 1934).

213   Drury, Francis K. W. *Drury's Guide to Best Plays*. Second Edition, by James M. Salem (Metuchen, New Jersey: Scarecrow Press, 1969)

   Synopses of plays, production information, and dates of first performance or publication.

214   Engle, Dorothy, and Hilary Carnell, eds. *The Oxford Literary Guide to the British Isles* (Oxford: Clarendon Press, 1977)

   Contains an index of authors, including many Irish dramatists.

215   *Enciclopedia Dello Spettacolo*, 10 vols. and appendix (Rome: Casa Editrice le Maschere, 1954-68)

   By far the most comprehensive work on all aspects of the stage, cinema, radio, and all related arts. Includes biographies and bibliographies. Coverage is universal.

216   *Encyclopedia of Ireland* (Dublin: Allen Figgis; New York: McGraw-Hill, 1968)

   Includes material on the Irish drama.

217   Esslin, Martin, ed. *Illustrated Encyclopaedia of World*

Theatre (London: Thames and Hudson, 1977)

Includes several entries on Irish drama.

218   Fay, W. G., comp. *A Short Glossary of Theatrical Terms* (London and New York: Samuel French, [1930]).

219   Fitzgerald, Thomas W. H. *Ireland and Her People* (Chicago: Fitzgerald Books, 1909-11), 5 vols.

Three of these volumes consist of biographies, though few are of literary figures.

220   Fleishmann, Wolfgang Bernard, ed. *Encyclopedia of World Literature in the 20th Century*, 3 vols. (New York: Frederick Ungar, 1969).

221   Freeman, William. *Dictionary of Fictional Characters* (London: J. M. Dent, 1967).

222   Gassner, John, and Edward Quinn, eds. *The Reader's Encyclopedia of World Drama* (New York: Thomas Y. Crowell, 1969)

Gives information on plays and playwrights and has an appendix containing "basic documents in dramatic theory."

223   Gillie, Christopher, ed. *Longman Companion to English Literature* (London: Longman, 1973).

224   Granville, Wilfred, comp. *A Dictionary of Theatrical Terms* (London: Andre Deutsch, 1952). American edition entitled *Theatre Dictionary* (New York: Oxford University Press, 1952)

Records technical, colloquial and slang terms.

225   Graves, A. P. "Anglo-Irish Literature," *The Cambridge History of English Literature*, vol. XIV, ed. A. W. Ward

and A. R. Waller (Cambridge: Cambridge University
Press, 1964), pp. 329-330.

226 *Green Room Book: Or Who's Who on the Stage; An Annual
Bibliographical Record of the Dramatic, Musical and
Variety World* (London: Pitman), 1906-1909. Con-
tinued as *Who's Who in the Theatre: A Biographical
Record of the Contemporary Stage* (London: Pitman),
1912 to the present

As well as biographies of all well-known living personalities in
the theatre includes genealogical tables, obituaries, and dates
of notable productions.

227 Grigson, Geoffrey, ed. *The Concise Encyclopedia of Modern
World Literature.* Second Edition (New York: Haw-
thorn Books, 1971)

Contains mini-essays on individual writers.

228 Hartnoll, Phyllis, ed. *The Oxford Companion to the Theatre.*
Third Edition (London: Oxford University Press,
1967)

Particular topics tend to be discussed under broad headings.

229 Harvey, Sir Paul, ed. *The Oxford Companion to English
Literature.* Fourth Edition Revised by Dorothy Eagle
(Oxford: Clarendon Press, 1973).

230 Hobson, Harold, ed. *International Theatre Annual* (London:
Calder), 1956-60

An attempt was made to group contributions round a particular
theme.

231 Holden, Michael. *The Stage Guide; Technical Information on
British Theatres* (London: Carson and Comerford,
1971)

A new and updated edition of the *Guide* published by the *The Stage* newspaper in 1912 and revised in 1946. Includes theatres in Ireland.

232   Hornstein, L. H., G. D. Percy, and S. A. Brown, eds. *The Reader's Companion to World Literature*, 2nd rev. and updated ed. (New York: New American Library, 1973).

233   International Theatre Institute. *World Premieres* (New York: UNESCO), 1949-1964

A list, arranged by country, of first productions, giving details of title, author, and cast.

Since 1965, this list has been incorporated in the Institute's periodical *World Theatre.*

234   Kienzle, Siegfried. *Modern World Theater: A Guide to Productions in Europe and the United States Since 1945.* Translated by Alexander and Elizabeth Henderson (New York: Frederick Ungar, 1970).

235   Kunitz, Stanley J., and Howard Haycraft, eds. *Twentieth Century Authors: A Biographical Dictionary of Modern Literature* (New York: H. W. Wilson, 1942); *First Supplement* (New York: H. W. Wilson, 1955).

236   Langnas, I. A., and J. A. List. *Major Writers of the World* (Paterson, New Jersey: Littlefield, Adams, 1963).

237   Lounsbury, Warren C. *Theatre Backstage from A to Z* (Seattle and London: University of Washington Press, 1967)

A dictionary of technical terms and methods.

238   *McGraw-Hill Encyclopedia of World Drama*, 4 vols. (New York: McGraw-Hill, 1972)

Includes articles on dramatists and summaries of their plays.

239 Magill, Frank N., ed. *Masterpieces of World Literature in Digest Form*. Four Series (New York and London: Harper & Row, 1949-1969)

Includes synopses of, and commentaries on, plays.

240 —, ed. *Cyclopedia of Literary Characters* (New York and London: Harper & Row, 1963)

Includes characters from Irish plays.

241 Matlaw, Myron. *Modern World Drama; An Encyclopedia* (New York: E. P. Dutton; London: Secker & Warburg, 1972).

242 May, Robin. *A Companion to the Theatre; The Anglo-American Stage from 1920* (London: Lutterworth Press, 1973)

Arranged alphabetically under dramatic categories.

243 —. *A Consice Encyclopedia of the Theatre* (Reading, Berkshire: Osprey Publishing Limited, 1974)

Includes chapters on Dramatists, Players, Famous Theatre Buildings, Companies and Organisations, and Theatre Terms.

244 Melchinger, Siegfried. *Drama Zwischen Shaw and Brecht: Ein Leitfaden Durch Das Zeitgenossische Schauspiel*, 2 vols. (Bremen: Schunemann, 1957)

A dictionary of both topics and dramatists.

245 —. *The Concise Encyclopedia of Modern Drama*. Foreword by Eric Bentley. Translated by George Wellwarth (New York: Horizon Press, 1964; London: Vision, 1966)

A dictionary of both topics and dramatists.

246   Morley, Sheridan, ed. *Theatre 71-*   (London: Hutchinson,
      1971-   )

> "The first of a series of annual volumes designed to give a con-
> tinuing picture of the theatre as it evolves during the 1970's";
> collection of essays on various aspects. Discontinued.

247   *New York Theatre Critics' Review* (New York: Critics'
      Theatre Review), 1940 to the present

> A periodical publication of the reviews of Broadway theatres
> reprinted from the seven major New York newspapers. Includes
> an index.

248   O'Donoghue, D. J. *The Poets of Ireland; A Biographical
      and Bibliographical Dictionary* (Dublin: Hodges,
      Figgis; London: Oxford University Press, 1912)

> "I confined myself to the Irish men and women who used the
> English language."

249   O'Mahony, Mathew. *Guide to Anglo-Irish Plays* (Dublin:
      Progress House, 1960)

> An up-to-date elaboration of the author's *Play Guide for Irish
> Amateurs*, published in 1947. "A survey of Anglo-Irish plays
> in suitable form for quick reference."

250   Pollard, Arthur, ed. *Webster's New World Companion to
      English and American Literature* (Salisbury: Compton
      Russell, 1973).

251   Pride, Leo B., ed. *International Theatre Directory: A World
      Directory of the Theatre and Performing Arts* (New
      York: Simon & Schuster, 1973)

> Include a list of the theatres in Ireland.

252 Queant, G. *Encyclopedie du Theatre Contemporain, 1850-1950*, 2 vols. (Paris: Publications de France, 1957-1959)

> This is not a true encyclopedia, but it contains a great deal of visual material in brilliant colour and monochrome.

253 Rae, Kenneth, and Richard Southern, eds. *International Vocabulary of Technical Theatre Terms in Eight Languages* (Brussels: Elsevier; New York: Reinhardt, 1959; Theatre Arts, 1960)

> Compiled for the International Theatre Institute. The eight languages are American, Dutch, English, French, German, Italian, Spanish, and Swedish.

254 Roberts, Peter. *Theatre in Britain; A Playgoer's Guide* (London: Pitman, 1973)

> Provides "rapid access to the background of what the British theatre has to offer."

255 Sampson, George. "Anglo-Irish Literature," *The Concise Cambridge History of English Literature* (Cambridge: Cambridge University Press, 1961), pp. 887-909

> Survey.

256 Seymour-Smith, Martin. "British Literature," *Guide to Modern World Literature* (London: Wolfe Publishing, 1973)

> Survey.

257 —. *Who's Who in Twentieth Century Literature* (London: Weidenfeld and Nicolson, 1976).

258 Shank, Theodore J., ed. "Irish Drama," *A Digest of 500 Plays: Plot Outlines and Production Notes* (New York:

Collier Books; London: Collier-Macmillan, 1966), pp. 409-418.

259   Share, Bernard. *Irish Lives* (Dublin: Allen Figgis, 1971)

Includes biographies of Lady Gregory, Bernard Shaw, W. B. Yeats, J. M. Synge, Jack B. Yeats, and James Joyce.

260   Sharp, Harold S., and Marjorie Z., comps. *Index to Characters in the Performing Arts; An Alphabetical Listing of 30,000 Characters.* Part I: Non-Musical Plays. 2 vols. (Metuchen, New Jersey: The Scarecrow Press, 1966)

Identifies characters with the play in which they appear, indicates the author of the play, and shows the year in which the play was written, produced, or published.

261   Shipley, Joseph T. *Guide to Great Plays* (Washington, D.C.: Public Affairs Press, 1956)

Includes synopses of plays and information on productions, casts, and reviews.

262   Sobel, Bernard, ed. *The New Theatre Handbook and Digest of Plays* (New York: Crown Publishers, 1959)

Contains synopses of plays, glossary of theatre terms, biographies, information on productions, and bibliographies.

263   Sprinchorn, Evert, ed. *20th-Century Plays in Synopsis* (New York: Thomas Y. Crowell, 1965)

Act-by-act synopses of plays and biographical information on the playwrights.

264   Stacey, R. *Plays: A Classified Guide to Play Selection 1957-1965* (Bromley, Kent: Stacey Publications, 1959-66)

Classified according to type, with details of cast, publisher, price, etc.

265 *The Stage and Television Today Year Book* (London: Carson and Comerford), 1908 to the present

Gives overall picture of the previous year in a few short articles and lists names of managements, professional organisations, etc.

266 *Stagecast: Irish Stage and Screen Directory*, ed. Derek Young (Dublin: Stagecast Publications), 1962 to the present

Also includes a reference section.

267 Taylor, John Russell. *The Penguin Dictionary of the Theatre* (Harmondsworth: Penguin Books, 1966; New York: Barnes and Noble, 1967)

Despite its title, this is really a miniature encyclopedia.

268 Temple, Ruth Z., and Martin Tucker, eds. *A Library of Literary Criticism; Modern British Literature*, 3 vols. (New York: Frederick Ungar, 1966)

Includes excerpts from criticism on several Irish dramatists.

269 *Theatre World Annual* (London: Barrie and Rockliff), 1949-1963; (London: Iliffe), 1964 to the present

Indexes the plays and players featured in its largely pictorial survey of the major London productions.

270 Thom, Alexander, *Thom's Irish Who's Who* (Dublin and London: Alexander Thom, 1923)

Contains life sketches of some 2,500 Irish men and women.

271 Vinson, James, ed. *Contemporary Dramatists*. With a preface by Ruby Cohn (London: St. James Press; New York: St. Martin's Press, 1973)

A bio-bibliographical encyclopedia on the most important living playwrights in the English language.

272   Ward, A. C. *Longman Companion to Twentieth Century Literature*. Second Edition (London: Longman, 1975)

A compact handbook.

273   *Who's Who in the Theatre*. See *Green Room Book*, above.

274   *Who's Who, What's What and Where in Ireland* (London and Dublin: Geoffrey Chapman Publishers, 1973).

275   *World Theatre*. See International Theatre Institute, above.

III

Books

276 "The Abbey Theatre," *The Ireland of Today. Reprinted, with Some Additions, from the London Times* (London: John Murray, 1913; Boston: Small, Maynard, 1915), pp. 131-137

   Survey.

277 *The Abbey Theatre Dramatic Festival of Plays and Lectures* (Dublin: Cahill, 1938)

   A 38-page souvenir brochure.

278 Adock, A. St. John. *The Glory That Was Grub Street; Impressions of Contemporary Authors* (London: Low, 1928)

   Includes impressions of Bernard Shaw and St. John Ervine.

279 Agate, James. "The Irish Players," *Buzz, Buzz! Essays of the Theatre* (London: W. Collins, [1917]), pp. 150-160

   On plays by J. M. Synge and Lady Gregory.

280 —. *At Half-Past Eight; Essays of the Theatre 1921-1922* (London: Jonathan Cape, 1923; rpt. New York: Benjamin Blom, 1969)

   Includes reviews from *The Saturday Review* of plays by St. John Ervine and Bernard Shaw.

281   --. *The Contemporary Theatre, 1925* (London: Leonard
      Parsons, 1926; rpt. New York: Benjamin Blom, 1969)

      Includes reviews from *The Sunday Times* of plays by Sean
      O'Casey, Lennox Robinson, and Bernard Shaw.

282   Allen, John. *Masters of British Drama* (London: Dennis
      Dobson, 1957; rpt. New York: Citadel, 1968)

      Includes chapters on Bernard Shaw and Sean O'Casey.

283   Allison, Alexander W., Arthur J. Carr, and Arthur M. East-
      man, eds. *Masterpieces of the Drama*, 3rd ed. (New
      York: Macmillan, 1974)

      Anthology including plays, with commentaries, by J. M. Synge,
      Bernard Shaw, Sean O'Casey, and Samuel Beckett.

284   Altenbernd, Lynn, and Leslie L. Lewis, eds. *Introduction to
      Literature: Plays* (New York: Macmillan, 1963)

      Anthology including plays, with commentaries, by W. B. Yeats
      and J. M. Synge.

285   Andrews, Charlton. *The Drama Today* (Philadelphia and
      London: J. B. Lippincott, 1913), pp. 160-168

      Survey.

286   Archer, William. *The Old Drama and the New; An Essay in
      Re-Valuation* (Boston: Small, Maynard, 1923; rpt.
      New York: Benjamin Blom, 1972)

      Includes studies of Bernard Shaw, J. M. Synge, W. B. Yeats,
      and Lennox Robinson.

287   Armstrong, William A. "The Irish Point of View: The Plays
      of Sean O'Casey, Brendan Behan, and Thomas Mur-
      phy," *Experimental Drama* (London: G. Bell, 1963;
      New York: Dufour, 1965), pp. 79-102.

288 ~ , ed. *Classic Irish Drama* (Harmondsworth: Penguin, 1964)

> Includes a survey, "The Irish Dramatic Movement," and plays, with commentaries, by W. B. Yeats, J. M. Synge, and Sean O'Casey.

289 Arns, Karl. *Grundriss der Geschichte der Englischen Literatur von 1832 bis zur Gegenwart* (Paderborn: Schoningh, 1941)

> Includes brief studies of George Russell, Padraic Colum, Lord Dunsany, Lady Gregory, Denis Johnston, James Joyce, George Moore, Sean O'Casey, Lennox Robinson, Bernard Shaw, J. M. Synge, and W. B. Yeats.

290 Ashley, Leonard R. N. *Mirrors for Man* (Cambridge, Massachusetts: Winthrop Publishers, 1974)

> Anthology including plays, with commentaries, by Bernard Shaw and J. M. Synge.

291 Bach, Bert C., and Gordon Browning, eds. *Drama for Composition* (Glenview, Illinois; Brighton, England: Scott, Foresman, 1973)

> Anthology including plays, with commentaries, by Bernard Shaw and J. M. Synge.

292 Balmforth, Ramsden. *The Problem-Play and Its Influence on Modern Thought and Life* (London: George Allen & Unwin; New York: Henry Holt, 1928)

> Includes discussions on plays by Bernard Shaw and St. John Ervine.

293 Barnet, Sylvan, Morton Berman, and William Burto, eds. *The Genius of the Irish Theater.* Mentor Books (New York: The New American Library, 1960)

Anthology including an introduction, "The Irish Theater;" and plays, with commentaries, by Bernard Shaw, Lady Gregory, J. M. Synge, W. B. Yeats, Jack B. Yeats, Frank O'Connor, and Sean O'Casey.

294   Bates, Katharine Lee, ed. *The New Irish Drama; Yeats, Synge, Lady Gregory and Others* ([Chicago] : The Drama League of America, 1911)

A 12-page pamphlet published on the occasion of the Abbey Theatre's first American tour.

295   Baxter, Beverley. *First Nights and Noises Off* (London and New York: Hutchinson, n. d.)

Includes reviews of plays by Micheál MacLiammóir and Bernard Shaw.

296   Beach, Joseph Warren. "The Drama in Ireland," *English Literature of the Nineteenth and the Early Twentieth Centuries* (New York: Oxford University Press, 1950; rpt. New York: Collier Books; London: Collier-Macmillan, 1962), pp. 221-230

Survey.

297   Beckerman, Bernard. *Dynamics of Drama; Theory and Method of Analysis* (New York: Alfred A. Knopf, 1970)

Includes analysis of plays by J. M. Synge, Sean O'Casey, and Bernard Shaw.

298   Beerbohm, Max. *Around Theatres, 1898-1910* (London: Heinemann, 1924; New York: Alfred A. Knopf, 1930; rpt. London: Rupert Hart-Davis; New York: British Book Centre, 1953)

Includes criticism on plays by Bernard Shaw, W. B. Yeats, and J. M. Synge.

299 —. *More Theatres, 1898-1903* (London: Rupert Hart-Davis, 1969)

> Includes criticism on plays by Bernard Shaw and W. B. Yeats.

300 —. *Last Theatres, 1904-1910* (London: Rupert Hart-Davis, 1970)

> Includes criticism on plays by Bernard Shaw, J. M. Synge, and Lady Gregory.

301 —. "In Dublin," *The Genius of the Irish Theater*, ed. Sylvan Barnet *et al*. (New York: The New American Library, 1960), pp. 345-348

> Review of plays by W. B. Yeats and Edward Martyn.

302 Bell, Sam Hanna. "Theatre," *Causeway: The Arts in Ulster*, ed. Michael Longley (Belfast: Arts Council of Northern Ireland; Dublin: Gill & Macmillan, 1971), pp. 83-94

> Survey.

303 —. *The Theatre in Ulster: A Survey of the Dramatic Movement in Ulster from 1902 Until the Present Day* (Dublin: Gill and Macmillan; Totowa, New Jersey: Rowman and Littlefield, 1972)

> The first account of any length about the Ulster stage since McHenry's 1931 volume. Also lists first productions of the Ulster Litearary Theatre, the Ulster Group Theatre, and the Lyric Players Theatre.

304 Bellinger, Martha Fletcher. "The Last Fifty Years in England and Ireland," *A Short History of the Drama* (New York: Henry Holt, 1927), pp. 343-346

> Survey.

305   Bentley, Eric. *The Playwright as Thinker; A Study of Drama
      in Modern Times* (New York: Reynal & Hitchcock,
      [1946]). British edition entitled *The Modern Theatre;
      A Study of Dramatists and the Drama* (London:
      Robert Hale, 1948)

      Includes studies of Bernard Shaw and W. B. Yeats.

306   —. *In Search of Theater* (New York: Alfred A. Knopf;
      Toronto: McClelland & Stewart, 1953; London:
      Dobson, 1954)

      Includes chapters on "The Poet in Dublin," "Bernard Shaw
      Dead," "Yeat's Plays," and "The Abbey Theatre".

307   —. *The Dramatic Event; An American Chronicle* (New York:
      Horizon Press, 1954; rpt. Boston: Beacon Press, 1956)

      Includes chapters on Sean O'Casey and W. B. Yeats.

308   Bergholz, Harry. *Die Neugestaltung des Modernen Englischen
      Theaters, 1870-1930* (Berlin: Bergholz, 1933)

      Includes discussion on the Abbey Theatre.

309   Bergonzi, Bernard, ed. *The Twentieth Century* (London:
      Sphere Books, 1970)

      Includes essays on W. B. Yeats and James Joyce; and a survey
      of the Irish drama.

310   Bickley, Francis. "The Irish Theatre," *J. M. Synge and the
      Irish Dramatic Movement* (London: Constable; Boston
      & New York: Houghton Mifflin, 1912), pp. 67-73

      Survey.

311   Black, Hester M. *The Theatre in Ireland: An Introductory
      Essay* (Dublin: Trinity College, 1957)

Survey.

312 Block, Haskell M., and Robert G. Shedd, eds. *Masters of Modern Drama* (New York: Random House, 1962)

 Anthology including plays, with commentaries, by Bernard Shaw, J. M. Synge, W. B. Yeats, Sean O'Casey, and Samuel Beckett.

313 Blunt, Jerry. "Irish," *Stage Dialects* (San Francisco: Chandler Publishing Co., 1967), pp. 75-90

 The phonetics of the Irish stage dialect.

314 Blythe, Ernest. *The Abbey Theatre* (Dublin: The National Theatre Society, [1965])

 A brochure on the Abbey's policies.

315 Bogard, Travis, and William I. Oliver, eds. *Modern Drama; Essays in Criticism* (New York: Oxford University Press, 1965)

 Includes essays on Bernard Shaw and W. B. Yeats.

316 Bonazza, Blaze O., and Emil Roy, eds. *Studies in Drama*, 2nd ed. (New York and London: Harper & Row, 1968)

 Anthology including plays, with commentaries, by J. M. Synge and Bernard Shaw.

317 Borsa, Mario. "The Irish National Theatre," *The English Stage of Today*. Translated by Selwyn Brinton (London and New York: John Lane, 1908), pp. 286-314.

 Survey.

318 Boyd, Ernest A. *Ireland's Literary Renaissance* (Dublin:

Talbot Press; New York: John Lane, 1916). New Revised Edition (New York: Alfred A. Knopf, 1922, rpt. Dublin: Allen Figgis, 1968)

Includes chapters on the Irish dramatic movement.

319   —. *Appreciations and Depreciations: Irish Literary Studies* (Dublin: Talbot Press, 1917; London: T. Fisher Unwin; New York: John Lane, 1918; rpt. Freeport, New York: Books for Libraries Press, 1968)

Includes chapters on George Russell, Lord Dunsany, and Bernard Shaw.

320   —. *The Contemporary Drama of Ireland* (Dublin: Talbot Press; London: T. Fisher Unwin, 1918; Boston: Little, Brown, 1928)

Survey and chapters on Edward Martyn, W. B. Yeats, J. M. Synge, Padraic Colum, Lady Gregory, William Boyle, George Fitzmaurice, Seamus O'Kelly, Lord Dunsany, Lennox Robinson, and the Ulster Literary Theatre.

321   Bradbrook, M. C. *English Dramatic Form: A History of Its Development* (London: Chatto & Windus; New York: Barnes & Noble, 1965)

Includes studies of W. B. Yeats and Samuel Beckett.

322   Brahms, Caryl. *The Rest of the Evening's My Own* (London: W. H. Allen, 1964)

Includes commentaries on plays by Bernard Shaw, J. M. Synge, and Samuel Beckett.

323   Brawley, Benjamin. *A Short History of the English Drama* (London: George G. Harrap, 1921; rpt. Freeport, New York: Books for Libraries Press, 1969)

Includes chapters on Bernard Shaw, Lady Gregory, W. B. Yeats, and J. M. Synge.

324 Bridgewater, Patrick. *Nietzsche in Anglosaxony: A Study of Nietzsche's Impact on English and American Literature* (Leicester: Leicester University Press, 1972)

Includes discussions on Bernard Shaw and W. B. Yeats.

325 Brockett, Oscar G. "The Irish Renaissance," *History of the Theatre* (Boston: Allyn and Bacon, 1968), pp. 576-578

Survey.

326 --, and Robert R. Findlay. *Century of Innovation: A History of European and American Theatre and Drama Since 1870* (Englewood Cliffs, New Jersey: Prentice-Hall, 1973), pp. 160-170, 479-484

Survey.

327 Brook, Donald. *The Romance of the English Theatre* (London: Rockliff, 1945; rev. ed., 1952), chap. XII

Includes studies of the Abbey Theatre, W. B. Yeats, J. M. Synge, and Sean O'Casey.

328 Brooks, Cleanth, and Robert B. Heilman. *Understanding Drama; Twelve Plays* (New York: Henry Holt, 1945; rpt., 1948)

Includes short studies of plays by Bernard Shaw and J. M. Synge.

329 -- *et. al.*, eds. *An Approach to Literature*, 5th ed. (Englewood Cliffs, New Jersey: Prentice-Hall, 1975)

Includes plays, with commentaries, by Bernard Shaw and Samuel Beckett.

330   Brooks, Van Wyck. "Impressions of Ireland," *From the Shadow of the Mountain; My Post-Meridian Years* (New York: E. P. Dutton, 1961), pp. 138-161

       Includes reflections on the Irish drama.

331   Brown, Ivor. *Theatre 1954-5* (London: Max Reinhardt, 1955)

       Includes studies of Sean O'Casey and Bernard Shaw.

332   Brown, Malcolm. *The Politics of Irish Literature: From Thomas Davis to W. B. Yeats* (London: George Allen & Unwin; Seattle: University of Washington Press, 1972)

       Touches on a few plays by W. B. Yeats, Lady Gregory, J. M. Synge, and Sean O'Casey.

333   Browne, E. Martin, ed. "Introduction," *Three Irish Plays* (Harmondsworth: Penguin, 1959)

       Anthology including an introduction and plays by Denis Johnston, Joseph O'Conor, and Donagh MacDonagh.

334   Brustein, Robert. *Seasons of Discontent; Dramatic Opinions 1959-1965* (New York: Simon and Schuster, 1965; London: Jonathan Cape, 1966)

       Includes criticism on plays by Samuel Beckett and Brendan Behan.

335   —. "Two Plays about Ireland," *The Culture Watch; Essays on Theatre and Society, 1969-1974* (New York: Alfred A. Knopf, 1975), pp. 53-56.

336   Bryant, Sophie. "The Gael in Literature," *The Genius of the Gael: A Study in Celtic Psychology and Its Manifestations* (London: T. Fisher Unwin, 1913), pp. 181-218

Background to the Irish drama.

337　Burton, E. J. *The Student's Guide to British Theatre and Drama* (London: Herbert Jenkins, 1963), pp. 150-156

Survey of the Irish drama.

338　Byrne, Dawson. *The Story of Ireland's National Theatre: The Abbey Theatre, Dublin* (Dublin: Talbot Press, 1929; rpt. New York: Haskell House, 1971)

Survey and chapters on J. M. Synge and Sean O'Casey.

339　Cahill, Susan, and Thomas Cahill. *A Literary Guide to Ireland* (New York: Charles Scribner's, 1973)

Includes background to the Irish drama.

340　Calderwood, James L., and Harold E. Toliver, eds. *Forms of Drama* (Englewood Cliffs, New Jersey: Prentice-Hall, 1969)

Anthology including plays, with commentaries, by W. B. Yeats, Bernard Shaw, and Samuel Beckett.

341　--, eds. *Forms of Tragedy* (Englewood Cliffs, New Jersey: Prentice-Hall, 1972)

Anthology including plays, with commentaries, by J. M. Synge and W. B. Yeats.

342　Canfield, Curtis, ed. *Plays of the Irish Renaissance 1880-1930* (London: Macmillan; New York: Ives Washburn, 1929; rpt. 1932, 1938, 1974)

Anthology of plays, with commentaries, by W. B. Yeats, George William Russell, Lady Gregory, Douglas Hyde, George Fitzmaurice, J. M. Synge, Padraic Colum, T. C. Murray, Padraic Pearse, Edward Martyn, Sean O'Casey, and Lennox Robinson.

343   –, ed. *Plays of Changing Ireland* (New York: Macmillan, 1936)

> Anthology of plays, with commentaries, by W. B. Yeats, Denis Johnston, Lennox Robinson, Lord Longford, George Shiels, Lady Longford, Mary Manning, and Rutherford Mayne.

344   Capan, Cevat. *Irlanda tiyatrosunda gercekcilik* (Istanbul: Istanbul Metbaasi, 1966)

> Irish dramatic realism, especially in J. M. Synge and Sean O'Casey.

345   Carpenter, Bruce. *The Way of the Drama; A Study of Dramatic Forms and Moods* (New York: Prentice-Hall, 1929)

> Includes studies of plays by J. M. Synge and W. B. Yeats.

346   Carroll, Paul Vincent. "The Irish Theatre (Post War)," *International Theatre*, ed. John Andrews and Ossia Trilling (London: Sampson Low, 1949), pp. 122-128

> Survey.

347   Chandler, Frank Wadleigh. "Irish Plays of Mysticism and Folk History" and "Irish Plays of the Peasantry," *Aspects of Modern Drama* (New York: Macmillan, 1914; rpt. 1916, 1924), chaps. XI and XII

> Also includes a chapter on Bernard Shaw.

348   Chanel [i. e. Clery, Arthur Edward]. *The Idea of a Nation* (Dublin: Duffy, 1907)

> Includes "After the Abbey Is Over", pp. 17-19 and "The Philosophy of an Irish Theatre," pp. 48-51.

349   Chew, Samuel C., and Richard D. Altick. "The Irish Literary Renaissance," *The Nineteenth Century and After*

(1789-1939), ed. Albert C. Baugh (New York: Appleton-Century-Crofts, 1948; 2nd ed., 1967), pp. 1507-
1515

Survey.

350   Chiari, J. *Landmarks of Contemporary Drama* (London:
Herbert Jenkins, 1965; New York: Hillary House,
1966; rpt. New York: Gordian Press, 1971)

Includes studies of Samuel Beckett and W. B. Yeats.

351   Chrisholm, Cecil. *Repertory: An Outline of the Modern
Theatre Movement* (London: Peter Davis, 1934)

Includes brief discussion on the Abbey Theatre and some of its
dramatists.

352   Chrislett, William, Jr. *Moderns and Near Moderns* (London:
Grafton Press; New York: Hitchcock, 1928)

Includes studies of J. M. Synge, Lady Gregory, W. B. Yeats,
Lord Dunsany, and Bernard Shaw.

353   Clark, Barrett H. *The British and American Drama of Today*
(New York: Henry Holt, 1915; rpt. AMS Press, 1971)

Includes study outlines of plays by Bernard Shaw, W. B. Yeats,
J. M. Synge, Lady Gregory, T. C. Murray, and St. John Ervine.

354   --. "The Irish Drama," *A Study of the Modern Drama*. New
Edition (New York and London: D. Appleton-Cen-
tury, 1936), pp. 329-357

A study of plays by W. B. Yeats, J. M. Synge, Lady Gregory,
Lord Dunsany, St. John Ervine, and Bernard Shaw.

355   —, ed. *Representative One-Act Plays by British and Irish
Authors* (Boston: Little, Brown, 1921)

Includes plays, with commentaries, by W. B. Yeats, J. M. Synge, Lady Gregory, St. John Ervine, and Lord Dunsany.

356   Clark, William S. "The Rise of the Irish Theater and Drama," *Chief Patterns of World Drama: Aeschylus to Anderson* (Boston: Houghton Mifflin, 1946), pp. 887-890

Survey.

357   Clarke, Austin. *Twice Round the Black Church; Early Memories of Ireland and England* (London: Routledge & Kegan Paul, 1962)

Includes background to the Irish drama.

358   Clayes, Stanley, ed. *Drama & Discussion* (New York: Appleton-Century-Crofts, 1967)

Anthology including plays, with commentaries, by J. M. Synge, Bernard Shaw, and Samuel Beckett.

359   —, and David Spencer, eds. *Contemporary Drama: 13 Plays* (New York: Charles Scribner's, 1962)

Anthology including plays, with commentaries, by Bernard Shaw and Sean O'Casey.

360   Cleaver, James. "The English Theatre of the Twentieth Century," *Theatre Through the Ages* (New York: Hart Publishing Co., 1967)

Includes studies of Bernard Shaw, the Abbey Theatre, Sean O'Casey, the Dublin Gate Theatre, and Irish actors.

361   Clurman, Harold. *Lies Like Truth; Theatre Reviews and Essays* (New York and London: Macmillan, 1958)

Includes reviews of plays by Sean O'Casey, Samuel Beckett, and Bernard Shaw.

362 —. *Seven Plays of the Modern Theater* (New York: Grove
Press, 1962)

> Anthology including an introduction and plays by Samuel
> Beckett and Brendan Behan.

363 —. *The Naked Image; Observations on the Modern Theatre*
(New York: Macmillan; London: Collier-Macmillan,
1966)

> Includes studies of Samuel Beckett and Brendan Behan.

364 —. *The Divine Pastime; Theatre Essays* (New York: Macmillan; London: Collier-Macmillan, 1974)

> Includes essays on Samuel Beckett and Bernard Shaw.

365 Chochran, Charles B. *Showman Looks On* (London: J. M.
Dent, 1945)

> Includes references to Samuel Beckett, Sean O'Casey, and
> Bernard Shaw.

366 Cohen, Helen Louise. "The Irish National Theatre," *One-
Act Plays by Modern Authors* (New York: Harcourt,
Brace, 1921), pp. xxvi-xxix

> Introductory survey. Anthology including plays, with commen-
> taries, by Lady Gregory, J. M. Synge, and Lord Dunsany.

367 Cohn, Ruby, and Bernard Dukore, eds. *Twentieth Century
Drama: England, Ireland and the United States* (New
York: Random House, 1966)

> Anthology including plays, with commentaries, by Bernard
> Shaw, J. M. Synge, W. B. Yeats, and Samuel Beckett.

368 Cole, Toby, ed. *Playwrights on Playwriting; The Meaning
and Making of Modern Drama from Ibsen to Ionesco*

(London: MacGibbon & Kee, 1960; New York: Hill &
Wang, 1961)

An anthology including writings by W. B. Yeats, Bernard Shaw,
J. M. Synge, and Sean O'Casey.

369   Collins, A. S. *English Literature of the Twentieth Century*
      (London: University Tutorial Press, 1951; rpt. 1965)

Includes a survey of the Irish drama and chapters on W. B.
Yeats, Bernard Shaw, and James Joyce.

370   Colum, Mary. *Life and the Dream* (London: Macmillan;
      Garden City, New York: Doubleday, 1947; rev. ed.
      Dublin: Dolmen Press; London: Oxford University
      Press, 1966)

Includes "Early Days of the Abbey Theatre," "Lady Gregory
of the Abbey Theatre," and "The Yeats I Knew."

371   Colum, Padraic. *My Irish Year* (London: Mills & Boon, 1912)

Contains background to the Irish drama.

372   —. *The Road Round Ireland* (New York: Macmillan, 1926)

Includes chapters on the Abbey Theatre and J. M. Synge.

373   Connery, Donald S. *The Irish* (New York: Simon and Schus-
      ter, 1968), pp. 234-238 and *passim*

The Abbey Theatre.

374   Coogan, Timothy Patrick. *Ireland Since the Rising* (New
      York and London: Frederick A. Praeger, 1966)

Background and references to the Irish drama.

375   Corkery, Daniel. "On Anglo-Irish Literature," *Synge and
      Anglo-Irish Literature; A Study* (Dublin and Cork:

Cork University Press; London: Longmans, Green, 1931; Cork: Mercier Press, 1966), pp. 1-27

Background to the Irish drama.

376 Corrigan, Robert W., ed. "England and Ireland," *The Modern Theatre* (New York: Macmillan, 1964), pp. 877-1072

Anthology including plays, with commentaries, by Samuel Beckett, W. B. Yeats, J. M. Synge, Sean O'Casey, and Bernard Shaw.

377 —, ed. *Masterpieces of the Modern Irish Theatre* (New York: Collier Books, 1967)

Anthology including an introduction, "The Irish Dramatic Flair," and plays, with commentaries, by W. B. Yeats, J. M. Synge, and Sean O'Casey.

378 —, ed. *Comedy: A Critical Anthology* (Boston: Houghton Mifflin, 1971)

Includes plays, with commentaries, by J. M. Synge and Bernard Shaw.

379 —. *The Theatre in Search of a Fix* (New York: Delacorte Press, 1973)

Includes studies of Bernard Shaw, Samuel Beckett, and J. M. Synge.

380 —, and James L. Rosenberg, eds. *The Context and Craft of Drama; Critical Essays on the Nature of Drama and Theatre* (San Francisco: Chandler Publishing Co., 1964)

An anthology including contributions by Bernard Shaw and Sean O'Casey.

381 Corsani, Mary. *Il Nuovo Teatro Inglese* (Milan: U. Mursia,

1970)

Includes studies of Samuel Beckett, Brendan Behan, and Sean O'Casey.

382   Costello, Peter. *The Heart Grown Brutal, The Irish Revolu-
       tion in Literature from Parnell to the Death of Yeats,
       1891-1939* (Dublin: Gill and Macmillan; Totowa,
       New Jersey: Rowman and Littlefield, 1977)

Includes discussions of Brendan Behan, Daniel Corkery, Oliver St. John Gogarty, Lady Gregory, James Joyce, Sean O'Casey, Frank O'Connor, Sean O'Faolain, Bernard Shaw, J. M. Synge, Jack B. Yeats, and W. B. Yeats.

383   Courtney, Marie-Thérèse. *Edward Martyn and the Irish
       Theatre* (New York: Vantage Press, 1956).

384   Cowell, Raymond. *Twelve Modern Dramatists* (Oxford:
       Pergamon Press, 1967)

Includes essays on Bernard Shaw, J. M. Synge, Sean O'Casey, and Samuel Beckett.

385   Coxhead, Elizabeth. *J. M. Synge and Lady Gregory*. Writers
       and Their Work No. 149 (London: Longmans, Green
       for the British Council and the National Book League,
       1962; rev. ed., 1969)

Introduction and select bibliography.

386   Cronin, Anthony. *Dead As Doornails; A Chronicle of Life*
       (Dublin: Dolmen Press; London: Calder & Boyars,
       1976)

Includes recollections of Brendan Behan and Brian O'Nolan.

387   Cunliffe, John W. "The Irish Movement," *English Literature
       During the Last Half-Century* (London and New York:

Macmillan, 1919; rpt. Freeport, New York: Books for Libraries Press, 1971)

Survey.

388 —. *Modern English Playwrights; A Short History of the English Drama from 1925* (New York and London: Harper, 1927; rpt. Port Washington, New York: Kennikat Press, 1969)

Includes chapters on Bernard Shaw, J. M. Synge, St. John Ervine, Lord Dunsany, and Sean O'Casey.

389 —. "The Irish Renaissance," *English Literature in the Twentieth Century* (New York: Macmillan, 1933)

Survey containing background to the Irish drama.

390 Curran, C. P. *Under the Receding Wave* (Dublin: Gill and Macmillan, 1970)

Includes an account of the early years of the Abbey Theatre.

391 Dace, Letitia, and Wallace Dace. *Modern Theatre and Drama* (New York: Richards Rosen Press, 1973)

Includes chapters on Bernard Shaw and The Abbey Theatre.

392 Dalgard, Olav. *Teatret i Det 20. Hundrearet* (Oslo: Norske Samlget, 1955)

Includes studies of W. B. Yeats, J. M. Synge, Bernard Shaw, and Sean O'Casey.

393 Darlington, W. A. *Through the Fourth Wall* (London: Chapman and Hall, 1922; rpt. New York: Brentano's, 1933)

Includes essays on Lord Dunsany and Bernard Shaw.

394   Daubeny, Peter. "Irish Theatre," *My World of Theatre*
      (London: Jonathan Cape, 1971), pp. 278-289

      Production of Irish plays.

395   Day, Martin S. "The Celtic Renaissance," *History of English
      Literature 1837 to the Present* (Garden City, New
      York: Doubleday, 1964), pp. 237-261

      Survey.

396   De Blácam, Aodh. *A First Book of Irish Literature* (Dublin
      and Cork: Talbot Press, [1934])

      Includes background to the Irish drama.

397   Dédéyan, Charles. *Le Nouveau Mal du Siècle*, vol. 2 (Paris:
      Société d Édition d' Enseignement Supérieur, 1972)

      Includes studies of J. M. Synge, W. B. Yeats, and Bernard
      Shaw.

398   Dent, Alan. "Notes at an Irish Festival," *Preludes and Studies*
      (London: Macmillan, 1942; rpt. Port Washington,
      New York: Kennikat Press, 1970), pp. 155-163

      In Dublin.

399   --. *Nocturnes and Rhapsodies* (London: Hamish Hamilton,
      1950)

      Includes reviews of plays by Sean O'Casey and Bernard Shaw.

400   Dickinson, P. L. "The Theatre," *The Dublin of Yesterday*
      (London: Methuen, 1929), pp. 82-98

      Covers the period 1904-1914.

401   Dickinson, Thomas H. *An Outline of Contemporary Drama*

(Boston: Houghton Mifflin, 1927; rpt. New York: Biblo and Tannen, 1969)

Includes studies of Bernard Shaw and of The Irish National Theatre.

402 —, ed. *Chief Contemporary Dramatists*. First Series (Boston: Houghton Mifflin, 1915)

Anthology including plays, with commentaries, by W. B. Yeats, J. M. Synge, and Lady Gregory.

403 *Did You Know That the Gate. . . ?* (Dublin: The Gate Theatre, 1940)

A 12-page pamphlet summarizing the history of the Theatre and giving a list of the productions of the first thirteen seasons.

404 Dietrich, Margret. *Das Moderne Drama: Stromungen-Gestalten-Motive* (Stuttgart: Alfred Kroner 1961)

Includes studies of St. John Ervine, Sean O'Casey, Bernard Shaw, J. M. Synge, Samuel Beckett, and W. B. Yeats.

405 Dietrich, R. F., William E. Carpenter, and Kevin Kerrane, eds. *The Art of Drama*, 2nd ed. (New York: Holt, Rinehart and Winston, 1976)

Anthology including plays, with commentaries, by Bernard Shaw and Samuel Beckett.

406 Dodson, Daniel, ed. *Twelve Modern Plays* (Belmont, California: Wadsworth Publishing Company, 1970)

Anthology including plays, with commentaries, by Bernard Shaw and J. M. Synge.

407 Dolan, Paul J., and M. Grace, eds. *Introduction to Drama* (New York: Wiley, 1974)

Includes plays, with commentaries, by W. B. Yeats and Bernard Shaw.

408 Dooley, Roger B. *Modern British and Irish Drama*. Monarch Review Notes & Study Guide Series, No. 624 (New York: Thor Publications, 1964)

Introductory.

409 Downer, Alan S. *The British Drama; A Handbook and Brief Chronicle* (New York: Appleton-Century-Crofts, 1950)

Includes chapters on Bernard Shaw and "The Abbey Theatre Dramatists."

410 Drescher, Horst W. "British Literature," *World Literature Since 1945*, ed. Ivar Ivask and Gero von Wilpert (New York: Frederick Ungar, 1973)

Includes brief discussions on Samuel Beckett, Brendan Behan, J. P. Donleavy, and Sean O'Casey.

411 Drew, Elizabeth. *Discovering Drama* (New York: W. W. Norton; London: Jonathan Cape, 1937)

Includes studies of Bernard Shaw and W. B. Yeats.

412 Drimba, Ovidiu. "Teatrul irlandez şi englez [The Irish and English Theatre]," *Teatrul de la origini şi pîna azi* (Bucharest: Albatros, 1973), pp. 342-344

Brief survey.

413 Drinkwater, John. *The Gentle Art of Theatre-Going* (London: Robert Holden; Boston and New York: Ernest Benn, 1927)

Includes studies of Sean O'Casey and Bernard Shaw.

414   Driver, Tom F. *Romantic Quest and Modern Query; A History of the Modern Theatre* (New York: Delacorte Press, 1970)

> Includes studies of Bernard Shaw, Samuel Beckett, J. M. Synge, and W. B. Yeats.

415   Duggan, G. C. *The Stage Irishman; A History of the Irish Play and Stage Characters from the Earliest Times* (Dublin and Cork: Talbot Press; London: Longmans, 1937)

> Survey.

416   Dukes, Ashley. *The Youngest Drama; Studies of Fifty Dramatists* (London: Ernest Benn, 1923; Chicago: Charles H. Sergel, 1924; rpt. Folcroft, Pennsylvania: Folcroft Press, 1969)

> Includes essays on Bernard Shaw, J. M. Synge, and St. John Ervine.

417   ⸺. *The Scene Is Changed* (London: Macmillan, 1942)

> Includes discussions on plays by J. M. Synge and Bernard Shaw.

418   Dukore, Bernard F., ed. "Nineteenth Century and Twentieth-Century England and Ireland," *Dramatic Theory and Criticism: Greeks to Grotowski* (New York: Holt, Rinehart and Winston, 1947), pp. 577-672

> Includes contributions by Bernard Shaw, W. B. Yeats, and J. M. Synge.

419   ⸺, ed. *17 Plays: Sophocles to Baraka* (New York: Thomas Y. Crowell, 1976)

> Anthology including plays, with commentaries, by J. M. Synge and Bernard Shaw.

420   Duncan, George A. *The Abbey Theatre in Pictures* (Dublin:
       National Press Service of Ireland, 1962).

421   Dunsany, Lord. "Dublin," *My Ireland* (Leipzig: Tauchnitz,
       1938), pp. 226-236

       On the Abbey.

422   Duprey, Richard A. *Just Off the Aisle: The Ramblings of a
       Catholic Critic* (Westminster, Maryland: Newman
       Press, 1962)

       Includes studies of Paul Vincent Carroll and Brendan Behan.

423   Eaton, Walter Prichard. *The Drama in English* (New York:
       Charles Scribner's, 1930; London: Charles Scribner's,
       1931)

       Includes studies of Bernard Shaw, J. M. Synge, and Sean
       O'Casey.

424   Edwards, Hilton. *The Mantle of Harlequin* (Dublin: Progress
       House, 1958)

       On the Dublin Gate Theatre, including a list of Gate produc-
       tions up to 1958.

425   —. "The Irish Theatre," *A History of the Theatre*, by George
       Freedley and John A. Reeves, 3rd rev. ed. (New York:
       Crown Publishers, 1968), pp. 735-748

       Survey.

426   Eglinton, John. *Irish Literary Portraits* (London: Macmillan,
       1935)

       Includes chapters on W. B. Yeats, George Russell, George
       Moore, and James Joyce.

427   Ellis, Havelock. *From Marlowe to Shaw* (London: Williams and Norgate, 1950)

> Includes essays on Bernard Shaw and George Moore.

428   Ellis-Fermor, Una. *The Irish Dramatic Movement* (London: Methuen, 1939; 2nd rev. ed., 1954; rpt. London: University Paperbacks, 1967)

> Survey and chapters on W. B. Yeats, Edward Martyn, George Moore, Lady Gregory, and J. M. Synge.

429   Ellmann, Richard, ed. *Edwardians and Late Victorians* (New York and London: Columbia University Press, 1960)

> Includes studies of Bernard Shaw, W. B. Yeats, and George Moore.

430   —. *Golden Codgers; Biographical Speculations* (New York: Oxford University Press, 1973)

> Deals with James Joyce and W. B. Yeats, *passim.*

431   Elton, Oliver. "Living Irish Literature," *Modern Studies* (London: Edward Arnold, 1907), pp. 285-320

> Includes studies of W. B. Yeats, J. M. Synge, and Lady Gregory.

432   Ervine, St. John. *Some Impressions of My Elders* (London: George Allen & Unwin, 1923)

> Includes chapters on George Russell, George Moore, Bernard Shaw, and W. B. Yeats.

433   Erzgräber, Willi, ed. *Interpretationen 7-9: Englische Literatur*, 3 vols. (Frankfurt: Fischer Bücherei, 1970)

> Includes essays on the main Irish dramatists.

434   Esslin, Martin. *An Anatomy of Drama* (London: Temple Smith, 1976)

> Includes discussions on plays by Samuel Beckett and Bernard Shaw.

435   Evans, Gareth Lloyd. *The Langauge of Modern Drama* (London: Dent; Totowa, New Jersey: Rowman and Littlefield, 1977)

> Includes chapters on Bernard Shaw and W. B. Yeats.

436   Evans, Sir Ifor. *English Literature between the Wars* (London: Methuen, 1948; repr. 1949, 1951)

> Includes chapters on James Joyce and W. B. Yeats.

437   —. *A Short History of English Drama* (Harmondsworth: Penguin, 1948; rev. ed. London: Staples Press, 1950; rev. and enl. ed. Boston: Houghton Mifflin, 1965)

> Includes a survey of the Irish dramatic movement.

438   Fallis, Richard. *The Irish Renaissance* (Syracuse, New York: Syracuse University Press, 1977)

> Includes a survey of Irish drama.

439   Fallon, Gabriel, ed. *Abbey Theatre—Dublin 1904-1966* (Dublin: The National Theatre Society, 1966)

> A brochure to mark the opening of the new Abbey Theatre building in 1966.

440   —. *The Abbey and the Actor* (Dublin: The National Theatre Society, 1969)

> A booklet on "the historical background to what has come to be known as the Abbey Theatre acting tradition."

441 Fay, Frank J. *Towards a National Theatre: The Dramatic Criticism of Frank J. Fay*, ed. Robert Hogan. Irish Theatre Series, No. 1 (Dublin: Dolmen Press; London: Oxford University Press, 1970)

Selections from his reviews and essays on the Irish dramatic movement which appeared in *The United Irishman* from 1899 to 1902.

442 Fay, Gerard. "The Irish Theatre—A Decline and Perhaps, in the End, a Fall," *Theatre in Review*, ed. Frederick Lumley (Edinburgh: Richard Paterson, 1956), pp. 80-89

It is questionable "whether such a thing as 'the Irish theatre' now exists."

443 —. *The Abbey Theatre, Cradle of Genius* (Dublin: Clonmore & Reynolds; London: Hollis & Carter, 1958)

A history by the son of the Abbey actor Frank Fay, concentrating on the period 1902-1908.

444 Fay, William George. *Merely Players* (London: Rich & Cowan, 1932)

Background to the Irish drama by a leading Irish actor.

445 —, and Catherine Carswell. *The Fays of the Abbey Theatre; An Autobiographical Record* (London: Rich & Cowan; New York: Harcourt, Brace, 1935)

Also contains "List of First Productions, with Casts."

446 Fechter, Paul. *Das Europaische Drama: Geist und Kultur im Spiegel des Theatres*, 3 vols. (Mannheim: Bibliographisches Institut Ag., 1956-58)

Includes studies of Sean O'Casey, T. C. Murray, W. B. Yeats, Bernard Shaw, J. M. Synge, and Samuel Beckett.

447   Fehse, Klaus-Dieter, and Norbert H. Platz, eds. *Dan Zeit-*
      genössische Englische Drama: Einführung, Interpre-
      tation, Dokumentation (Frankfurt: Athenäum, 1975)

      Includes studies of plays by Brendan Behan and Samuel Beck-
      ett.

448   Figgis, Darrell. *Studies and Appreciations* (London: J. M.
      Dent; New York: Dutton, 1912)

      Includes studies of J. M. Synge and W. B. Yeats.

449   Findlater, Richard. *The Unholy Trade* (London: Victor
      Gollancz, 1952)

      Includes studies of Sean O'Casey and Bernard Shaw.

450   Flanagan, Hallie. "Erin," *Shifting Scenes of the Modern*
      European Theatre (New York: Coward-McCann,
      1928; London: Harrap, 1929; rpt. New York: Ben-
      jamin Blom, 1972), pp. 19-43

      Reflections on the Irish drama.

451   Flannery, James W. *Miss Annie F. Horniman and the Abbey*
      Theatre. Irish Theatre Series, No. 3 (Dublin: Dolmen
      Press; London: Oxford University Press, 1970).

452   —. *W. B. Yeats and the Idea of a Theatre; The Early Abbey*
      Theatre in Theory and Practice (New Haven and Lon-
      don: Yale University Press, 1976)

      Analyses the development of Yeats's aesthetic of the theatre
      and his intention that the Abbey be the matrix of an indigenous
      Irish national culture.

453   Ford, Boris, ed. *The Pelican Guide to English Literature*,
      vol. 7: *The Modern Age*, 3rd ed. (Harmondsworth:
      Penguin, 1973)

Contains material on James Joyce, W. B. Yeats, and the Irish Theatre.

454 Franzen, Erick. *Formen des Modernen Dramas; Von der Illusions-buehne zum Antitheater* (Munich: C. H. Beck, 1961)

Includes references to Bernard Shaw and W. B. Yeats.

455 Fraser, G. S. "The Irish Dramatic Revival," *The Modern Writer and His World* (London: Derek Verschoyle, 1953; rev. ed. London: Andre Deutsch; Pelican Books, 1964; rpt., 1967), pp. 204-211

Survey.

456 Freedley, George. "Irish Drama," *A History of Modern Drama*, ed. Barrett H. Clark and George Freedley (New York: Appleton-Century-Crofts, 1947), pp. 216-232

Survey.

457 —, and John A. Reeves. "The Irish National Theatre (1899-1940)," *A History of the Theatre*. Third Revised Edition (New York: Crown Publishers, 1968), pp. 481-494

Survey.

458 Freedman, Morris, ed. *Essays in the Modern Drama* (Boston: D. C. Heath, 1964)

Includes essays on Bernard Shaw, Sean O'Casey, and Samuel Beckett.

459 —. *The Moral Impulse; Modern Drama from Ibsen to the Present* (Carbondale and Edwardsville: Southern Illinois University Press; London and Amsterdam: Feffer & Simon, 1967)

Includes studies of Bernard Shaw and Sean O'Casey.

460   Freyer, Grattan. "The Irish Contribution," *The Modern Age*. The Pelican Guide to English Literature 7, ed. Boris Ford (Harmondsworth: Penguin, 1961; rpt., 1966), pp. 196-208

Survey.

461   Fricker, Robert. *Das Moderne Englische Drama* (Göttingen: Vandenhoeck & Ruprecht, 1964)

Includes studies of Denis Johnston, James Joyce, Sean O'Casey, Bernard Shaw, J. M. Synge, W. B. Yeats, Samuel Beckett, and Brendan Behan.

462   Frow, Gerald, ed. *The Mermaid Theatre; The First Ten Years* (London: The Mermaid Theatre, 1969)

Includes records of productions of plays by Bernard Shaw and Sean O'Casey, 1959-1969.

463   Gaffney, Sylvester. *The Burning of the Abbey Theatre (or The Lament for the Queen's)* (Dublin: Walton, 1951)

Ballad set to music.

464   *Gaiety Theatre, 1871-1971: One Hundred Years of Gaiety* (Dublin: Gaiety Theatre, 1971) [A 36-page booklet.] Previous books on this Theatre include the 70th Anniversary volume (1941) [A 32-page booklet]; and the 75th anniversary one (1946) [A 46-page booklet.]

465   Garzilli, Enrico. *Circles Without Center: Paths to the Discovery and Creation of Self in Modern Literature* (Cambridge, Massachusetts: Harvard University Press, 1972)

Deals in part with Samuel Beckett and James Joyce.

466   Gascoigne, Bamber. *Twentieth-Century Drama* (London: Hutchinson University Library, 1962; New York: Barnes & Noble, 1968)

Includes studies of Brendan Behan and Samuel Beckett.

467   Gaskell, Ronald. *Drama and Reality: The Euorpean Theatre Since Ibsen* (London: Routledge & Kegan Paul, 1972)

Includes studies of plays by J. M. Synge and Samuel Beckett.

468   Gassner, John. *Masters of the Drama*. Third Revised and Enlarged Edition (New York: Dover Publications, 1954)

Includes chapters on J. M. Synge, Bernard Shaw, Sean O'Casey, and Paul Vincent Carroll.

469   —. *The Theatre in Our Times; A Survey of the Men, Materials and Movements in the Modern Theatre* (New York: Crown Publishers, 1954)

Includes studies of Bernard Shaw, J. M. Synge, W. B. Yeats, and the Dublin Gate Theatre.

470   —. *Theatre at the Crossroads; Plays and Playwrights of the Mid-Century American Stage* (New York: Holt, Rinehart and Winston, 1960)

Includes studies of Bernard Shaw, Sean O'Casey, Samuel Beckett, and James Joyce.

471   —. *Dramatic Soundings; Evaluations and Retractions Culled from 30 Years of Dramatic Criticism*, ed. Glenn Loney (New York: Crown Publishers, 1968)

Includes studies of Bernard Shaw and Samuel Beckett.

472 —, and Ralph G. Allen. *Theatre and Drama in the Making*
     (Boston: Houghton Mifflin, 1964)

>   Anthology of dramatic method including contributions by
>   W. B. Yeats, J. M. Synge, and Bernard Shaw.

473 —, and Bernard F. Dukore, eds. *A Treasury of the Theatre,
     Vol. II: From Henrik Ibsen to Robert Lowell* (New
     York: Simon and Schuster, 1970)

>   Anthology including plays, with commentaries, by Bernard
>   Shaw, J. M. Synge, Sean O'Casey, and W. B. Yeats.

474 —, and Morris Sweetkind, eds. *Introducing the Drama* (New
     York: Rinehart and Winston, 1963)

>   Anthology including plays, with commentaries, by Lord Dun-
>   sany and Bernard Shaw.

475 Gilder, Rosamond, *et al*, eds. *Theatre Arts Anthology; A
     Record and a Prophecy* (New York: Theatre Arts
     Books, 1950)

>   Includes articles on W. B. Yeats, Sean O'Casey, and Bernard
>   Shaw.

476 Gill, Richard. *Happy Rural Seat: The English Country
     House and the Literary Imagination* (New Haven:
     Yale University Press, 1972)

>   Deals in part with Bernard Shaw, W. B. Yeats, and Lady Greg-
>   ory.

477 Gilliatt, Penelope. *Unholy Fools; Wits, Comics, Disturbers
     of the Peace: Film and Theatre* (London: Secker &
     Warburg; New York: Viking Press, 1973)

>   Includes criticism on plays by Samuel Beckett and Bernard
>   Shaw.

478 Gillie, Christopher. "Drama 1900-1940," *Movements in English Literature 1900-1940* (Cambridge: Cambridge University Press, 1975), pp. 164-177

Includes discussions on Bernard Shaw, W. B. Yeats, J. M. Synge, and Sean O'Casey.

479 Goetsch, Paul, ed. *English Dramatic Theories; 20th Century* (Tübingen: Max Niemeyer, 1972)

An anthology including dramatic writings by Bernard Shaw, W. B. Yeats, J. M. Synge, and Sean O'Casey.

480 Gogarty, Oliver St. John. *As I Was Going Down Sackville Street* (London: Reynal; New York: Ryerson Press, 1937; rpt. London: Sphere Books, 1968)

Includes reflections on the Irish drama.

481 Goldman, Emma. *The Social Significance of the Modern Drama* (Boston: Richard G. Badger; Toronto: Copp Clark, 1914)

Includes chapters on Bernard Shaw, W. B. Yeats, Lennox Robinson, and T. C. Murray.

482 Goldman, Mark, and Isadore Traschen, eds. *The Drama: Traditional and Modern* (Boston: Allyn and Bacon, 1968)

Anthology including plays, with commentaries, by Bernard Shaw and Samuel Beckett.

483 Goldstone, Richard H., and Abraham H. Lass, eds. *The Mentor Book of Short Plays* (New York: The New American Library, 1969)

Anthology including plays, with commentaries, by J. M. Synge and Lady Gregory.

484 Gottfried, Martin. *Opening Nights; Theater Criticism of the Sixties* (New York: G. P. Putnam's 1969)

> Includes criticism on plays by Samuel Beckett and Bernard Shaw.

485 Gowda, H. H. Anniah. *Dramatic Poetry from Mediaeval to Modern Times* (Madra: Macmillan, 1972), pp. 273-293

> Deals with J. M. Synge, W. B. Yeats, Sean O'Casey, and James Joyce.

486 Gozenpud, A. *Puti i Pereput'ya. Angliiskaya i Frantszskaya Dramaturgiya xxv.* [Roads and cross-roads. English and French 20th century drama] (Leningrad: Iskusstvo, 1967)

> Includes studies of James Joyce, Sean O'Casey, Bernard Shaw, Samuel Beckett, and Brendan Behan.

487 Graves, A. P. "Anglo-Irish Literature," *The Cambridge History of English Literature*, ed. A. W. Ward and A. R. Waller (Cambridge: Cambridge University Press, 1964), pp. 14, 329-330

> Survey.

488 Gray, Tony. *The Irish Answer: An Anatomy of Modern Ireland* (London: Heinemann, 1966), pp. 255-256

> A note on the "dreary but comfortable routine" at the Abbey Theatre.

489 Grebanier, Bernard D. N. *The Essentials of English Literature, vol. 2: The Nineteenth Century to the Present* (Woodbury, New York: Barron's 1948)

> Includes studies of James Joyce, W. B. Yeats, Bernard Shaw, J. M. Synge, and Sean O'Casey.

490 Greene, David H., ed. "Introduction," *An Anthology of Irish Literature* (New York: Modern Library, 1954; New York: University Press, 1971)

>Includes discussion on the Irish drama.

491 Gregory, Anne. *Me and Nu: Childhood at Coole* (Gerrards Gross, Buckinghamshire: Colin Smythe, 1970)

>Describes visits to Coole Park by W. B. Yeats, Jack B. Yeats, George Russell, Douglas Hyde, Sean O'Casey, J. M. Synge, and Bernard Shaw.

492 Gregory, Lady [Isabella Augusta]. *Our Irish Theatre* (New York and London: G. P. Putnam, 1914; rpt. New York: Capricorn Books, 1965; rev. enl. ed. with foreword by Roger McHugh, New York: Oxford University Press, 1973)

>Survey and chapters on Synge.

493 —. *Journals 1916-1930*, ed. Lennox Robinson (London: G. P. Putnam, 1946; New York: Macmillan, 1947)

>Includes material on the Irish drama, particularly pp. 51-126 "The Abbey Theatre."

494 —. *Seventy Years 1852-1922*, ed. Colin Smythe (Gerrards Cross, Buckinghamshire: Colin Smythe, 1974)

>Includes material on the Irish drama.

495 Griffin, Gerald. *The Wild Geese; Pen Portraits of Famous Irish Exiles* (London: Jarrolds, [1938])

>Includes chapters on Bernard Shaw, James Joyce, George Moore, W. B. Yeats, Padraic Colum, and Sean O'Casey.

496 Groom, Bernard. *A Literary History of England* (London

and New York: Longmans, 1929)

Includes studies of Bernard Shaw and J. M. Synge.

497   Guerrero Zamora, Juan. *Historia del Teatro Contemporaneo*, 4 vols. (Barcelona: Juan Flors, 1961-67)

Includes chapters on W. B. Yeats, J. M. Synge, Sean O'Casey, Bernard Shaw, and Brendan Behan.

498   Guthrie, Tyrone. "Belfast" and "Ireland," *A Life in the Theatre* (London: Hamish Hamilton; New York: McGraw-Hill, 1960), chaps. 3 and 19

Reflections on the Irish drama.

499   Gwynn, Denis. "The Irish Literary Theatre," *Edward Martyn and the Irish Revival* (London: Jonathan Cape, 1930), pp. 109-170

Survey.

500   Gwynn, Stephen. "The Gaelic League and the Irish Theatre," *Today and Tomorrow in Ireland; Essays on Irish Subjects* (Dublin: Hodges, Figgis, London: Macmillan, 1903), pp. 87-96.

501   —. "The Irish Theatre," *Irish Literature*, ed. Justin Mac-Carthy (Chicago: John D. Morris, 1904)

Survey.

502   —. "Beginnings of the Irish Drama," *Irish Literature and Drama in the English Language; A Short History* (London: Thomas Nelson, 1936; rpt. Folcroft, Pennsylvania: Folcroft Press, 1969), chap. IX

Survey.

503   —. *Dublin Old and New* (New York: Macmillan, 1938), pp. 49-53

> On the Abbey Theatre.

504   Hale, John, ed. *Post-War Drama* (London: Faber & Faber, 1966)

> Includes extracts from plays, with commentaries, by Samuel Beckett and Brendan Behan.

505   Hamilton, Clayton. "The Irish National Theatre," *Studies in Stagecraft* (London: Grant Richards; New York: Henry Holt, 1914), pp. 123-144. Reprinted from *The Bookman* (New York), XXXIV (January 1912), 508-516

> Discusses the aims and achievements of the Irish National Theatre Society.

506   —. *The Theory of the Theatre and Other Principles of Dramatic Criticism* (New York: Henry Holt, 1939)

> Includes chapters on Bernard Shaw, St. John Ervine, Lord Dunsany, and the Irish National Theatre.

507   Haney, J. L. *English Literature* (New York: Harcourt, Brace, 1920)

> Includes discussions on Bernard Shaw, W. B. Yeats, J. M. Synge, and Lord Dunsany.

508   Harper, George Mills. *The Mingling of Heaven and Earth: Yeats's Theory of Theatre* (Dublin: The Dolmen Press, 1975), passim.

509   Harris, Frank. *Contemporary Portraits*. Four Series (New York: Privately printed, 1915-23)

Includes essays on Bernard Shaw, George Moore, and Lord Dunsany.

510   Hatcher, Harlan, ed. *A Modern Repertory* (New York: Harcourt, Brace & World, 1953)

Anthology including plays, with commentaries, by Bernard Shaw and Sean O'Casey.

511   Hatlen, Theodore W., ed. *Drama: Principles & Plays* (New York: Appleton-Century-Crofts, 1967)

Anthology including plays, with commentaries, by Bernard Shaw and Samuel Beckett.

512   Heffner, Hubert, ed. *The Nature of Drama* (Boston: Houghton Mifflin, 1959)

Anthology including plays, with commentaries, by Bernard Shaw and Sean O'Casey.

513   Heiney, Donald, and Lenthiel H. Downs. *Contemporary British Literature* (Woodbury, New York: Barron's Educational Series, 1974)

Includes introductory discussions on James Joyce, W. B. Yeats, J. M. Synge, Lady Gregory, Sean O'Casey, Brendan Behan, Lord Dunsany, Paul Vincent Carroll, Bernard Shaw, and Louis MacNeice.

514   Henderson, W. A. *1909: The Irish National Theatre Movement: A Year's Work at the Abbey Theatre* (Dublin: Privately printed, 1909)

Told in press-cuttings.

515   Henn, T. R. *The Harvest of Tragedy* (London: Methuen, 1956; University Paperbacks; New York: Barnes & Noble, 1966)

Includes chapters on Bernard Shaw and on "The Irish Tragedy".

516 —. *Last Essays* (Gerrards Cross, Buckinghamshire: Colin Smythe, 1976)

Includes essays on W. B. Yeats, George Russell, George Moore, and J. M. Synge.

517 Hewitt, Barnard. *History of the Theatre from 1800 to the Present* (New York: Random House, 1970), pp. 69-70, 76-77

Brief survey of the Abbey Theatre.

518 Hickey, Des, and Gus Smith. *A Paler Shade of Green* (London: Leslie Frewin, 1972). American edition entitled *Flight from the Celtic Twilight* (Indianapolis: Bobbs-Merrill, 1973)

Includes interviews with, or recollections of Padraic Colum, Denis Johnston, Micháel MacLiammóire, Hilton Edwards, Cyril Cusack, Sean O'Casey, Brendan Behan, F. J. McCormick, Siobhan McKenna, Dan O'Herlihy, Jack MacGowran, Tyrone Guthrie, Anna Manahan, Richard Harris, Donal Donnelly, T. P. McKenna, Norman Rodway, Milo O'Shea, Hugh Leonard, Sean Kenny, Tom Murphy, Brian Friel, and Conor Cruise O'Brien.

519 Hinchcliffe, Arnold P. *Modern Verse Drama* (London: Methuen, 1977)

Includes discussions of plays by Samuel Beckett, Louis MacNeice, J. M. Synge, and W. B. Yeats.

520 Hind, C. Lewis. *Authors and I* (London: John Lane, 1920)

Includes essays on Lord Dunsany, George Moore, Bernard Shaw, and W. B. Yeats.

521 —. *More Authors and I* (London: John Lane, 1922)

Includes essays on St. John Ervine, George Russell, and J. M. Synge.

522   Hobson, Bulmer, ed. *The Gate Theatre, Dublin* (Dublin: Gate Theatre, 1934)

On the productions of the Dublin Gate Theatre since 1928.

523   Hobson, Harold. *Theatre* (London and New York: Longmans, Green, 1948)

Includes criticism on plays by Sean O'Casey, Bernard Shaw, Denis Johnston, and St. John Ervine.

524   —. *Verdict at Midnight; Sixty Years of Dramatic Criticism* (London and New York: Longmans, Green, 1952)

Includes criticism on plays by Bernard Shaw and Sean O'Casey.

525   Hobson, James Landsdale. *No Phantoms Here* (London: Faber and Faber, 1932)

Includes essays on Sean O'Casey and Bernard Shaw.

526   Hogan, Robert. *After the Irish Renaissance; A Critical History of the Irish Drama Since "The Plough and the Stars"* (Minneapolis: University of Minnesota Press, 1967; rpt. London: Macmillan, 1968)

An "informal critical account". Includes chapters on Paul Vincent Carroll, Brendan Behan, John B. Keane, Sean O'Casey, Michael J. Molloy, Denis Johnston, George Fitzmaurice, the Dublin Gate Theatre, and the theatre in Ulster.

527   —. ed. *Seven Irish Plays, 1946-1964* (Minneapolis: University of Minnesota Press, 1967)

Anthology including an introduction, "Pull Back the Green Curtains;" and plays, with commentaries, by John O'Donovan, John B. Keane, and James Douglas.

528 —. "Where Have All the Shamrocks Gone?" *Aspects of the Irish Theatre,* ed. Patrick Rafroidi, Raymonde Popot, and William Parker (Lille: Publications de l'Université de Lille; Paris: Editions Universitaires, 1972), pp. 261-271

> Argues that the Irishness of Irish drama will become extinct.

529 —, and James Kilroy, eds. *Lost Plays of the Irish Renaissance* (Newark, Delaware: Proscenium Press; Gerrards Cross, Buckinghamshire: Colin Smythe, 1970)

> This volume exemplifies "the chief alternatives that were arising to challenge Yeats' idea of a poetic drama." Includes plays by P. T. McGinley, Fred Ryan, James H. Cousins, Lady Gregory, Padraic Colum, and Maud Gonne MacBride.

530 —, and James Kilroy. *The Modern Irish Drama: The Irish Literary Theatre 1899-1901* (Dublin: Dolmen Press; Atlantic Highlands, New Jersey: Humanities Press, 1975)

> Survey through letters, memoirs, and reviews.

531 —, and James Kilroy. *The Modern Irish Drama: Laying the Foundations, 1902-1904* (Dublin: Dolmen Press; Atlantic Highlands, New Jersey: Humanities Press, 1976)

> Survey through letters, memoirs, and reviews.

532 —, and Sven Eric Molin, eds. *Drama: The Major Genres; An Introductory Critical Anthology* (New York: Dodd, Mead, 1967)

> Includes plays, with commentaries, by Bernard Shaw and Sean O'Casey.

533 Holloway, Joseph. *Joseph Holloway's Abbey Theatre; A*

Selection from His Unpublished Journal "Impressions of a Dublin Playgoer," ed. Robert Hogan and Michael J. O'Neill (Carbondale and Edwardsville: Southern Illinois University Press; London and Amsterdam: Feffer & Simons, 1967)

The history of Dublin and the Abbey Theatre "has been considerably enlivened by the fact that Mr. Holloway trundled home every day to record in detail his reactions to plays and players and his comments about and conversations with literary and theatrical people." Covers the years 1899-1926.

534   —. *Joseph Holloway's Irish Theatre, 1926-1944.* 3 vols., ed. Robert Hogan and Michael J. O'Neill (Dixon, California: Proscenium Press, 1968-70)

Selections from the later years of Holloway's journal.

535   Hortmann, Wilhelm. *Englische Literatur im 20. Jahrundert* (Bern: A. Francke, 1965)

Includes studies of Sean O'Casey, Denis Johnston, Bernard Shaw, W. B. Yeats, James Joyce, Louis MacNeice, Brendan Behan, and Samuel Beckett.

536   Houghton, Norris. *The Exploding Stage; An Introduction to Twentieth Century Drama* (New York: Weybright and Tally, 1971; Delta Books, 1973)

Includes criticism on plays by Samuel Beckett and Bernard Shaw.

537   Howarth, Herbert. *The Irish Writers, 1880-1940: Literature Under Parnell's Star* (London: Rockliff, 1958; New York: Hill & Wang, 1959)

Includes chapters on George Moore, Lady Gregory, W. B. Yeats, George Russell, J. M. Synge, and James Joyce.

538   Howe, P. P. *The Repertory Theatre: A Record and a*

Criticism (London: Martin Secker, 1910: New York: Mitchell Kennerley, 1911), pp. 42-51

The Abbey Theatre.

539   Hubbell, Jay B., and John O. Beaty. "Irish Dramatists," *An Introduction to Drama* (New York: Macmillan, 1929), pp. 522-524

Survey.

540   Hudson, Lynton. "The Little Theatre: The Irish Movement," *The Twentieth Century Drama* (London: George G. Harrap, 1946), pp. 37-44

Survey.

541   Hughes, Glenn. "The Free Theatre in Ireland," *The Story of the Theatre; A Short History of Theatrical Art from Its Beginnings to the Present Day* (New York and London: Samuel French, 1944), pp. 269-271

Introductory survey.

542   Huneker, James Gibbons. *The Pathos of Distance; A Book of A Thousand and One Moments* (New York: Charles Scribner's, 1913; London: T. Werner Laurie, 1922)

Includes studies of George Moore, J. M. Synge, and W. B. Yeats.

543   Hunt, Hugh. *The Theatre and Nationalism in Ireland* (Swansea, Wales: University College of Swansea, 1974)

The Professor W. D. Thomas Memorial Lecture delivered at the University College of Swansea on 19 November 1974.

544   Hurtik, Emil, and Robert Yarber. *An Introduction to Drama and Criticism* (Waltham, Massachusetts: Xerox College Publishing, 1971)

Anthology including plays, with commentaries, by J. M. Synge and Bernard Shaw.

545   *Irish Art Handbook* (Dublin: Cahill, 1943)

Includes: Lord Longford, "Irish Drama Today," pp. 81-83; Micheál MacLiammóir, "We Start a Theatre the Gate Theatre," pp. 85-92.

546   Jacquot, Jean, ed. *Le Théâtre Moderne; Hommes et Tendances* (Paris: Éditions du Centre National de la Recherche Scientifique, 1965), pp. 321-336

Survey of the Irish drama.

547   Jameson, Storm. *Modern Drama in Europe* (London: W. Collins; New York: Harcourt, Brace, 1920)

Includes discussions on Bernard Shaw, Lord Dunsany, and J. M. Synge.

548   Jeffares, A. Norman. *The Circus Animals* (London: Macmillan, 1970)

Includes essays on W. B. Yeats and Oliver St. John Gogarty.

549   —. "Ireland," *Literatures of the World in English*, ed. Bruce King (London and Boston: Routledge & Kegan Paul, 1974), pp. 98-115

Survey partially dealing with the modern Irish drama.

550   Jones, Margo. *Theatre-in-the-Round* (New York: Rinehart, 1951)

Includes criticism of plays by Sean O'Casey and Bernard Shaw.

551   Jones, Robert Edmond. *The Dramatic Imagination* (New York: Theatre Arts Books, 1941), pp. 29-30

Recollections of seeing the Abbey Players.

552 Jordan, John. "The Irish Theatre—Retrospect and Premonition," *Contemporary Theatre*, ed. John Russell Brown and Bernard Harris. Stratford-upon-Avon Studies, 4 (London: Edward Arnold, 1961; New York: St. Martin's Press, 1962), pp. 165-183

Survey from the beginnings to about 1960.

553 Joyce, James. "The Day of the Rabblement," *The Critical Writings of James Joyce*, ed. Ellsworth Mason and Richard Ellmann (London: Faber & Faber, 1959), pp. 68-72

Condemns the Irish Literary Theatre for its parochialism.

554 Kain, Richard M. *Dublin in the Age of William Butler Yeats and James Joyce* (Norman: University of Oklahoma Press, 1962; rpt., 1967)

Includes background to the Irish drama.

555 Kane, Whitford. *Are We All Met?* (London: E. Mathews & Marrot, 1931)

Includes information on the Ulster theatre.

556 Kaufman, Stanley. *Persons of the Drama; Theater Criticism and Comment* (New York and London: Harper and Row, 1976)

Includes reviews of plays by Samuel Beckett, James Joyce, J. M. Synge, and Bernard Shaw.

557 Kavanagh, Patrick. *Collected Pruse* (London: MacGibbon & Kee, 1967)

Includes essays on W. B. Yeats, George Moore, James Joyce, and Samuel Beckett.

558   Kavanagh, Peter. *The Irish Theatre; Being A History of the Drama in Ireland from the Earliest Period Up To the Present Day* (Tralee, Ireland: Kerryman, 1946)

Includes chapters on Bernard Shaw, The Abbey Theatre, and The Dublin Gate Theatre.

559   —. *The Story of the Abbey Theatre, from Its Origins in 1899 to the Present* (New York: Devin-Adair, 1950)

Survey.

560   Kelly, Blanche Mary. "Stage Directions," *The Voice of the Irish* (New York: Sheed & Ward, 1952), pp. 253-276

Survey of the Irish dramatic movement.

561   Kennedy, Andrew. *Six Dramatists In Search of a Language* (Cambridge: Cambridge University Press, 1975)

Includes essays on Bernard Shaw and Samuel Beckett.

562   Kennedy, David. "The Drama in Ulster," *The Arts in Ulster; A Symposium*, ed. Sam Hanna Bell *et al* (London: George G. Harrap, 1951), pp. 47-68

Survey.

563   Kennedy, J. M. *English Literature 1880-1905* (London: Stephen Swift, 1912)

Includes sections on Bernard Shaw and W. B. Yeats.

564   Kenny, Herbert A. "Modern Times," *Literary Dublin; A History* (Dublin: Gill & Macmillan; New York: Taplinger, 1974), pp. 243-318

Survey.

565 Kernodle, George R. "Poetic Drama of Ireland," *Invitation to the Theatre* (New York: Harcourt, Brace and World, 1967), pp. 229-231

> J. M. Synge, Sean O'Casey, and W. B. Yeats.

566 Kidd, Walter E., ed. *British Winners of the Nobel Literary Prize* (Norman: University of Oklahoma Press, 1973)

> Includes essays on W. B. Yeats, Bernard Shaw, and Samuel Beckett.

567 Kitchin, Laurence. *Mid-Century Drama* (London: Faber and Faber, 1960; New York: Humanities Press, 1961; 2nd rev. ed., 1962)

> Includes criticism on Samuel Beckett and Brendan Behan.

568 —. *Drama in the Sixties; Form and Interpretation* (London: Faber and Faber, 1966)

> Includes criticism on Sean O'Casey and Samuel Beckett.

569 Knight, G. Wilson. *The Golden Labyrinth; A Study of British Drama* (London: Phoenix House; New York: W. W. Norton, 1962; University Paperbacks, 1965)

> Includes a survey of the Irish dramatic movement and a chapter on Bernard Shaw.

570 Kraft, Irma. "Ireland—The Rebellions," *Plays, Players, Playhouses: International Drama of Today* (New York: Dobsevage, 1928), pp. 146-151.

571 Kronenberger, Louis. *The Thread of Laughter; Chapters on English Stage Comedy from Jonson to Maugham*

(New York: Alfred A. Knopf, 1952; rpt. New York: Hill & Wang Dramabook, 1970)

Includes chapters on Bernard Shaw and J. M. Synge.

572 —, ed. *Cavalcade of Comedy* (New York: Simon and Schuster, 1953)

Includes plays, with commentaries, by Bernard Shaw, J. M. Synge, and Sean O'Casey.

573 Krutch, Joseph Wood. *"Modernism" in Modern Drama; A Definition and an Estimate* (Ithaca, New York: Cornell University Press, 1953; London: Oxford University Press, 1954; Cornell Paperbacks, 1966)

Includes chapters on Bernard Shaw and J. M. Synge.

574 Lamm, Martin. *Modern Drama*. Translated by Karin Elliott (Oxford: Basil Blackwell, 1952; New York: Philosophical Library, 1953; rpt. Folcroft, Pennsylvania: Folcroft Library Editions, 1971)

Includes chapters on Bernard Shaw and on "Irish Drama".

575 Lane, Yoti. *The Psychology of the Actor* (London: Secker & Warburg, 1959; New York: John Day, 1960; rpt. Westport, Connecticut: Greenwood Press, 1973), p. 201

The Abbey Players.

576 Law, Hugh Alexander. "Dramatists," *Anglo-Irish Literature* (Dublin: Talbot Press; London: Longmans, 1926), pp. 250-271

Survey.

577 Lawson, John Howard. *Theory and Technique of Playwriting*

(New York: Hill & Wang, 1960)

Includes studies of Bernard Shaw and Sean O'Casey.

578 Leal, Rine, ed. *Teatro irlandès* (Habana: Consejo Nacional de Cultura, 1966)

Anthology including plays, with commentaries, by W. B. Yeats, Lady Gregory, Sean O'Casey, J. M. Synge, Paul Vincent Carroll, and Brendan Behan.

579 Leblanc, Gerard. "L'Abbey Theatre: Une difficile naissance," *Actes du Congrès de Nancy*, S. A. E. S. (Paris: Didier, 1975), pp. 291-305

The beginnings of the Abbey Theatre.

580 Lennartz, Franz, ed. *Ausländische Dichter und Schriftsteller unserer Zeit* [Foreign Poets and Writers of Our Time.] 4th rev. ed. (Stuttgart: Kröner, 1971)

Includes essays on contemporary Irish dramatists.

581 Lenson, David. *Achilles' Choice; Examples of Modern Tragedy* (Princeton and London: Princeton University Press, 1975)

Includes discussions on plays by W. B. Yeats and Samuel Beckett.

582 Letts, Winifred. "For Sixpence," *Songs from Leinster* (London: Smith, Elder, 1914), pp. 40-41

A poem commemorating the old days at the Abbey Theatre.

583 Levin, Harry, ed. *Perspectives of Criticism* (Cambridge, Massachusetts: Harvard University Press, 1950)

Includes studies of W. B. Yeats and J. M. Synge.

584   Lewis, Allan. *The Contemporary Theatre; The Significant Playwrights of Our Time* (New York: Crown Publishers, 1962)

> Includes chapters on Bernard Shaw, Sean O'Casey, and Samuel Beckett.

585   Lewisohn, Ludwig. *The Modern Drama; An Essay in Interpretation* (New York: B. W. Huebsch, 1915; London: Secker, 1916; New York: Viking Press, 1931)

> Includes studies of Bernard Shaw, W. B. Yeats, J. M. Synge, and Lady Gregory.

586   *Literary Ideals of Ireland* (London: T. Fisher Unwin, 1899; rpt. New York: Lemma Publishing Corporation, 1973)

> Contents: John Eglinton, "What Should be the Subject of a National Drama?"; W. B. Yeats, "A Note on National Drama"; John Eglinton, "National Drama and Contemporary Life"; and A. E. [George Russell], "Literary Ideals in Ireland."

587   Long, William J. "The Celtic Revival," *English Literature: Its History and Its Significance for the Life of the English Speaking World* (Boston: Ginn, 1964), pp. 610-620

> Introductory survey.

588   *Longford Productions: Dublin Gate Souvenir, 1939* (Dublin: Corrigan & Wilson, [1939])

> A brochure including a short essay by Lord Longford and a list of the first 126 plays produced by the Theatre.

589   Lucas, F. L. *The Drama of Chekhov, Synge, Yeats and Pirandello* (London: Cassell; New York: Dufour, 1963)

> Chapters on individual plays.

590 Lumley, Frederick. *Trends in 20th Century Drama: A Survey Since Ibsen and Shaw* (London: Barrie and Rockliff, 1956; rev. ed., 1960). Updated ed. entitled *New Trends in 20th Century Drama: A Survey Since Ibsen and Shaw* (London: Barrie and Rockliff, New York: Oxford University Press, 1967)

Includes studies of Samuel Beckett, Sean O'Casey, and Brendan Behan.

591 Lunari, Gigi. *Il Movimento Drammatico Irlandese (1899-1922)* (Bologna: Cappelli, 1960)

Survey of the Abbey movement.

592 —, ed. *Teatro Irlandese* (Milano: Nuova Accademia, 1961)

Anthology including plays, with commentaries, by W. B. Yeats, Lady Gregory, J. M. Synge, Lennox Robinson, Sean O'Casey, and Maurice Meldon.

593 Lynd, Robert. "Literature and Music," *Home Life in Ireland* (London: Mills & Boon, 1909), pp. 305-317

Reflections on the Irish drama.

594 —. *Old and New Masters* (London: T. Fisher Unwin; New York: Scribner's, 1919; rpt. Freeport, New York: Books for Libraries Press, 1970)

Includes chapters on J. M. Synge, Bernard Shaw, W. B. Yeats, and Lady Gregory.

595 —. *Books and Writers* (London: J. M. Dent, 1952)

Includes essays on W. B. Yeats, Bernard Shaw, and James Joyce.

596 *The Lyric Players 1951-1959* (Belfast: Lyric Players, 1960)

Brochure to launch an appeal for financial support.

597   *Lyric Theatre 1951-1968* (Belfast: Lyric Theatre, [1968])

       Survey of the famous Theatre in Northern Ireland.

598   Mabley, Edward. *Dramatic Construction; An Outline of
       Basic Principles* (Philadelphia: Chilton Book Co.,
       1972)

       Includes analyses of plays by Bernard Shaw, Sean O'Casey, and
       Samuel Beckett.

599   MacAnna, Tomas. "Nationalism from the Abbey Stage,"
       *Theatre and Nationalism in Twentieth-Century Ire-
       land*, ed. Robert O'Driscoll (Toronto: University of
       Toronto Press, 1971), 89-101.

600   McBrien, Peter F. "Anglo-Irish Drama," *Higher English:
       Drama* (Dublin: Intermediate & University College,
       n. d.), pp. 205-208

       Introductory survey.

601   McCann, Sean, ed. *The Story of the Abbey Theatre*. A Four
       Square Book (London: New English Library, 1967)

       Contents: Sean McCann, "The Beginnings"; Anthony Butler,
       "The Guardians"; Sean McCann, "The Theatre Itself"; Cather-
       ine Rynne, "The Playwrights"; Gabriel Fallon, "The Abbey
       Theatre Acting Tradition"; and Donal Dorcey, "The Big Oc-
       casions".

602   MacCarthy, Desmond. *Drama* (London and New York:
       G. P. Putnam, 1940; rpt. New York: Benjamin Blom,
       1971)

       Includes criticism on plays by James Joyce, Sean O'Casey, and
       Bernard Shaw.

603   MacDonagh, Thomas. *Literature in Ireland; Studies Irish and
       Anglo-Irish* (Dublin: Talbot Press; New York: Stokes,

1916; rpt. Port Washington, New York: Kennikat Press, 1970)

Survey.

604 Macgowan, Kenneth, and William Melnitz. "The Irish National Theatre," *The Living Stage; A History of the World Theater* (Englewood Cliffs, New Jersey: Prentice-Hall, 1955), pp. 419-424

Survey.

605 McGrory, Kathleen, and John Unterecker, eds. *Yeats, Joyce, and Beckett: New Light on Three Modern Irish Writers* (Lewisburg: Bucknell University Press: London: Associated University Presses, 1976)

Essays and recollections by various hands.

606 McHenry, Margaret. *The Ulster Theatre in Ireland* (Philadelphia: University of Pennsylvania, 1931)

Survey, with list of first productions.

607 MacKenna, Stephen. *Journal and Letters*, ed. E. R. Dodds (London: Constable; New York: William Morrow, 1936)

Includes background to the Irish Drama.

608 Mac Liammóir, Micheál. *All for Hecuba; An Irish Theatrical Autobiography* (London: Methuen, 1946; rpt. Dublin: Progress House, 1961)

Relates the story of the Dublin Gate Theatre.

609 —. *Theatre in Ireland* (Dublin: Three Candles, for the Cultural Relations Committee of Ireland, 1950; rpt. with "Sequel"; 1964)

A monograph describing the rise of Irish theatre movements other than the Abbey.

610 —. *Each Actor on His Ass* (London: Routledge & Kegan Paul, 1961)

Includes details of his acting experiences and an account of a Dublin Gate tour to Egypt.

611 —. "Dramatic Accidents," *Theatre 72*, ed. Sheridan Morley (London: Hutchinson, 1972), pp. 37-49

The Irish theatre in the twentieth century, viewed by its most distinguished actor-manager.

612 McQuillan, Deirdre, comp. *The Abbey Theatre Dublin 1966-1976; A commemorative Record* (Dublin: The Abbey Theatre, 1976)

A booklet celebrating the 10th anniversary of the new Abbey Theatre.

613 Mais, S. P. B. *Some Modern Authors* (London: Grant Richards, 1923; rpt. Freeport, New York: Books for Libraries Press, 1970)

Includes essays on St. John Ervine and Bernard Shaw.

614 Malone, Andrew E. *The Irish Drama* (London: Constable; New York: Scribner's, 1929; rpt. New York: Benjamin Blom, 1965)

Survey, with chapters on W. B. Yeats, Lady Gregory, Edward Martyn, and George Moore.

615 Malye, Jean. *La Littérature Irlandaise Contemporaine* (Paris: Bibliothèque Internationale d'Édition, [1913])

Includes a survey of the Irish dramatic movement.

616 Marcus, Phillip L. "The Theater Movement and Beyond," *Yeats and the Beginnings of the Irish Renaissance* (Ithaca, New York and London: Cornell University Press, 1970), chap. 6

    Survey.

617 Marowitz, Charles, Tom Milne, and Owen Hale, eds. *The Encore Reader; A chronicle of the New Drama* (London: Methuen, 1965)

    Includes reviews of plays by Brendan Behan and Samuel Beckett.

618 Marriott, J. W. *The Theatre* (London: George G. Harrap, 1931)

    Includes studies of Bernard Shaw, Sean O'Casey, and St. John Ervine.

619 —. *Modern Drama* (London and New York: Thomas Nelson, [1934]; Folcroft, Pennsylvania: Folcroft Library Editions, 1973)

    Includes chapters on Bernard Shaw and on the "Irish Dramatists."

620 Matthews, Brander. "Irish Plays and Irish Playwrights," *The Principles of Playmaking and Other Discussions of the Drama* (New York: Scribner's, 1919), pp. 196-213. Reprinted from *Scribner's Magazine*, LXI (January 1917), 85-90

    Survey.

621 Mercier, Vivian. *The Irish Comic Tradition* (London and New York: Oxford University Press, 1962; paperback ed., 1969)

    Shows that an unbroken comic tradition may be traced in Irish literature.

622   —, and David H. Greene, eds. "Introduction," *1000 Years of Irish Prose: The Literary Revival* (New York: Devin Adair, 1952; rpt. Grosset & Dunlop, 1961), pp. ix-xxix

Includes background material.

623   Metwally, Abdalla A. *Studies in Modern Drama*, Vol. 1 (Beirut: Beirut Arab University, 1971)

Includes essays on Bernard Shaw and J. M. Synge.

624   Mikhail, E. H., ed. *J. M. Synge: Interviews and Recollections* (London: Macmillan: New York: Barnes and Noble, 1977)

Includes material on the Irish drama.

625   —, ed. *W. B. Yeats: Interviews and Recollections* (London: Macmillan; New York: Barnes and Noble, 1977)

Includes material on the Irish drama.

626   —, ed. *Lady Gregory: Interviews and Recollections* (London: Macmillan, Totowa, New Jersey: Rowman and Little-field, 1977)

Includes material on the Irish drama.

627   —, and John O'Riordan, eds. *The Sting and the Twinkle: Conversations with Sean O'Casey* (London: Macmillan; New York: Barnes and Noble, 1974)

Includes material on the Irish drama.

628   Miller, Anna Irene. "The National Theatre of Ireland," *The Independent Theatre in Europe, 1887 to the Present* (New York: Ray Long and Richard R. Smith, 1931; rpt. New York: Benjamin Blom, 1966), pp. 255-310

Survey.

629 Miller, Nellie Burget. "The New Theater of Ireland," *The Living Drama* (New York and London: Century, 1924), pp. 330-353

Includes discussions on plays by W. B. Yeats, Lady Gregory, J. M. Synge, Lord Dunsany, St. John Ervine, and Lennox Robinson.

630 Millett, Fred B. "The Irish Drama," *Contemporary British Literature* (New York: Harcourt, Brace, 1944), pp. 59-62

Survey.

631 —. *Reading Drama; A Method of Analysis with Selections for Study* (New York: Harper; London: Hamish Hamilton, 1950; rpt. Freeport, New York: Books for Libraries Press, 1970)

Includes commentaries on plays by W. B. Yeats and J. M. Synge.

632 Monahan, Michael. *Nova Hibernia: Irish Poets and Dramatists of Today and Yesterday* (New York: Mitchell Kennerley, 1914)

Includes studies of W. B. Yeats and J. M. Synge.

633 Montague, C. E. *Dramatic Values* (London: Methuen, 1911; rev. ed. Garden City, New York: Doubleday, 1925)

Includes chapters on J. M. Synge and Bernard Shaw.

634 Moody, William Vaughan, and Robert Morss Lovett. "The Irish Drama," *A History of English Literature*, 8th ed. by Fred B. Millett (New York: Charles Scribner's, 1964), pp. 398-401, 456-460

Introductory survey.

635   Moore, Alfred S. *The Little Theatre; Its Story and Aims*
      (Belfast: Ulster & Dramatic Art, n. d.)

      Ulster's only repertory theatre.

636   Moore, George. *Hail and Farewell* (London: Heinemann;
      New York: D. Appleton, 1911-14; ed. Richard Cave
      (Gerrards Cross, Buckinghamshire: Colin Smythe,
      1976)

      Reminiscences including background to the Irish drama.

637   Morgan, A. E. *Tendencies of Modern English Drama* (Lon-
      don: Constable; New York: Scribner's, 1924; rpt.
      Freeport, New York: Books for Libraries Press, 1969)

      Includes chapters on Bernard Shaw, W. B. Yeats, Edward
      Martyn, Lady Gregory, J. M. Synge, Padraic Colum, Lennox
      Robinson, T. C. Murray, St. John Ervine, and Lord Dunsany.

638   Morris, Lloyd R. "The Drama," *The Celtic Dawn: A Survey
      of the Renascence in Ireland 1889-1916* (New York:
      Macmillan, 1917; rpt. New York: Cooper Square
      Publications, 1970), pp. 88-172

      Survey.

639   Moses, Montrose J., ed. "The Irish School of Playwrights,"
      Representative British Dramas, Victorian and Modern
      (Boston: Heath, 1931), pp. 889-897

      Survey.

640   Na Mainistreach, Amharchann, ed. *The Creation of the
      Abbey Theatre* (Dublin: Irish Tourist Board, 1966)

      A 20-page pamphlet issued to mark the opening of the new
      building.

641   Nathan, George Jean, ed. "Foreword," *Five Great Modern*

Irish Plays (New York: Modern Library, 1941), pp. ix-xiii

Reflections on the Irish drama.

642 —. "The Contribution of the Irish," *The Entertainment of a Nation* (New York: Alfred A. Knopf, 1942), pp. 68-75

Argues that, except for Sean O'Casey, "the quondam rich vein appears to have run dry."

643 —. *The Magic Mirror; Selected Writings on the Theatre*, ed. Thomas Quinn Curtiss (New York: Alfred A. Knopf, 1960)

Includes essays on Bernard Shaw and Sean O'Casey.

644 National Theatre Society. *Rules of the National Theatre Society Limited* (Dublin: Cahill, [1903]).

645 Nevinson, H. W. "Irish Plays of 1904," *Books and Personalities* (London and New York: John Lane, 1905), pp. 245-250

Includes discussion on plays by W. B. Yeats, J. M. Synge, and Padraic Colum.

646 Newman, Evelyn. *The International Note in Contemporary Drama* (New York: Kingsland Press, 1931)

Includes brief discussions on Sean O'Casey and Bernard Shaw.

647 Nichols, Beverley. *Are They the Same at Home?* (London: Jonathan Cape; New York: Doubleday, 1929)

Includes chapters on George Moore and Sean O'Casey.

648   Nicoll, Allardyce. *British Drama; An Historical Survey from
       the Beginnings to the Present Time*. Fourth Revised
       Edition (London: George G. Harrap, 1947)

> Includes studies of St. John Ervine, J. M. Synge, Bernard Shaw
> and a survey of the Irish dramatic movement.

649   —. *World Drama from Aeschylus to Anouilh*. Second Revised
       and Enlarged Edition (London: Harrap, 1976)

> Critical survey. Includes chapters on Bernard Shaw and Sean
> O'Casey and a survey of the Irish drama.

650   Nic Shiubhlaigh, Maire. *The Splendid Years: Recollections of
       Maire Nic Shiubhlaigh, As Told to Edward Kenny*.
       With a Foreword by Padraic Colum (Dublin: James
       Duffy, 1955)

> The detailed memoir of one of the Abbey's first leading actress-
> es, covering the period 1899-1916.

651   Nowaczyński, Adolf. "Teatr irlandzki," *Szkice literackie*
       (Poznań: Nakladem spólki wydawniczelj ostoja, 1918),
       pp. 59-70

> Survey.

652   Nünning, Josefa, ed. *Das Englische Drama* (Darmstadt:
       Wissenschaftliche Buchgesellschaft, 1973)

> Includes discussions on Bernard Shaw, J. M. Synge, W. B. Yeats,
> Sean O'Casey, Samuel Beckett, Brendan Behan, St. John Ervine,
> Lady Gregory, and Denis Johnston.

653   O'Casey, Sean. *Autobiographies*, 6 vols. in 2 (London: Mac-
       millan, 1963)

> Contains Background to the Irish drama.

654 O Cearnaigh [Kearney], Peadar. "The Abbey Theatre" and "Abbey on Tour—1911," *The Soldier's Song*, by Seamus de Burca (Dublin: P. J. Bourke, 1957), pp. 34-39 and 63-67

Recollections by the author of the National Anthem of Ireland.

655 O'Connor, Frank. "All the Olympians," *The Backward Look; A Survey of Irish Literature* (London: Macmillan, 1967), pp. 183-193. American edition entitled *A Short History of Irish Literature; A Backward Look* (New York: G. P. Putnam, 1967; Capricorn Books, 1968), pp. 183-193. Reprinted from *Saturday Review* (New York), XLIX (10 December 1966), 30-32, 99

Includes discussions on J. M. Synge, W. B. Yeats, and Lady Gregory.

656 —. "The Abbey Theatre," *My Father's Son* (London: Macmillan, 1968), pp. 145-178; (New York: Aflred A. Knopf, 1969), pp. 169-208

Recollections.

See also the chapter entitled "The Death of Yeats."

657 O'Conor, Norreys Jephson. *Changing Ireland: Literary Backgrounds of the Irish Free State, 1889-1922* (London: Oxford University Press; Cambridge, Massachusetts: Harvard University Press, 1924)

Includes background to the Irish drama and studies of W. B. Yeats, Lord Dunsany, and Lady Gregory.

658 O'Donnel, F[rank], Hugh. *The Stage Irishman of the Pseudo-Celtic Drama* (London: John Long, 1904).

659 O'Driscoll, Robert, ed. *Theatre and Nationalism in*

Twentieth-Century Ireland (Toronto: University of Toronto Press; London: Oxford University Press, 1971)

Contents: Robert O'Driscoll, "Introduction"; Ann Saddlemyer, "Stars of the Abbey's Ascendancy"; George Mills Harper, " 'Intellectual Hatred' and 'Intellectual Nationalism': the Paradox of Passionate Politics"; Robert O'Driscoll, "Two Lectures on the Irish Theatre by W. B. Yeats"; Thomas Macanna, "Nationalism from the Abbey Stage"; Roger McHugh, "The Rising"; David Krause, "Sean O'Casey and the Higher Nationalism"; David R. Clark, "Yeats, Theatre, and Nationalism"; M. J. Sidnell, "Hic and Ille: Shaw and Yeats"; and Francis Warner, "The Absence of Nationalism in the Works of Samuel Beckett".

660   Ó Broighneáin, Muiris. "An 'Irish Literary Theatre'," *Taighde i gComhair stair litridheachta na nua-Ghaedhilge ó 1882 annas* (Baile Átha Cliath: Oifig díolta foilleseacháin rialtais, 1936), pp. 94-97

Survey.

661   O'Faolain, Sean. "Preface," *She Had to Do Something: A Comedy in Three Acts* (London: Cape, 1938), pp. 7-24

Sums up his thoughts on the Abbey Theatre.

662   —. "The Writers," *The Irish; A Character Study* (New York: Devin-Adair, 1949), pp. 156-180

Background to the Irish drama.

663   —. *Vive moi!* (Boston: Little, Brown, 1964; London: Hart-Davis, 1965)

Autobiography including background to the Irish drama.

664   O'Farachain, Roibeard. "The Second Spring: A Manifesto for

the New Abbey Theatre," in the souvenir programme to mark the occasion of the opening of the new Abbey Theatre, 1966.

665 O'Hagan, Thomas. "The Irish Dramatic Movement," *Essays on Catholic Life* (Baltimore: John Murphy, 1916; rpt. Freeport, New York: Books for Libraries Press, 1965), pp. 57-73

Survey.

666 O hAodha, Micheál. *Plays and Places* (Dublin: Progress House, 1961)

Includes chapters on T. C. Murray, Padraic Fallon, Edward Martyn, and amateur drama festivals.

667 —. *The Abbey—Then and Now* (Dublin: Abbey Theatre, 1969)

A monograph bringing the Abbey Theatre's history up to 1969.

668 —. *Theatre in Ireland* (Oxford: Basil Blackwell, 1974; Totowa, New Jersey: Rowman and Littlefield, 1975)

Traces the formative processes which have shaped Irish drama from the opening of the first theatre in Ireland in 1637 to the re-opening of the Gate Theatre on a subsidized basis in 1971.

669 Oliver, D. E. *The English Stage; Its Origins and Modern Developments—A Critical and Historical Survey*, 2nd ed. (London: John Ouseley, 1912), pp. 118-121

Survey of the Irish dramatic movement.

670 O'Neill, James J. *Irish Theatrical History: A Biographical Essay* (Dublin: Browne & Nolan, 1910)

Survey.

671 Oppel, Horst, ed. *Das Moderne Englische Drama: Interpretationen* (Berlin: Erich Schmidt, 1963; 2nd rev. ed., 1971)

> Includes studies of plays by Bernard Shaw, W. B. Yeats, J. M. Synge, and Sean O'Casey.

672 —. *Das Englische Drama der Gegenwart; Interpretationen* (Berlin: Erich Schmidt, 1976)

> Includes studies of plays by Brendan Behan, Brian Friel, and Samuel Beckett.

673 O'Sullivan, Seamus. "The Irish National Theatre," *The Rose and the Bottle and Other Essays* (Dublin: Talbot Press, 1946), pp. 116-126. Also includes recollections, *passim.*

674 Ould, Hermon. *The Art of the Play* (London: Isaac Pitman, 1938)

> Includes discussions on Bernard Shaw and Sean O'Casey.

675 Palmer, D. J. "Drama," *The Twentieth-Century Mind: History, Ideas, and Literature in Britain, Vol. 1: 1900-1918,* ed. C. B. Cox and A. E. Dyson (London and New York: Oxford University Press, 1972), pp. 447-474

> Includes discussions on Bernard Shaw and J. M. Synge.

676 Palmer, John. *The Future of the Theatre* (London: G. Bell, 1913), pp. 167-172

> Survey of the Irish National Theatre.

677 Pasquier, Marie-Claire, Nicole Rougier, and Bernard Brugière. *Le Nouveau Théâtre Anglais* (Paris: Armand Colin, 1969)

Includes material on Brendan Behan and Samuel Beckett.

678   Paul-Dubois, L. "The Literary Awakening," *Contemporary Ireland* (Dublin: Maunsel; New York: Baker & Taylor, 1908), pp. 420-430

Includes a survey of the Irish drama.

679   Peacock, Ronald. *The Poet in the Theatre* (London: Routledge; New York: Harcourt, Brace, 1946; rpt. London: MacGibbon & Kee; New York: Hill & Wang, 1960)

Includes chapters on Bernard Shaw, J. M. Synge, and W. B. Yeats.

680   —. *The Art of Drama* (London: Routledge & Kegan Paul, 1957; Westport, Connecticut: Greenwood Press, 1974)

Includes discussion on Bernard Shaw, J. M. Synge, and W. B. Yeats, *passim.*

681   Pellizzi, Camillo. "In Ireland," *English Drama; the Last Great Phase*. Translated by Rowan Williams (London and New York: Macmillan, 1935), pp. 204-240

Survey.

682   Perry, Henry Ten Eyck. "Modern Times," *Masters of Dramatic Comedy and Their Social Themes* (Cambridge, Massachusetts: Harvard University Press, 1939; rpt. Port Washington, New York: Kennikat Press, 1968)

Includes studies of W. B. Yeats, Lady Gregory, J. M. Synge, and Bernard Shaw.

683   Pinter, Harold. *Mac* (London: Pendragon Press, 1968)

Includes experiences of two seasons touring with Anew

McMaster's company in the Irish provinces.

684   Plunkett, Grace. *Twelve Nights at the Abbey Theatre; A Book of Drawings* (Dublin: At the Sign of the Three Candles, 1929).

685   —. *Doctors Recommend It: An Abbey Theatre Tonic in 12 Doses* (Dublin: At the Sign of the Three Candles, 1930).

686   Pogson, Rex. *Miss Horniman and the Gaiety Theatre, Manchester* (London: Rockliff, 1952), pp. 8-13

Miss Horniman's association with the Abbey Theatre.

687   Porter, Raymond J., and James D. Brophy, eds. *Modern Irish Literature; Essays in Honor of William York Tindall* (New York: Twayne Publishers, 1972)

Includes essays on W. B. Yeats, Lady Gregory, George Moore, Frank O'Connor, Oliver St. John Gogarty, James Joyce, and Samuel Beckett.

688   Power, Patrick C. *A Literary History of Ireland* (Cork: Mercier Press, 1969)

Includes an introductory survey of the Irish drama.

689   Prior, Moody E. *The Language of Tragedy* (New York: Columbia University Press, 1947; rpt. Bloomington and London: Indiana University Press, 1966)

Includes studies of plays by W. B. Yeats and J. M. Synge.

690   Rafroidi, Patrick. "Aspects du Théâtre Irlandais—Anglais," *L'Irlande: vol. 2 Littérature* (Paris: Armand Colin, 1970), pp. 76-107

An outline from Shaw to the present.

691 —, Raymonde Popot, and William Parker, eds. *Aspects of the Irish Theatre* (Lille: Publications de l'Université de Lille; Paris: Éditions Universitaires, 1972)

> Contents: Patrick Rafroidi, "The Funny Irishman"; Bernard Escarbelt, "Sheridan's Debt to Ireland"; William Parker, "Broadbent and Doyle, Two Shavian Archetypes"; Gérard Leblanc, "Ironic Reversal as Theme and Technique in Synge's Shorter Comedies"; Patrick Rafroidi, "Plays for Ireland"; Jeanne Lezon, "The Easter Rising Seen from the Tenements"; Bernard Mathelin, "From the Shadow of War to the Broken Tassie"; Bernard Leroy, "Two Committed Playwrights: Wesker and O'Casey"; Françoise Borel, "Alas, Poor Brendan!"; Jean-Michel Pannecoucke, "John Brendan Keane and the New Irish Rural Drama"; Patrick Rafroidi, "Nation of Myth-Makers"; Pascale Mathelin-Gastebois, "Irish Myths in the Theatre of W. B. Yeats"; Raymonde Popot, "The Hero's Light"; Mireille Schodet, "The Theme of Diarmuid and Grainne"; Bernard Hibon, "Samuel Beckett: Irish Tradition and Irish Creation"; Nigel Deacon, "Racial Conflicts and Related Themes in *Murderous Angels* by Conor Cruise O'Brien"; Robert Hogan, "Where Have All the Shamrocks Gone?"; and Christiane Thilliez, "From one Theatrical Reformer to Another: W. B. Yeats's Unpublished Letters to Gordon Craig."

692 Rao, B. Ramachandra. *Six One-Act Plays* (Patiala: Punjabi University, 1974)

> Includes plays, with commentaries, by St. John Ervine and Lady Gregory.

693 Reid, B. L. *The Man from New York: John Quinn and His Friends* (New York: Oxford University Press, 1968)

> Includes several references to the Abbey Theatre, Padraic Colum, St. John Ervine, Oliver St. John Gogarty, Lady Gregory, Douglas Hyde, James Joyce, Edward Martyn, George Moore, Lennox Robinson, George Russell, Bernard Shaw, James Stephens, J. M. Synge, Jack B. Yeats, and W. B. Yeats.

694 Reinert, Otto, ed. *Drama; An Introductory Anthology*

(Boston: Little, Brown, 1961)

Includes plays, with commentaries, by W. B. Yeats and Bernard Shaw.

695   —, ed. *Modern Drama; Nine Plays* (Boston: Little, Brown, 1962)

Anthology including plays, with commentaries, by Bernard Shaw and W. B. Yeats.

696   —, ed. *Drama; An Introductory Anthology*. Alternate Edition (Boston: Little, Brown, 1964)

Includes plays, with commentaries, by Bernard Shaw and J. M. Synge.

697   —, ed. *Modern Drama*. Alternate Edition (Boston: Little, Brown, 1966)

Anthology including plays, with commentaries, by Bernard Shaw, J. M. Synge, and W. B. Yeats.

698   —, ed. *Classic Through Modern Drama: An Introductory Anthology* (Boston: Little, Brown, 1970)

Includes plays, with commentaries, by Bernard Shaw and J. M. Synge.

699   Reiter, Seymour. *World Theater; The Structure and Meaning of Drama* (New York: Horizon Press, 1973; rpt. Delta Books, 1974)

Includes studies of plays by Sean O'Casey and Samuel Beckett.

700   Rest, Jaime. "El teatro irlandés," *El Teatro Inglés* (Buenos Aires: Centro Editor de América Latina, 1968), pp. 72-82

Introductory survey.

701 Reynolds, Ernest. *Modern English Drama; A Survey of the Theatre from 1900* (London: George G. Harrap; New York: British Book Centre, 1949; Norman, Oklahoma: University of Oklahoma Press, 1951)

> Includes studies of Bernard Shaw, J. M. Synge, St. John Ervine, and W. B. Yeats.

702 Rice, Elmer. *The Living Theatre* (New York: Harper, 1959; London: Heinemann, 1960), pp. 75-78

> Examines the decline of the Abbey Theatre.

703 Richards, Stanley, ed. *Best Short Plays of the World Theatre 1958-1967* (New York: Crown Publishers, 1968)

> Includes short plays, with commentaries, by Brendan Behan and Sean O'Casey.

704 Rivoallan, Anatole. *Littérature Irlandaise Contemporaine* (Paris: Hachette, 1939), chap. 6

> Survey of the Irish drama.

705 Robinson, Lennox. *Curtain Up: An Autobiography* (London: Michael Joseph, 1942)

> Contains background to the Irish drama.

706 —. *Pictures in a Theatre; A Conversation Piece* (Dublin: Abbey Theatre, [1947])

> Contains background to the Irish drama.

707 —. *Ireland's Abbey Theatre; A History 1899-1951* (London: Sidgwick & Jackson, 1951; rpt. Port Washington, New York: Kennikat Press, 1968)

> The official history commissioned by the Abbey Theatre authorities.

708   —. *I Sometimes Think* (Dublin: Talbot Press, 1956)

>   Includes chapters on Bernard Shaw, J. M. Synge, and W. B.
>   Yeats.

709   —, ed. *The Irish Theatre: Lectures Delivered During the
Abbey Theatre Festival Held in Dublin in August
1938* (London: Macmillan, 1939; rpt. New York:
Haskell House, 1971)

>   Contents: Andrew E. Malone, "The Early History of the Abbey
>   Theatre"; Frank O'Connor, "Synge"; Lennox Robinson, "Lady
>   Gregory"; F. R. Higgins, "Yeats and Poetic Drama in Ireland";
>   Andrew E. Malone, "The Rise of the Realistic Movement";
>   T. C. Murray, "George Shiels, Brinsley MacNamara, etc.";
>   Walter Starkie, "Sean O'Casey"; and Ernest Blythe, "Gaelic
>   Drama".

710   Rodgers, W. R., ed. *Irish Literary Portraits* (London: British
Broadcasting Corporation, 1972)

>   Broadcast conversations with those who knew some of the
>   greatest Irish writers, including W. B. Yeats, J. M. Synge, Ber-
>   nard Shaw, James Joyce, George Moore, Oliver St. John Gogar-
>   ty, F. R. Higgins, and George Russell.

711   Ronsley, Joseph, ed. *Myth and Reality in Irish Literature*
(Waterloo, Ontario: Wilfrid Laurier University Press,
1977)

>   Includes essays on Lady Gregory, W. B. Yeats, Samuel Beckett,
>   J. M. Synge, James Joyce, Sean O'Casey, Denis Johnston, and
>   Brian O'Nolan.

712   Roston, Murray. "The Modern Era," *Biblical Drama in England from the Middle Ages to the Present Day* (Lon-
don: Faber and Faber; Evanston, Illinois: Northwest-
ern University Press, 1968)

>   Includes discussions on Bernard Shaw and W. B. Yeats.

713 Rowe, Kenneth Thorpe. *Write That Play* (New York and London: Frank & Wagnalls, 1939; rpt., 1968)

> Includes detailed analyses of plays by Lord Dunsany and J. M. Synge.

714 Roy, Emil. *British Drama Since Shaw* (Carbondale: Southern Illinois University Press; London and Amsterdam: Feffer & Simons, 1972)

> Includes chapters on Bernard Shaw, W. B. Yeats, J. M. Synge, and Sean O'Casey.

715 Russell, Caro Mae Green. "Ireland," *Modern Plays and Playwrights*. University of North Carolina Liberal Extension Publications, Vol. 2, No. 6 (Chapel Hill: University of North Carolina Press, 1936)

> Includes studies of Lennox Robinson and Sean O'Casey.

716 Russell, Diarmuid, ed. "Introduction," *The Portable Irish Reader* (New York: Viking Press, 1946), pp. xi-xxx

> Includes background to the Irish drama.

717 Rust, Adolf. *Beitraege Zu Einer Geschichte der Neu-Keltischen Renaissance* (Bueckeburg: Grimme, 1922)

> Includes studies of W. B. Yeats, Edward Martyn, Alice Milligan, George Moore, Douglas Hyde, and J. M. Synge.

718 Ryan, John. *Remembering How We Stood; Bohemian Dublin at the Mid-Century* (Dublin: Gill and Macmillan, 1975)

> Includes background to the Irish drama.

719 Ryan, W. P. "Ireland at the Play," *The Pope's Green Island* (London: Nisbet, 1912), pp. 299-307

> Reflections on the Irish drama.

720   Sahal, N. *Sixty Years of Realistic Irish Drama (1900-1960)*
      (Bombay: Macmillan, 1971)

> Includes chapters on W. B. Yeats, Lady Gregory, J. M. Synge,
> Padraic Colum, William Boyle, W. F. Casey, T. C. Murray, R. J.
> Ray, Lennox Robinson, St. John Ervine, Sean O'Casey, George
> Shiels, Teresa Deevy, Paul Vincent Carroll, Joseph Tomelty,
> Michael J. Molloy, and Walter Macken.

721   Salem, Daniel. *La Révolution Théâtrale Actuelle en Angle-
      terre* (Paris: Deonoël, 1969)

> Includes studies of Brendan Behan and Samuel Beckett.

722   Salerno, Henry F., ed. *English Drama in Transition 1880-
      1920* (New York: Pegasus, 1968)

> Anthology including plays, with commentaries, by Bernard
> Shaw, W. B. Yeats, and J. M. Synge.

723   Samachson, Dorothy, and Joseph Samachson. "Dublin,
      1907," *The Dramatic Story of the Theatre* (London
      and New York: Abelard-Schuman, 1955), pp. 128-
      134

> Includes highlights of the Irish drama.

724   Saul, George Brandon. "Introduction," *Age of Yeats: The
      Golden Age of Irish Literature* (New York: Dell,
      1964)

> Includes background to the Irish drama.

725   Schaff, Harrison Hale, ed. *Three Irish Plays* (Boston: Inter-
      national Pocket Library, 1936)

> Anthology of plays, with commentaries, by W. B. Yeats, Doug-
> las Hyde, and J. M. Synge.

726   Scott-James, R. A. *Personality in Literature* (London:

Secker, 1931; New York: Henry Holt, 1932)

Includes studies of Bernard Shaw and J. M. Synge.

727 —. "The Irish Literary Movement," *Fifty Years of English Literature 1900-1950* (London: Longmans, 1951; 2nd ed., 1956), chap. 9

Survey.

728 Setterquist, Jan. *Ibsen and the Beginnings of Anglo-Irish Drama*. Upsala Irish Studies (Dublin: Hodges, Figgis; Cambridge, Massachusetts: Harvard University Press, 1952)

On the influence of Ibsen.

729 Sharp, R. Farquharson. "The Dublin Theatres," *A Short History of the English Stage from Its Beginnings to the Summer of the Year 1908* (New York: Walter Scott, 1909), chap. xx

Survey.

730 Shaw, Bernard. *A Note on the Irish Theatre by Theodore Roosevelt and an "Interview" on the Irish Players in America* (New York: Mitchell Kennerley, 1912)

On the occasion of the Irish Players' first American tour in 1911.

731 —. "The Irish Players," *The Matter with Ireland,* ed. David H. Greene and Dan H. Laurence (London: Rupert Hart-Davis; New York: Hill & Wang, 1972), pp. 61-68

The Abbey Theatre's first American tour, 1911.

732 Sheehy, Michael. *Is Ireland Dying? Culture and the Church in Modern Ireland* (London: Hollis & Carter, 1968)

Includes discussions on Samuel Beckett, Brendan Behan, James Joyce, Micheal MacLiammóir, George Moore, Sean O'Casey, George Russell, Bernard Shaw, J. M. Synge, and W. B. Yeats.

733 Short, Ernest. *Theatrical Cavalcade* (London: Eyre & Spottiswoode, 1942), pp. 205-210. Reprinted in *Sixty Years of Theatre* (London: Eyre & Spottiswoode, 1951), pp. 374-378

Deals with J. M. Synge and Sean O'Casey.

734 Simpson, Alan. *Beckett and Behan and a Theatre in Dublin* (London: Routledge and Kegan Paul, 1962)

On the Pike Theatre productions.

735 Skelton, Robin, and David R. Clark, eds. *Irish Renaissance; A Gathering of essays, Memoirs, and Letters from "The Massachusetts Review"* (Dublin: Dolmen Press; London: Oxford University Press, 1965)

Includes essays on W. B. Yeats, Lady Gregory, J. M. Synge, Bernard Shaw, and Sean O'Casey.

736 —, and Ann Saddlemyer, eds. *The World of W. B. Yeats: Essays in Perspective* (Victoria, British Columbia: Adelphi Bookshop, for University of Victoria, 1965; rev. ed. Seattle: University of Washington Press, 1967)

Includes articles on W. B. Yeats, the Abbey Theatre, poetic drama in Yeats' time, Lady Gregory, Edward Martyn, J. M. Synge, and George Moore.

737 Slater, Derek. *Plays in Action; A Six-Term Course in Drama* (Oxford: Pergamon Press, 1964)

Includes studies of plays by Bernard Shaw and J. M. Synge.

738 Sorell, Walter. "Irish Humor and Eloquence," *Facets of Comedy* (New York: Grosset & Dunlap, 1972), pp.

114-125 [Deals with W. B. Yeats, Lady Gregory, J. M. Synge, and Sean O'Casey] ; pp. 287-291 [Samuel Beckett.]

739 Speaight, Robert. *Drama Since 1939* (London: Longmans, Green for The British Council, 1947), pp. 25-28

Deals with Sean O'Casey, Paul Vincent Carroll, and Denis Johnston.

740 Spinner, Kaspar. *Die Alte Dame Sagt: Nein! Drei Irische Dramatiker: Lennox Robinson, Sean O'Casey, Denis Johnston.* Swiss Studies in English (Bern: A. Francke, 1961)

Detailed study of their plays.

741 *Stage Design at the Abbey Theatre: An Exhibition* (Dublin: Peacock Theatre, 1967)

741a Stalder, Hans-Georg. *Anglo-Irish Peasant Drama: The Motifs of Land and Emigration* (Bern and Frankfurt: Peter Land, 1977)

Includes discussions of the Abbey Theatre, the Ulster Literary Theatre, Rutherford Mayne, John B. Keane, Padraic Colum, Michael J. Molloy, Lennox Robinson, and John Murphy.

742 Stamm, Rudolf. *Zwischen Vision und Wirklichkeit* (Bern: A. Francke, 1964)

Includes essays on Bernard Shaw and W. B. Yeats.

743 Stanford, Derek, ed. *Landmarks* (London and Camden, New Jersey: Thomas Nelson, 1969)

Includes excerpts from plays, with introductory notes, by Samuel Beckett and Brendan Behan.

744 Stein, Walter. "Drama," *The Twentieth-Century Mind: History, Ideas, and Literature in Britain, Vol. II:*

1918-1945, ed. C. B. Cox and A. E. Dyson (London and New York: Oxford University Press, 1972), pp. 417-456

Includes discussions of Bernard Shaw and Sean O'Casey.

745   Steinberg, M. W., ed. *Aspects of Modern Drama* (New York: Holt, Rinehart and Winston, 1960)

Anthology including plays, with commentaries, by Bernard Shaw, J. M. Synge, and W. B. Yeats.

746   Stephens, James. *James, Seumas and Jacques*, ed. Lloyd Frankenberg (London: Macmillan, 1964)

Includes essays on J. M. Synge, W. B. Yeats, George Russell, Bernard Shaw, James Joyce, and Geroge Moore.

747   Stewart, J. I. M. *Eight Modern Writers*. Oxford History of English Literature, Vol. XII (London and New York: Oxford University Press, 1963; paperback, 1973)

Includes chapters on Bernard Shaw, W. B. Yeats, and James Joyce.

748   Strong, L. A. G. "An Old Woman Outside the Abbey The- atre," *Dublin Days* (Oxford: Blackwell, 1921), p. 9. Reprinted in *The Body's Imperfection: The Collected Poems* (London: Methuen, 1957), p. 20.

749   —. *Personal Remarks* (London: Peter Nevill; New York: Liveright, 1953)

Includes essays on W. B. Yeats, J. M. Synge, Padraic Colum, and James Joyce.

750   —. *Green Memory* (London: Methuen, 1961)

Includes background to the Irish drama.

751 Styan, J. L. *The Elements of Drama* (Cambridge: Cambridge University Press, 1960)

> Includes analyses of plays by J. M. Synge, Bernard Shaw, and Sean O'Casey.

752 —. *The Dark Comedy; The Development of Modern Comic Tragedy* (Cambridge: Cambridge University Press, 1962; 2nd ed., 1968)

> Includes studies of Bernard Shaw, J. M. Synge, Sean O'Casey, and Samuel Beckett.

753 —. *The Dramatic Experience; A Guide to the Reading of Plays* (Cambridge: Cambridge University Press, 1965)

> Includes studies of plays by Samuel Beckett, Sean O'Casey, Bernard Shaw, and J. M. Synge.

754 —. *Drama, Stage and Audience* (Cambridge: Cambridge University Press, 1975)

> Includes studies of plays by Samuel Beckett and Bernard Shaw.

755 Sühnel, Rudolf, and Dieter Riesner, eds. *Englische Dichter der Moderne: Ihr Leben und Werk* [Modern English Writers: Their Lives and Works] (Berlin: Erich Schmidt, 1971)

> Includes essays on Samuel Beckett, James Joyce, Sean O'Casey, Bernard Shaw, J. M. Synge, and W. B. Yeats.

756 Sutherland, James, ed. *The Oxford Book of Literary Anecdotes* (Oxford: Clarendon Press, 1975)

> Includes anecdotes on Bernard Shaw, W. B. Yeats, J. M. Synge, Oliver St. John Gogarty, James Joyce, Frank O'Connor, and George Moore.

757 Sweetkind, Morris, ed. *Ten Great One Act Plays* (New York:

Bantam Books, 1968)

Anthology including plays, with commentaries, by Bernard Shaw, Lady Gregory, and J. M. Synge.

758   Swinnerton, Frank. *The Georgian Literary Scene 1910-1935* (London and New York: Hutchinson, 1935; rev. ed., 1969)

Includes studies of George Moore, St. John Ervine, W. B. Yeats, and James Joyce.

759   Symons, Arthur. *Plays, Acting, and Music; A Book of Theory* (London: Constable, 1909)

Includes discussions of Bernard Shaw and W. B. Yeats.

760   Synge, J. M. *Collected Works, Vol. 2: Prose*, ed. Alan Price (London: Oxford University Press, 1966)

Includes critical material on the Irish drama.

761   Taylor, Estella Ruth. *The Modern Irish Writers; Cross Currents of Criticism* (Lawrence, Kansas: University of Kansas Press, 1954; rpt. New York: Greenwood Press, 1969)

Includes studies of the main Irish dramatists.

762   Téry, Simone. *L'Île des Bardes* (Paris: Ernest Flammarion, 1925)

Contains chapters on the Irish legends; and on W. B. Yeats, George Russell, J. M. Synge, George Moore, and James Joyce.

763   Tetzeli von Rosador, Kurt. *Das Englische Geschichtsdrama Seit Shaw* (Heidelberg: Carl Winter, 1976)

Includes chapters on Bernard Shaw, Lady Gregory, and W. B. Yeats.

764 Thompson, David, ed. *Theatre Today* (London: Longmans, 1965)

> Anthology including plays, with commentaries, by Bernard Shaw and Sean O'Casey.

765 Thompson, William Irwin. *The Imagination of an Insurrection: Dublin, Easter 1916; A Study of an Ideological Movement* (New York: Oxford University Press, 1967)

> Includes chapters on W. B. Yeats, George Russell, and Sean O'Casey.

766 Thorndike, Ashley H. *English Comedy* (New York: Macmillan, 1929; rpt. New York: Cooper Square Publishers, 1965)

> Includes studies of Bernard Shaw and J. M. Synge.

767 Tindall, William York. *Forces in Modern British Literature 1885-1956* (New York: Random House, 1947; 2nd ed., 1956), chap. 3, part II

> Survey of the Irish drama.

768 Tracy, Robert. "Ireland: The Patriot Game," *The City of Home: Cultural Nationalism and the Modern Writer*, ed. E. Ernest Lewald (Knoxville, Tennessee: University of Tennessee Press, 1972), pp. 39-57

> Includes discussions on nationalism in modern Irish drama.

769 Trewin, J. C. *The English Theatre* (London: Paul Elek, 1948)

> Includes introductory discussions on Bernard Shaw, St. John Ervine, and Sean O'Casey.

770 —. *We'll Hear a Play* (London: Carroll & Nicholson, 1949)

> Includes criticism on plays by Bernard Shaw, Sean O'Casey,

and Denis Johnston.

771 —. *The Theatre Since 1900* (London: Andrew Dakers, 1951)

> Includes studies of the Abbey Theatre; and of W. B. Yeats, J. M. Synge, Bernard Shaw, and Sean O'Casey.

772 —. *Dramatists of Today* (London: Staples Press, 1953)

> Includes studies of Bernard Shaw, Sean O'Casey, St. John Ervine, Paul Vincent Carroll, and Denis Johnston.

773 —. *The Gay Twenties; A Decade of the Theatre* (London: Macdonald, 1958)

> Includes discussions on Bernard Shaw and Sean O'Casey.

774 —. *Drama in Britain 1951-1964* (London: Longmans, Green, for the British Council, 1965)

> Includes brief discussions on Brendan Behan, Samuel Beckett, and Sean O'Casey.

775 Trilling, Lionel, ed. *The Experience of Literature: Drama; A Reader with Commentaries* (New York: Holt, Rinehart and Winston, 1967)

> Includes plays, with commentaries, by Bernard Shaw and W. B. Yeats.

776 Truninger, Annelise. *Paddy and the Paycock: A Study of the Stage Irishman from Shakespeare to O'Casey.* The Cooper Monographs, vol. 24/Theatrical Physiognomy Series (Bern: Francke Verlag, 1976)

> Includes general view and studies of plays by Padraic Colum, T. C. Murray, J. M. Synge, and Sean O'Casey.

777 Tucker, S. M., and Alan S. Downer, eds. *Twenty-Five Modern*

Plays. Third Edition (New York and London: Harper, 1953)

Anthology including plays, with commentaries, by J. M. Synge, Sean O'Casey, and St. John Ervine.

778 Tynan, Katharine. *Twenty-Five Years: Reminiscences* (London: John Murrary; New York: Devin-Adair, 1913)

Includes background to the Irish drama.

779 Tynan, Kenneth. *Curtains* (New York: Atheneum; London: Longmans, 1961)

Includes reviews of plays by Bernard Shaw, Sean O'Casey, Samuel Beckett, and Brendan Behan.

780 ---. *Tynan Right & Left* (London: Longmans; New York: Atheneum, 1967)

Includes reviews of plays by Bernard Shaw, J. M. Synge, and Samuel Beckett.

781 —. *A View of the English Stage 1944-1963* (London: Davis-Poynter, 1975)

Includes reveiws of plays by Samuel Beckett, Brendan Behan, and Bernard Shaw.

782 Ulanov, Barry, ed. *Makers of the Modern Theater* (New York: McGraw-Hill, 1961)

Anthology including plays, with commentaries, by Bernard Shaw, W. B. Yeats, J. M. Synge, and Sean O'Casey.

783 Ure, Peter. *Yeats and Anglo-Irish Literature; Critical Essays,* ed. C. J. Rawson (Liverpool: University of Liverpool Press; New York: Harper, 1974)

Includes studies of W. B. Yeats, Bernard Shaw, and George Moore.

784 Ussher, Arland. *Three Great Irishmen: Shaw, Yeats, Joyce* (London: Victor Gollancz, 1952).

785 Van Doren, Carl, and Mark Van Doren. "Irish Drama," *American and British Literature Since 1890* (New York: Appleton-Century-Crofts, 1939; rev. and enl. ed., 1967), pp. 324-340

Survey.

786 Vernon, Frank. *The Twentieth-Century Theatre* (London: George G. Harrap, 1924)

Includes discussions on plays by Bernard Shaw, J. M. Synge, Lady Gregory, and Lord Dunsany.

787 Vickery, John. *The Literary Impact of the Golden Bough* (Princeton, New Jersey: Princeton University Press, 1973)

Includes discussions on James Joyce and W. B. Yeats.

788 Vines, Sherard. *A Hundred Years of English Literature* (London: Duckworth, 1950; New York: Macmillan, 1951), pp. 215-219

Survey.

789 Walbrook, H. M. *Nights at the Play* (London: W. J. Ham-Smith, 1911)

Includes reviews of plays by Bernard Shaw, Lady Gregory, J. M. Synge, and Lennox Robinson.

790 Walkley, A. B. *Drama and Life* (London: Methuen, 1907; New York: Brentano's, 1908; rpt. Freeport, New

York: Books for Libraries Press, 1967)

Includes chapters on Bernard Shaw and "The Irish National Theatre".

791 Ward, A. C. *Twentieth-Century English Literature 1901-1960* (London: Methuen, 1964)

Includes chapters on Bernard Shaw and on "The Irish Theatre".

792 —, ed. *Specimens of English Dramatic Criticism XVII-XX Centuries* (London: Oxford University Press, 1945)

Includes criticism of plays by Bernard Shaw and J. M. Synge.

793 Warnock, Robert, ed. *Representative Modern Plays: British* (Chicago: Scott, Foresman, 1953)

Anthology including plays, with commentaries, by Bernard Shaw, J. M. Synge, and Sean O'Casey.

794 —. *Representative Modern Plays: Ibsen to Tennessee Williams* (Chicago: Scott, Foresman, 1964)

Anthology including plays, with commentaries, by Bernard Shaw, J. M. Synge, and Sean O'Casey.

795 Watson, E. Bradlee, and Benfield Pressey, eds. *Contemporary Drama* (New York: Charles Scribner's, 1931)

Anthology including plays, with commentaries, by J. M. Synge, Lady Gregory, Lord Dunsany, and Sean O'Casey.

796 —, and Benfield Pressey, eds. *Contemporary Drama: 15 Plays* (New York: Charles Scribner's, 1959)

Anthology including plays, with commentaries, by Bernard Shaw, J. M. Synge, and Sean O'Casey.

797 Wauchope, George Armstrong. *The New Irish Drama.*

Bulletin of the University of South Carolina, No. 168
(Columbia: University of South Carolina, 1925)

Survey.

798 Weland, Hermann J., ed. *Insight IV: Analyses of Modern
     British and American Drama* (Frankfurt: Hirsch-
     graben, 1975)

Includes analyses of plays by Samuel Beckett, Sean O'Casey,
Bernard Shaw, J. M. Synge, and W. B. Yeats.

799 Weiss, Samuel A., ed. *Drama in the Modern World* (Boston:
     D. C. Heath, 1964)

Anthology including plays, with commentaries, by Bernard
Shaw, J. M. Synge, and Samuel Beckett.

800 —, ed. *Drama in the Western World* (Boston: D. C. Heath,
     1968)

Anthology including plays, with commentaries, by Bernard
Shaw and Samuel Beckett.

801 —. *Drama in the Modern World: Plays and Essays; Alter-
     nate Edition* (Lexington, Massachusetts: D. C. Heath,
     1974)

Includes plays, with commentaries, by Bernard Shaw, J. M.
Synge, and Samuel Beckett.

802 Wellwarth, George E. *The Theater of Protest and Paradox;
     Developments in the Avant-Garde Drama* (New York:
     New York University Press; London: MacGibbon and
     Kee, 1964)

Includes studies of Samuel Beckett and Brendan Behan.

803 Weygandt, Cornelius. *Irish Plays and Playwrights* (London:

Constable; Boston and New York: Houghton Mifflin, 1913; rpt. Port Washington, New York: Kennikat Press, 1966)

> Survey. Includes chapters on W. B. Yeats, Edward Martyn, George Moore, George Russell, Lady Gregory, J. M. Synge, Padraic Colum, William Boyle, T. C. Murray, Lennox Robinson, Rutherford Mayne, "Norreys Connell", St. John Ervine, Joseph Campbell, and William Sharp.

804 —. *Tuesdays at Ten; Dramatists and Essayists* (Philadelphia: University of Pennsylvania Press, 1928; London: Oxford University Press, 1929)

> Includes talks on Lord Dunsany and W. B. Yeats.

805 Whitaker, Thomas R. *Fields of Play in Modern Drama* (New Jersey: Princeton University Press, 1977)

> Includes discussions of plays by Samuel Beckett and Bernard Shaw.

806 White, Harold. *Souvenir of Theatre Royal, July 24th 1903* (Dublin: Theatre Royal, 1903).

807 White, Terence de Vere. *The Anglo-Irish* (London: Victor Gollancz, 1972)

> Includes discussions of Bernard Shaw, George Russell, Oliver St. John Gogarty, Lady Gregory, Edward Martyn, George Moore, Sean O'Casey, J. M. Synge, and W. B. Yeats.

808 Whitfield, George. *An Introduction to Drama* (London: Oxford University Press, 1938; 2nd ed., 1963)

> Includes studies of plays by Bernard Shaw and Samuel Beckett.

809 Whiting, Frank M. "Ireland," *An Introduction to the Theatre*, 3rd ed. (New York and London: Harper, 1969), pp. 98-100

Introductory survey.

810   Whiting, John. *The Art of the Dramatist* (London: London Magazine Editions, 1970)

Includes studies of Bernard Shaw and Samuel Beckett.

811   Wieczorek, Hubert. *Irische Lebenshaltung im Neuen Irishen Drama* (Breslau: Priebatsch, 1937)

Deals with Irish way of life in the Irish drama.

812   Wild, Friedrich. *Die Englische Literatur der Gegenwart Seit 1870: Drama und Roman* (Wiesbaden: Dioskuren-Verlag, 1928)

Includes a chapter on Anglo-Irish drama.

813   Williams, Harold. "The Irish Literary Theatre" and "The Irish Playwrights," *Modern English Writers; Being A Study of Imaginative Literature 1890-1914* (London: Sidgwick & Jackson, 1925; rpt. Port Washington, New York: Kennikat Press, 1970), pp. 193-196 and 197-220

Survey.

814   Williams, Raymond. *Drama from Ibsen to Eliot* (London: Chatto & Windus, 1952). Revised and enlarged ed. entitled *Drama from Ibsen to Brecht* (London: Chatto & Windus, 1968; Harmondsworth: Penguin Books, 1973)

Includes studies of W. B. Yeats, J. M. Synge, James Joyce, Sean O'Casey, Bernard Shaw, and Samuel Beckett.

815   Williamson, Audrey. *Theatre of Two Decades* (London:

Rockliff, 1951)

> Includes discussions on Bernard Shaw, J. M. Synge, Sean O'Casey, Denis Johnston and Paul Vincent Carroll.

816 —. *Contemporary Theatre 1953-1956* (London: Rockliff, 1956)

> Includes criticism of plays by Bernard Shaw, Samuel Beckett, and Sean O'Casey.

817 Wilson, A. E. *Playwrights in Aspic; Some Variations Upon an Unoriginal Theme* (London: Home & Van Thal, 1946)

> Includes parodies of plays by Bernard Shaw and J. M. Synge.

818 Winkler, Elizabeth Hale. *The Clown in Modern Anglo-Irish Drama* (Frankfurt: Peter Lang; Bern: Herbert Lang, 1977)

> Includes studies of Bernard Shaw, Lady Gregory, J. M. Synge, Sean O'Casey, and Samuel Beckett.

819 Worsley, T. C. *The Fugitive Art; Dramatic Commentaries 1947-1951* (London: John Lehmann, 1952)

> Includes criticism on plays by Bernard Shaw and James Joyce.

820 Worth, Katharine J. *Revolutions in Modern English Drama* (London: G. Bell; Toronto: Clarke, Irwin, 1973)

> Includes criticism on Bernard Shaw, Sean O'Casey, James Joyce, and Samuel Beckett.

821 Yamamoto, Shuji. *Airurando Engeki Kenkyu* (Kyoto: Aporon-sha, 1968)

> The story of the Irish drama.

822   Yeats, W. B. "A Note on National Drama." *Literary Ideals in Ireland* (London: T. Fisher Unwin, 1899).

823   —. "The Literary Movement in Ireland," *Ideals in Ireland*, ed. Lady Gregory (London: Unicorn, 1901), pp. 87-102.

824   —. *The Cutting of an Agate* (London and New York: Macmillan, 1912). Reprinted in *Essays* (London: Macmillan, 1924) and in *Essays and Introductions* (London: Macmillan, 1961).

825   —. "The Irish Dramatic Movement 1901-1919," *Plays and Controversies* (London: Macmillan, 1923), pp. 1-218.

826   —. "The Celtic Element in Literature," *Essays* (London: Macmillan, 1924), pp. 213-231. Reprinted in *Essays and Introductions* (London: Macmillan, 1961), pp. 173-189.

827   —. *The Irish National Theatre* (Rome: Reale Academia d'Italia, 1935).

828   —. *Dramatis Personae* (London: Macmillan, 1936). Reprinted in *Autobiographies* (London: Macmillan, 1955).

829   —. *Autobiographies* (London: Macmillan, 1955).

830   —. *Explorations* (London: Macmillan, 1962).

831   —. *Memoirs*, ed. Denis Donoghue (New York: Macmillan, 1972)

> Includes Yeats's Journal, begun in December 1908; and the first draft of his Autobiography, begun in 1915.

832   —. *Uncollected Prose*, vol. 1, ed. John P. Frayne (London: Macmillan; New York: Columbia University Press,

1970); vol. 2, ed. John P. Frayne and Colton Johnson (London: Macmillan; New York: Columbia University Press, 1975)

Includes several articles and letters on the Irish drama.

833 Young, Cecilia Mary. "The Irish Theatre," *Ring Up the Curtain* (St. Paul: Library Service Guild, 1941), pp. 134-152

Only Catholic dramatists understand the Irish.

834 Young, Ella. "Eire," *Flowering Dusk; Things Remembered Accurately and Inaccurately* (New York: Longmans, 1945; London: Dennis Dobson, 1947), pp. 3-200

Background to the Irish drama, including amateur productions in the early 1900s.

835 Young, Stark. *Immortal Shadows; A Book of Dramatic Criticism* (New York and London: Scribner's, 1948; London: MacGibbon & Kee, 1958)

Includes criticism on plays by Bernard Shaw and W. B. Yeats.

IV

Periodical Articles

836   "The Abbey," *The Irish Times* (Dublin), (12 August 1938), p. 6

> Editorial. This issue and the preceding and the following issues carry reports on the speeches and lectures made at the Abbey Theatre Festival.

837   "The Abbey," *The Irish Times* (Dublin), (20 February 1963), p. 7

> Editorial on the disgraceful state of affairs.

838   "The Abbey," *Newsweek* (Dayton, Ohio), LXVIII, No. 5 (1 August 1966), 82

> On the opening of the new Abbey Theatre.

839   "The Abbey Theatre," *Theatre Arts Monthly* (New York), XVI, No. 9 (September 1932), 692, 695

> Announcing the Abbey Theatre's new American tour.

840   "The Abbey Theatre," *The Irish Times* (Dublin), (1 April 1919), p. 4

> Praise of its work.

841   "The Abbey Theatre," *The Irish Times* (Dublin), (28 July 1944), p. 3

> Letters to the Editor on the general condition of the Irish National Theatre.

842   "The Abbey Theatre," *Boston Evening Transcript*, (7 October 1911), Part 3, p. 4

Lady Gregory on its ways and methods.

843   "Abbey Theatre and Irish Plays," *Evening Telegraph* (Dublin), (3 November 1910), p. 6

Correspondence taking the Abbey Theatre to task for not producing plays in the Irish language.

844   "Abbey Theatre, Dublin," *Building* (New York), CCXII (23 September 1966), 81-88.

845   "The Abbey Theatre: Its Origins and Accomplishments," *The Times* (London), (17 March 1913): Irish Number, p. 15

Survey.

846   "Abbey Theatre Players," *The Irish American* (New York), (14 October 1911), pp. 1, 4

Abbey Theatre's first American tour.

847   "Abbey Theatre Subsidy," *The Literary Digest* (New York), LXXXVI (12 September 1925), 29-30

By the Irish Free State.

848   "The Abbey Theatre: What Is Wrong with the Drama," *Manchester Guardian Weekly*, XXXII (19 April 1935), 318

On the Theatre's plans to produce more foreign plays for lack of Irish ones.

849   "Abbey's New Policy," *The Evening Herald* (Dublin), (13 August 1935), p. 7. Reprinted in *The Literary Digest*

(New York), CXIX (1 June 1935), 24

Some of the best classical, Continental, and American drama will be given when new Irish plays are not available.

850 "Acting of the Irish Players," *The New York Times* (25 November 1911), p. 3

Abbey Theatre's first American tour.

851 Adams, J. Donald. "The Irish Dramatic Movement," *The Harvard Monthly* (Cambridge, Massachusetts), LIII (November 1911), 44-48

Survey.

852 "AE talked to Shaw without Knowing It," *The New York Times*, (7 February 1928), p. 12

Recollections, by George Russell, of Bernard Shaw, James Joyce, W. B. Yeats, George Moore, and Lord Dunsany.

853 Alldridge, John. "What's Wrong with the Abbey?" *The Irish Digest* (Dublin), XXIX, No. 4 (February 1948), 17-19

An attack on the directors of the Abbey Theatre.

854 Allen, Percy. "Ulster Drama; Modern Developments," *The Daily Telegraph* (London), (25 March 1926), p. 65. Reprinted as "The Theatre in Ulster," *The Living Age* (Boston), CCCXXIX (29 May 1926), 467-469

Brief history of the Ulster Literary Theatre and the Northern Drama League.

855 Allgood, Sara. "The National Theatre: An Autobiographical Sketch," *Weekly Freeman* (Dublin), XCIII (20 March 1909), 11

The Abbey Theatre.

856   Al-Malih, Ghassan. "Al-Harakah al-Masrahiyah al-Irlandiyah"
      [The Irish Dramatic Movement], *Al-Ma'rifah,* III, No.
      34 (December 1964), 376-384

      Survey in Arabic.

857   "Aloysius Truth Society Bitterly Denounces Irish Plays,"
      The Washington Times, (16 November 1911), p. 10

      Abbey Theatre's first American tour.

858   Andrews, Irene Dwen. "The Irish Literary Theatre," *Poet-
      Lore* (Boston), XXXIX (Spring 1928), 94-100

      Striking features of modern Irish drama.

859   Ansorge, Peter. "Ireland," *Plays and Players* (London), XV,
      No. 8 (May 1968), 60-62

      On the Abbey Theatre's offerings at the World Theatre Season
      in London.

860   Archer, Kane. "What Really Happened," *Plays and Players*
      (London), XXII, No. 3 (December 1974), 32-34

      Survey of the Dublin Theatre Festival.

861   —. "Dublin," *Plays and Players* (London), XXII, No. 10
      (July 1975), 40-41

      Survey of play productions.

862   Archer, William. "Things in General: The Irish Theatre,"
      Morning Leader (London), (5 December 1908), p. 4

      Describes the building of the Abbey Theatre.

863 Arnold, Sidney. "The Abbey Theatre," *Arts and Philosophy* (London), I (Summer 1950), 25-30

> "It is as yet an infant that is nearer to Homer rather than an adolescent who is ignorant of the soul of the poet".

864 "The Art of the Irish Players," *Everybody's Magazine* (New York), XXVI (February 1912), 231-240

> The Abbey Theatre's first American tour.

865 "At Least Better Than Riot," *The New York Times*, (19 January 1912), p. 10

> Editorial on the Abbey Theatre's first American tour.

866 "Au Revoir to the Abbey Theatre," *The Sunday Times* (London), (25 January 1959), p. 9

> To preserve a record of the Abbey Theatre before it is pulled down for rebuilding, some of its former illustrious members visited it to make a film.

867 "Aviation, Animals and 'The Abbey'; From A Dublin Tragedy to a Flying Delta," *The Illustrated London News*, CCXIX (28 July 1951), 153

> On the fire which gutted the Abbey Theatre on 18 July 1951.

868 Ayling, Ronald. "The Theatre That Shook the World," *Tribune* (London), (28 November 1958), p. 10

> Review article on the Abbey Theatre.

869 —. "W. B. Yeats on Plays and Players," *Modern Drama*, IX, No. 1 (May 1966), 1-10.

870 B. "The Irish Players," *T. P.'s Weekly* (London), (16 July 1911), 744

The Irish National Theatre Society season at the Court Theatre, London.

871 B., E. M. "Festival Standards," *Drama* (London), No. 42 (Autumn 1956), 60-61

A note on the drama festival in Ulster.

872 B., J. P. "Give the People Theatres!" *The Irish Digest* (Dublin), XXIII, No. 2 (December 1945), 71-72

The provincial theatre movment in Ireland "may accomplish big things".

873 Barrington, Maeve. "Home of Many Stars," *The Irish Digest* (Dublin), L, No. 1 (March 1954), 76-78

Theatre in Galway.

874 —. "Queen of the Abbey Theatre," *The Irish Digest* (Dublin), LIV, No. 4 (October 1955), 29-31

Maureen Delany and recollections of the Abbey Theatre.

875 Bartley, J. O. "The Stage Irishman," *The Irish Digest* (Dublin), XIX, No. 1 (July 1944), 56-58

Survey.

876 Baughan, E. A. "The Irish Players," *The Daily News and Leader* (London), (14 July 1913), p. 6

"No progress has been made either in the writing or acting of these Irish plays".

877 Bennett, James O'Donnell. "Lessons of the Abbey Company's Engagement," *Record Herald* (Chicago), (3 March 1912), Part 7, p. 1

Abbey Theatre's first American tour.

878 Bentley, Eric. "World Theatre: 1900-1950," *Theatre Arts* (New York), XXXIII (December 1949), 22-27

> *Passim.*

879 —. "Irish Theatre: Splendeurs et Misères," *Poetry* (Chicago), LXXIX, No. 4 (January 1952), 216-232. Reprinted in *In Search of Theater* (New York: Vintage Books, 1953), pp. 307-321

> Blasts the Abbey as one of the world's most overrated theatres, but sees "real glory" in J. M. Synge, Sean O'Casey, and W. B. Yeats.

880 Bessey, Mabel A. "There Are No Stars," *Scholastic* (Pittsburgh), XXVI, No. 6 (9 March 1935), 8-9, 14

> 'Team Work' has made the Abbey Theatre and the Irish Players a national institution.

881 Bewley, Charles. "The Irish National Theatre," *The Dublin Review,* CLII, No. 304 (January 1913), 132-144. Reprinted in *The Living Age* (Boston), CCLXXVI (15 February 1913), 410-418

> "The present stage of the Abbey Theatre is a continuous source of disappointment."

882 Bickley, Francis. "Deirdre," *The Irish Review* (Dublin), II, No. 17 (July 1912), 252-255

> The theme as treated by W. B. Yeats, J. M. Synge, and George Russell.

883 Birmingham, George A. "The Literary Movement in Ireland," *The Fortnightly Review* (London and New York), LXXXII, New Series (December 1907), 947-957

> The last part of the article surveys the Irish Dramatic Movement.

884   Bissing, Toska. "Dublin Gate Theatre Productions," *Theatre Arts* (New York), XXV, No. 1 (January 1941), 49-51

Survey.

885   Black, Hester. "The Theatre in Ireland before 1900," *Threshold* (Belfast), I, No. 2 (Summer 1957), 20-23

Background to the modern period.

886   Blake, Warren Barton. "Irish Plays and Players," *Independent* (New York), LXXIV (6 March 1913), 515-519

Review article.

887   "Boston Culture Impressed Yeats," *The New York Times*, (26 November 1911), Section III, p. 3

Abbey Theatre's first American tour.

888   Bowen, Evelyn. "The Abbey and the Gate," *The Bell* (Dublin), IV, No. 3 (June 1942), 188-189

Survey of play productions.

889   —. "Gate and Gaiety," *The Bell* (Dublin), IV, No. 5 (August 1942), 364-368

Survey of play productions.

890   —. "Plays and Personalities," *The Bell* (Dublin), IV, No. 6 (September 1942), 438-440

Survey of play productions.

891   —. "The Theatre: Dublin," *The Bell* (Dublin), V, No. 3 December 1942), 236-238

Survey of play productions.

892 Boyd, Ernest A. "The Irish National Theatre; A Criticism," *The Irish Times* (Dublin), (27 December 1912), p. 5

> "Unless good plays are produced and past successes revived, the Abbey Theatre will continue to decline until it is scarely distinguishable from the ordinary commercial theatre".
>
> See correspondence in the following issues.

893 —. "The Abbey Theatre," *The Irish Review* (Dublin), II, No. 24 (February 1913), 628-634

> Some radical change must be made in the conduct of the Abbey Theatre.

894 —. "Le Théâtre irlandais," *Revue de Paris*, V (1 September 1913), 191-205

> Survey, with a stress on J. M. Synge.

895 —. "The Irish Renaissance—Renascent," *The Dial* (Chicago), LXVII (26 July 1919), 53-55

> On the Abbey Theatre.

896 Brereton-Barry, R. "The Need for a State Theatre," *The Irish Statesman* (Dublin), III, No. 7 (25 October 1924), 210-212

> Points out the limitations of the Abbey and suggests the French state theatre as a model for Ireland.

897 Breslin, Sean. "Mary O'Malley's Lyric Theatre," *Hibernia* (Dublin), (16 November 1973), p. 15

> The story of the Lyric Theatre, Belfast.

898   Bridges-Adams, W. "A National Theatre," *Drama* (London),
      No. 51 (Winter 1958), 27-30

      Review article on the Abbey Theatre.

899   Brien, Alan. "Stage Irish," *The Spectator* (London), CCV
      (23 September 1960), 441-442

      Review of the Dublin Theatre Festival.

900   Brodzky, Leon. "The Irish National Theatre," *Lone Hand*
      (Australia), (1 May 1908), 105-110

      Mostly on the plays of W. B. Yeats, J. M. Synge, and Lady
      Gregory.

901   Bromage, Mary Cogan. "Literature of Ireland Today,"
      South Atlantic Quarterly (Durham, North Carolina),
      XLII, No. 1 (January 1943), 27-37

      Notes that Irish drama had moved from the romantic, imagin-
      ative, lyrical plays of a period when nationhood was a dream to
      the "drama of disillusionment" when nationhood became a
      reality.

902   Brooks, Benjamin Gilbert. "The Irish Theatre," *The Nine-
      teenth Century and After* (London), CXXVIII (Aug-
      ust 1940), 196-200

      Review article.

903   Brooks, Sydney. "The Irish Peasant As a Dramatic Issue,"
      Harper's Weekly (New York), LI (9 March 1907),
      344

      Deplores the fact that sometimes "mob opinion rules" in
      Ireland.

904   Brosnan, Gerald. "Dublin's Abbey—the Immortal Theatre,"

Theatre Arts (New York), XXXV, No. 10 (October 1951), 36-37

Recollections by a playwright who happened to be in Dublin and to see the ruins of the Abbey Theatre, which went up in flames on 18 July 1951.

905 B[rown], I[vor]. "The Allgood Sisters," *Drama* (London), No. 77 (Summer 1965), 45-47

Review article on Sara Allgood and Maire O'Neill.

906 Burke, Michael. "The Irish Theatre: Forty Years After," *New Alliance* (Edinburgh), I, No. 2 (Autumn 1939), 70-77

An outline.

907 Burke-Kennedy, Declan. "A Theatre Is Born," *Hibernia* (Dublin), (October 1967), p. 25

Dublin Focus Theatre.

908 Burrowes, Wesley. "Writers Are Not Encouraged," *The Irish Times* (Dublin), (18 March 1968), p. 10

There is nothing in Ireland "to encourage anybody to write a play, except his own dedication".

909 Byars, John A. "The Brief and Troublesome Reign of Cathleen Ni Houlihan (1902-1907)," *South Atlantic Bulletin*, (May 1975), 40-46

In the plays of W. B. Yeats, Lady Gregory, and J. M. Synge.

910 Byrne, John Keyes. "Dublin," *Plays and Players* (London), IV, No. 4 (January 1957), 32; IV, No. 5 (February 1957), 33; IV, No. 6 (March 1957), 32; IV, No. 7 (April 1957), 32; IV, No. 8 (May 1957), 32; V, No. 3

(December 1957), 33; V, No. 4 (January 1958), 32; V, No. 5 (February 1958), 33; V, No. 7 (April 1958), 32; V, No. 10 (July 1958), 32; V, No. 11 (August 1958), 32; VI, No. 6 (March 1959), 33; VI, No. 8 (May 1959), 32; VI, No. 9 (June 1959), 32

Survey.

911   —. "Clean, If Not Clever," *Plays and Players* (London), VII, No. 2 (November 1959), 9

Survey of the Dublin Theatre Festival productions.

912   C., C. "The Theatre," *The Bell* (Dublin), III, No. 5 (February 1942), 362; V, No. 2 (November 1942), 140-146; No. 4 (January 1943), 308-314; VI, No. 1 (April 1943), 72-74; No. 2 (May 1943), 155-161; No. 3 (June 1943), 251-257, No. 4 (July 1943), 346-348; No. 5 (August 1943), 434-438; No. 6 (September 1943), 530-533; VII, No. 2 (November 1943), 171-175; VIII, No. 2 (May 1944), 151-157; IX, No. 2 (November 1944), 168-170

Survey of play productions.

913   Campbell, John. "The Rise of the Drama in Ireland," *The New Liberal Review* (London), VII (April 1904), 291-307

Discusses the activities of the Irish National Theatre Society.

914   Carroll, Donald. "Contemporary Irish Theatre," *Drama* (London), No. 66 (Autumn 1962), 34-36

Current Irish Theatre "is stale and lifeless".

915   Carroll, Paul Vincnet. "Can the Abbey Theatre Be Restored?" *Theatre Arts* (New York), XXXVI, No. 1 (January 1952), 18-19, 79

The Abbey Theatre has been "in retreat" as a result of: 1. "unofficial interference of the Government" 2. "very powerful unofficial clerical censorship" 3. "deplorable policy of the Abbey Directorate".

916 Carter, William. "Lament for the Province without Playwrights," *Ireland Today* (Dublin), I, No. 7 (December 1936), 68-69

On the scanty dramatic output in Ulster.

917 —. "The Drama in Ulster," *Ireland Today* (Dublin), II, No. 1 (January 1937), 73

Survey of play productions.

918 Caswell, Robert W. "Unity and the Irish Theatre," *Studies; An Irish Quarterly Review* (Dublin), IL (Spring 1960), 63-67

Suggests the amalgamation of "the various splinter groups" since petty quarrels have ruined what the Abbey has achieved.

919 "A Celtic Theatre," *The Freeman's Journal* (Dublin), (22 March 1900), p. 4

Editorial.

920 Chambers, E. K. "The Experiments of Mr. Yeats," *The Academy and Literature* (London), LXIV (9 May 1903), 465-466

On plays given by the Irish National Theatre Society at the Queen's Gate Hall. See Yeats's reply, "Irish Plays and Players," LXIV (16 May 1903), 495 Letter to the Editor.

921 Chanel [i. e. Clery, Arthur Edward]. "The Deserted Abbey," *The Leader* (Dublin), XII, No. 10 (28 April 1906), 151-152

The reasons behind the declining attendance at the Abbey Theatre.

922   Clark, James M. "The Irish Literary Movement," *Englische Studien* (Leipzig), IL (July 1915), 50-98

The last part of the article surveys the modern Irish theatre.

923   Clarke, Austin. "My First Visit to the Abbey," *The Irish Digest* (Dublin), LXVI, No. 3 (September 1959), 77-79

Recollections.

924   Clarke, Michael. "The Abbey Theatre," *The Irish Times* (Dublin), (11 August 1944), p. 3

Letter to the Editor on the "disintegration" of the Theatre.

925   Coffey, Brian. "In Dublin," *The Commonweal* (New York), XLVI, (3 October 1947), 597-598

Survey of the season at the major theatres.

926   Cohen, Helen Louise. "The Irish National Theatre," *Scholastic* (Pittsburgh), XXIV (17 March 1934), 7-8

Survey.

927   "A Cold Eye Cast on the Abbey Theatre," *The Arts in Ireland*, II, No. 4 (Autumn 1974), 18-27

A symposium in which Denis Johnston, Mary Manning, Hugh Leonard, Joe Dowling, and others assess the present state of the Abbey Theatre.

928   Cole, Alan. "The Gate Influence on Dublin Theatre," *The Dublin Magazine*, XXIX, No. 3 (July-September 1953), 6-14

Compares the philosophies of the Abbey Theatre and the Dublin Gate Theatre, established by Micheál Mac Liammóir and Hilton Edwards in 1928.

929 —. "Acting at the Abbey," *University Review* (Dublin), II, No. 13 (1961), 37-52.

930 Colgan, Gerald. "Ibsen, Joyce and Kafka," *Plays and Players* (London), IX, No. 2 (November 1961), 9

Survey of the Dublin Theatre Festival.

931 —. "Threadbare Harlequin," *Plays and Players* (London), X, No. 5 (February 1963), 20-24

Praises new companies like Orion, Gemini, Libra, and Envoy Productions, which filled the void left by the disbanding of old independent companies like the Pike and the Globe.

932 —. "Dublin 1964," *Plays and Players* (London), XII, No. 1 (October 1964), 11-12

Preview of Dublin Theatre Festival.

933 —. "Dublin: Second Festival Week," *Plays and Players* (London), XII, No. 3 (December 1964), 18

Survey.

934 —. "Dublin 1965," *Plays and Players* (London), XIII, No. 1 (October 1965), 15

Survey of Dublin Theatre Festival.

935 —. "Dublin Theatre Festival," *Plays and Players* (London), XIV, No. 1 (October 1966), 54

Looks at the preparations for the Festival.

936 —. "Dublin Preview," *Plays and Players* (London), XV, No. 1 (October 1967), 43

Looks ahead to the Dublin Theatre Festival.

937 —. "Operation Survival," *Plays and Players* (London), XV, No. 3 (December 1967), 50, 58

Survey of the 1966 Dublin Theatre Festival.

938 —. "Dublin," *Plays and Players* (London), IX, No. 5 (February 1962), 27; IX, No. 6 (March 1962), 27; IX, No. 7 (April 1962), 27-28; IX, No. 9 (June 1962), 44; IX, No. 10 (July 1962), 48; XVI, No. 1 (October 1968), 66; XVI, No. 3 (December 1968), 62-64; XVI, No. 6 (March 1969), 46-47, XVI, No. 8 (May 1969), 57-58; XVII, No. 3 (December 1969), 52-54; XVII, No. 9 (June 1970), 56-57; XVIII, No. 3 (December 1970), 56; XVIII, No. 6 (March 1971), 58; XVIII, No. 8 (May 1971), 52-53; XIX, No. 6 (March 1972), 56; XIX, No. 8 (May 1972), 38-40; XX, No. 8 (May 1973), 62-63; XX, No. 9 (June 1973), 65; XXI, No. 3 (December 1973), 62-64

Survey.

939 Colum, Padraic. "The Irish Literary Movement," *The Forum* (New York and London), III (January 1915), 133-148

The last part of the article surveys the modern Irish theatre.

940 —. "The Irish Theatre in America," *The American Review of Reviews* (New York), LI (February 1915), 244-245

The tendencies and ideals of the Abbey Theatre.

941 —. "Youngest Ireland," *The Seven Arts Magazine* (New York), II, No. 11 (September 1917), 608-623

The last part of the article deals briefly with the Irish theatre.

942 —. "The Abbey Theatre Comes of Age," *Theatre Arts Monthly* (New York), X, No. 9 (September 1926), 580-584

Recalls the Abbey's early successful days.

943 —. "Ibsen in Irish Writing," *Irish Writing* (Cork), No. 7 (February 1949), 66-70

Ibsen does not seem to have had much influence on Irish dramatists.

944 —. "Theatre: Dublin," *Theatre Arts* (New York), XLIV, No. 2 (February 1960), 24-25

Survey underlining "the necessity for the opening of a regular national theatre".

945 "The Coming Irish Players," *Boston Evening Transcript*, (8 September 1911), p. 12

The Abbey Theatre's First American Tour.

946 Conachar, W. M. "The Irish Literary Movement," *Queen's Quarterly*, XLV (Spring 1938), 56-65

Calls attention to certain marked characteristics.

947 Connell, Vivian. "The Theatre," *The Bell* (Dublin), XIII, No. 3 (June 1944), 240-245; No. 4 (July 1944), 344-349; No. 5 (August 1944), 440-443

Survey of play productions.

948 Connolly, James. "National Drama," *The United Irishman* (Dublin), X (24 October 1903), 2

On the Irish National Theatre.

949   Connolly, Peter. "Missing Men of the Theatre," *Hibernia* (Dublin), (16 October 1959), p. 8

The need for the presence of the priest in the Irish Theatre.

950   Conway, Thomas G. "Women's Work in Ireland," *Éire-Ireland* (St. Paul, Minnesota), VII, No. 1 (Spring 1972), 10-17

Includes background to the Irish drama.

951   Cooper, Bryan. "The Drama in Ireland," *The Irish Review* (Dublin), III (May 1913), 140-143

Examines the Abbey as a repertory theatre.

952   Corkery, Daniel. "Peasant Plays Made the Abbey," *The Irish Digest* (Dublin), XXVIII, No. 2 (August 1947), 35-36

By their "unique contribution to world drama".

953   Correy, Percy. "Ireland's National Theatre," *Tabs* (London), XXIV, No. 3 (September 1966), 6-12

Description of the New Abbey Theatre building.

954   Coulter, John. "The Canadian Theatre and the Irish Exemplar," *Theatre Arts Monthly* (New York), XXII (July 1938), 503-509

Argues that the Canadian Theatre should emulate the example of the Abbey Theatre.

955   Coxe, Louis. "Letter from Dublin," *The Nation* (New York), CXC, No. 13 (26 March 1960), 282

"I have seen little Irish drama, new or old, that I would call really good".

956 Craig, May. "My Abbey Debut," *The Irish Digest* (Dublin), XXXIV, No. 1 (July 1949), 53-55

Recollections of the Abbey Theatre by an Irish actress.

957 —. "I'm the Last of the Original 'Playboy' Cast," *The Irish Digest* (Dublin), LXIX, No. 1 (July 1960), 68-72

Recollections of the Abbey Theatre.

958 Crawford, Mary Caroline. "The Irish Players," *The Theatre Magazine* (New York), XIV (November 1911), 157-158, ix

Abbey Theatre's first American tour.

959 Cronin, Anthony. "Theatre," *The Bell* (Dublin), XVII, No. 3 (June 1951), 54-57; No. 4 (July 1951), 43-46; No. 5 (August 1951), 56-57; No. 6 (September 1951), 56-58; No. 7 (October 1951), 58-60; No. 8 (November 1951), 62-64

Survey of play productions.

960 Cronin, Colm. "Festival Preview," *Hibernia* (Dublin), (October 1968), p. 21

The 11th Dublin International Theatre Festival.

961 Crowe, Eileen. "Eileen Crowe Tells Her Story," *The Irish Digest* (Dublin), XX, No. 2 (December 1944), 51-53

Recollections of the Abbey Theatre.

962 Cusack, Cyril. "The Value of a Vital Irish Theatre," *The Irish Digest* (Dublin), LXV, No. 3 (September 1959),

10-14

The Irish actor examines the present unsatisfactory situation and suggests a remedy.

963   —. "Priests at the Theatre," *Hibernia* (Dublin), (23 October 1959), p. 8

The need for the presence of the priest in the Irish Theatre.

964   —. "In Terms of Theatre," *Iris Hibernia* (Fribourg, Switzerland), IV, No. 3 (1960), 20-26

Comments on the Irish Theatre, past and present.

965   D., E. K. "The Irish Theatre Society," *The Dial* (Chicago), (16 December 1911), 521

Letter to the Editor.

966   Dantanus, Ulf. "Time for a New Irish Playwright?" *Moderna Sprak* (Stockholm), LXXI, No. 1 (February-March 1977), 37-47

An assessment of Irish drama today, including a study of John B. Keane, Thomas Murphy, Hugh Leonard, and Brian Friel.

967   Davie, Donald. "The Dublin Theatre Festival," *The Twentieth Century* (London), CLXII (July 1957), 71-73

Survey of the first Dublin Theatre Festival.

968   Dean, Basil. "The Abbey Theatre," *The Twentieth Century* (London), CLXIV (December 1958), 600-603

Review article.

969   De Blacam, Aodh. "What Do We Owe the Abbey?" *The Irish Monthly* (Dublin), LXIII (March 1935), 191-200

"Both happiness in youth and a great advance in the cultivation of letters."

970 —. "Yeats and the Nation; A Surrender to Subjectivity: Why the Abbey Idea Failed," *The Irish Times* (Dublin), (13 June 1935), pp. 6-7

An attack on W. B. Yeats and the Abbey Theatre.

971 De Blaghd, Earnan [i. e. Blythe, Ernest]. "The Abbey Theatre and the Irish Language," *Threshold* (Belfast), II, No. 2 (Summer 1958), 26-33

The Abbey Theatre's policy of producing plays in Irish.

972 —. "Amharclann na Mainistreach," *Iris Hibernia* (Fribourg, Switzerland), IV, No. 3 (1960), 43-45

Survey of Gaelic drama.

973 De Burca, Seamus. "The Queen's Royal Theatre 1929-1966," *Dublin Historical Record*, XXVII (December 1973), 10-26

Blends history, anecdote, and personal recollections of the Queen's Theatre, Dublin.

974 "The Decadence of the Abbey," *Saturday Herald* (Dublin), (19 July 1913), Magazine Page

Condemns the "protracted absences of the Abbey Company" abroad.

975 DeFoe, Louis V. "Visitors from Across the Sea Who Are Victims of Too Much Adulation," *The World* (New York), (26 November 1911), p. 6M

Abbey Theatre's first American tour.

976   Delany, Maureen. "Meet Maureen Delany," *The Irish Digest*
      (Dublin), XIX, No. 2 (August 1944), 55-56

>   Recollections of the Abbey Theatre.

977   De Lury, A. T. "The Irish Drama: Once More the Soul of
      Eire Throbs in Tara's Tragic Muse," *Celtic Forum*
      (Toronto), I, No. 2 (March 1935), 10-11

>   Observations.

978   —. "Literature in Ireland," *The Canadian Bookman* (Tor-
      onto), XX (August-September 1938), 25-29

>   Reflections on what is implied in a national literature, including
>   references to Irish dramatists.

979   Dent, Alan. "Abbey Theatre Drama Festival," *The Spectator*
      (London), CLXI (19 August 1938), 299

>   Survey of play productions.

980   De Paor, Seoram. "The Ulster Literary Theatre," *Ulad:
      A Literary and Critical Magazine* (Belfast), I, No. 4
      (September 1905), 5-10

>   Survey of the Theatre's productions.

981   de Smet, Robert. "Le théâtre anglais depuis la guerre,"
      Revue de Paris, (1 December 1931), 616-634

>   Survey.

982   —. "Le mouvement dramatique en angleterre," *Revue de
      Paris,* (15 September 1932), 456-470

>   Survey.

983   —. "Le mouvement dramatique en angleterre," *Revue de Paris*, (1 September 1933), 682-699; (1 October 1934), 185-201; (1 October 1935), 688-704

> Survey.

984   —. "La littérature dramatique en angleterre," *Revue de Paris*, (1 November 1936), 190-209

> Survey.

985   —. "Le théâtre en Irlande," *Revue de Paris*, (15 October 1937), 903-919

> Survey.

986   —. "Le théâtre en angleterre," *Revue de Paris*, (1 December 1937), 658-674

> Survey.

987   —. "Le théâtre en angleterre," *Revue de Paris*, (1 December 1939), 969-983

> Survey.

988   Desmond, Shaw. "The Irish Renaissance," *The Outlook* (New York), CXXXVIII (15 October 1924), 247-249

> Answers the questions: "*Whence* sprang the Irish Renaissance? *Why* its existence? *Whither* is it trending?".

989   "De Valera As Play Censor, " *The Manchester Guardian Weekly*, XXX, No. 15 (13 April 1934), 296

> The President of the Irish Republic "held strong views on the plays to be presented".

990   Digges, Dudley. "A Theatre Was Made," *The Irish Digest* (Dublin), IV, No. 4 (October 1939), 11-14

The famous Irish actor recollects how the Abbey Theatre started.

991   "Discussion on Irish Theatre Misfired," *The Irish Times* (Dublin), (27 February 1961), p. 5

Report on discussion by Brendan Behan, John B. Keane, Ray MacAnally, and Seamus Kelly.

992   Ditsky, John M. "All Irish Here: The 'Irishman' in Modern Drama," *Dalhousie Review* (Halifax), LIV, No. 1 (Spring 1974), 94-102

Certain British and American playwrights have attached special abilities and responsibilities to characters filling "Irish" roles.

993   Donn, Brian, "The Dublin Actors in London," *Inis Fáil* (London), No. 34 (July 1907), 9

The Abbey Theatre is not nationalistic enough.

994   Donn, Uilliam [W. B. Reynolds]. "The Ulster Literary Theatre," *Uladh: A Literary and Critical Magazine* (Belfast), I, No. 1 (November 1904), 7-8

Survey of play productions in Belfast.

995   Donoghue, Denis. "Irish Writing," *The Month* (London), XVII (March 1957), 180-185

General characteristics.

996   —. "Dublin Letter," *The Hudson Review* (New York), XIII, No. 4 (Winter 1960), 579-585

Discusses the highlights of the Dublin International Theatre Festival.

997 Dowling, John. "The Abbey Theatre Attacked," *Ireland Today* (Dublin), II, No. 1 (January 1937), 35-43 [For not presenting nationalistic plays.] The attack is continued in the following two issues by Sean O Meadhra and Pat [Patrick D. Kenny].

998 "Drama," *The Nation* (New York), XCIII (30 November 1911), 528-529

Abbey Theatre's first American tour.

999 "Dublin," *Plays and Players* (London), I, No. 1 (October 1953), 25

Survey of play productions.

1000 "Dublin: Theatretown," *Focus: A Monthly Review* (Belfast), IV (October 1961), 239-244

Survey of play productions.

1001 "Dublin's Abbey Players Set for Coast-to-Coast Tour," *Newsweek* (Dayton, Ohio), IV, No. 21 (24 November 1934), 25.

1002 Duffus, R. L. "Dublin—Story of Two Cities. St. Patrick's Day Finds the Old Poetry of the City Co-Existing with a New Vitality," *The New York Times Magazine* (17 March 1957), 28, 39, 41.

1003 Dukes, Ashley. "The Irish Scene: Dublin Plays and Playhouses," *Theatre Arts Monthly* (New York), XIV, No 5 (May 1930), 378-384

Survey.

1004 "Dull Gaelic Plough," *Newsweek* (Dayton, Ohio), XXX, No. 21 (24 November 1947), 84

Result of the policy that "Gaelic plays and Gaelic-speaking actors and actresses have precedence over all else at the Abbey".

1005   Duncan, Ellen. "The Irish National Theatre," *The Speaker* (London), New Series, XV (26 January 1907), 496-497.

1006   —. "The Irish National Theatre," *The Irish Times* (Dublin), (28 December 1912), p. 9

Letter to the Editor.

1007   Dunne, John J. "I Treasure Those Theatre Programmes," *The Irish Digest* (Dublin), LXXV, No. 2 (August 1962), 81-82

"The footlights gleam again in these souvenirs of exciting nights".

1008   Dunsany, Lord. "Romance and the Modern Stage," *National Review* (London), LVII (July 1911), 827-835

Realism "has come in romance's place".

1009   —. "Some Irish Writers Whom I Have Known," *Irish Writing* (Cork), Nos. 20-21 (November 1952), 78-82

Recollections of J. M. Synge, Lady Gregory, W. B. Yeats, George Russell, James Stephens, George Moore, and Oliver St. John Gogarty.

1010   Eaton, Walter Prichard. "Viewing Irish Players in the Light of Reason," *The Sunday Record-Herald* (Chicago), (17 December 1911), Part VII, p. 3

Abbey Theatre's first American tour.

1011   —. "Some Plays Worth While," *The American Magazine* (New York), LXXIII (February 1912), 491-492

Abbey Theatre's first American tour.

1012 —. "The Literary Drama," *The American Magazine* (New York), LXXIII (March 1912), 625

Abbey Theatre's first American tour.

1013 Eberhart, Richard. "Memory of Meeting Yeats, AE, Gogarty, James Stephens," *The Literary Review* (Teaneck, New Jersey), I, No. 1 Autumn (1957), 51-56.

1014 Edwards, Hilton. "How I Plan to Run R. E. Television Drama," *The Irish Digest* (Dublin). LXXII, No. 3 (September 1961), 19-21

Interview.

1015 Edwards, James. "Dublin," *Plays and Players* (London), I, No. 10 (July 1954), 22

Survey.

1016 Eglinton, John. "Irish Letter," *The Dial* (Chicago), LXXXI (December 1926), 496-499

On the Abbey Theatre.

1017 Ellis-Fermor, Una. "Dramatic Notes: The Abbey Theatre Festival (7-20 August 1938)," *English* (London), II, No. 9 (Autumn 1938), 174-177

Survey.

1018 Ervine, St. John. "The Irish Dramatist and the Irish People," *The Forum* (New York), LI (June 1914), 940-948

"The Irish dramatist writes his plays round peasant characters because peasant life is the national life".

1019   —. "The Abbey—Past, Present, and Future," *The Observer*
         (London), (15 September 1935), p. 15; (22 Septem-
         ber 1935), p. 17.

1020   —. "We Don't Want State Aid for the Theatre," *Drama*
         (London), No. 19 (July 1942), 2-4

         Argues that the State's subsidy to the Abbey Theatre should be
         unconditional.

1021   —. "Peasant Plays and Kitchen Comedies," *The Irish Digest*
         (Dublin), XIX, No. 4 (October 1944), 27-29

         On the Group Theatre, Belfast.

1022   Everson, Ida G. "Young Lennox Robinson and the Abbey
         Theatre's First American Tour (1911-1912)," *Modern
         Drama*, IX, No. 1 (May 1966), 74-89

         Also includes the itenerary of the tour.

1023   —. "Lennox Robinson and Synge's *Playboy* (1911-1930):
         Two Decades of American Cultural Growth," *The New
         England Quarterly* (Baltimore), XLIV (March 1971),
         3-21

         The changing attitudes of American audiences toward Irish
         plays.

1024   F., I. "Actors Without a Stage," *The Irish Digest* (Dublin),
         LVII, No. 3 (September 1956), 87-89

         On Radio Eireann Players.

1025   Fallon, Gabriel. "More About a Catholic Theatre," *Irish
         Rosary* (Dublin), XXXIX, No. 11 (November 1935),
         810-814.

1026   —. "Abbey Interlude: Being Passages from a Pastiche in

Progress," *Capuchin Annual* (Dublin), VIII (1937), 95-102.

1027 —. "Drama of Lost Leaders," *The Irish Monthly* (Dublin), LXV (November 1937), 769-776

Criticism of a "Dictatorial Yeats".

1028 —. "The Ageing Abbey," *The Irish Monthly* (Dublin), LXVI, No. 778 (April 1938), 265-272; LXVI, No. 779 (May 1938), 339-344

"The decline of the Abbey Theatre in things of the theatre . . . began with the going out of the Fays and their players".

1029 —. "Subsidies, Cinemas and Theatre Festivals," *The Irish Monthly* (Dublin), LXVI (August 1938), 553-558.

1030 —. "And Now This Abbey Theatre," *The Leader* (Dublin), LXXVI (20 August 1938), 562-564 [Is it a national theatre?]. See correspondence in the following issues.

1031 —. "Festival Fanfare," *Hibernia* (Dublin), (September 1938), pp. 11, 19-20

A collection of pronouncements concerning the Abbey Theatre Festival.

1032 —. "Words on a National Theatre," *The Irish Monthly* (Dublin), XLVI (September 1938), 631-638

There is no Irish national theatre despite the Abbey Theatre Festival.

1033 —. "That After-Festival Feeling," *The Irish Monthly* (Dublin), LXVI (October 1938), 698-704

A big hangover.

1034 —. "Tribute to the Fays," *The Irish Monthly* (Dublin), LXXIII (January 1945), 18-24

> The contribution of William G. and Frank Fay to the Abbey Theatre.

1035 —. "The Abbey Theatre Speaks," *The Irish Monthly* (Dublin), LXXVI (February 1948), 88-92.

1036 —. "The Fays Made Abbey History," *The Irish Digest* (Dublin), XXX, No. 1 (March 1948), 50-52

> "They created a unique style of acting".

1037 —. "Maritain Was Wrong," *The Commonweal* (New York), LII (26 May 1950), 175-176

> Defends Seamus Byrne's *Design for a Headstone* against conservative Catholic demonstrators who found the play anticlerical and Marxist.

1038 —. "Abbey Theatre Today," *America* (New York), LXXXVII (4 October 1952), 14-16. Reprinted in *The Tablet* (London), CC (11 October 1952), 302-303.

1039 —. "A Critic Defends the Abbey," *The Irish Digest* (Dublin), XLIV, No. 2 (February 1953), 41-43

> "Today it is more firmly established than ever in its tenuous and adventurous career".

1040 —. "Why Is There No Irish Claudel or Mauriac?" *Evening Press* (Dublin), (5 Februry 1955), p. 5

> Irish dramatists do not concern themselves specifically with religious or spiritual themes.

1041 —. "The Future of the Irish Theatre," *Studies; An Irish Quarterly Review* (Dublin), XLIV (Spring 1955),

92-100

> "It is possible that we will return to the first principles of Yeats and use them as he intended they should be used—to bring upon the stage the deeper thoughts and emotions of Ireland".

1042 —. "Dublin Letter," *America* (New York), XCVIII, No. 2 (12 October 1957), 46-47

Survey of play productions.

1043 —. "Dublin International Theatre Festival," *Threshold* (Belfast), I, No. 3 (Autumn 1957), 75-81

Review of the first Dublin International Theatre Festival.

1044 —. "The Achievements and Problems of the Irish Theatre," *International Theatre Annual* (London), No. 2 (1957), 53-63

Survey of dramatic activities since the Abbey Theatre.

1045 —. "Alas, My Hilton and My Micheál," *International Theatre Annual* (Lodnon), No. 3 (1958), 42-52

Survey of play productions in Dublin, 1957-1958.

1046 —. "Dublin International Theatre Festival, 1959," *Threshold* (Belfast), III (Autumn 1959), 63-75

Review of Dublin's second annual Festival.

1047 —. "The Abbey Theatre Today," *Threshold* (Belfast), III (Winter 1959), 24-32

Reflections on the Abbey Theatre during its fifty-six years.

Reprinted in *Irish Hibernia* (Fribourg, Switzerland), IV, No. 3 (1960), 46-54.

1048   —. "All This and the Abbey Too," *Studies: An Irish Quarter-ly Review* (Dublin), XLVIII, No. 192 (Winter 1959), 434-442

>   Implies that only an upsurge of Irish dramatic talent will effect the rebirth of the Irish theatre.

1049   —. "Dublin's Fourth Theatre Festival," *Modern Drama*, V, No. 1 (May 1962), 21-26

>   Survey of play productions.

1050   —. "Alan Simpson's Story of the Pike," *Hibernia* (Dublin), (December 1962), p. 28

>   Review article on the Pike Theatre, Dublin.

1051   —. "Focus on the Peacock Theatre," *Hibernia* (Dublin), (14 July 1972), p. 20

>   Observations on the Abbey Theatre.

1052   Farrell, James T. "The Irish Cultural Renaissance in the Last Century," *Irish Writing* (Cork), No. 25 (December 1953), 50-53

>   "Synge, Yeats, Lady Greogry and their contemporaries helped bring a note of reality into Irish writing".

1053   Farrell, Michael. "The Country Theatre, *The Bell* (Dublin), I, No 1 (October 1940), 78-82

>   Report on theatrical activities.

1054   —. "Plays for the Country Theatre," *The Bell* (Dublin), I, No. 3 (December 1940), 58, 64; II, No. 1 (April 1941), 78-84; No. 2 (May 1941), 31-38

>   Suggestions for play productions.

1055 —. "More Country Theatre," *The Bell* (Dublin), I, No. 4 (January 1941), 78-86

Survey of theatre festivals.

1056 —. "A Famous Country Theatre," *The Bell* (Dublin), I, No. 2 (November 1940), 76-84

Birr Little Theatre.

1057 —. "Another Little Theatre," *The Bell* (Dublin), I, No. 6 (March 1941), 83-88

In Dundalk.

1058 —. "Drama at the Sligo Feis," *The Bell* (Dublin), II, No. 3 (June 1941), 88-95

Survey of play productions.

1059 —. "Drama in Ulster Now," *The Bell* (Dublin), II, No. 4 (July 1941), 82-88

Survey of play productions.

1060 —. "Our Only Regional Drama," *The Bell* (Dublin), II, No. 5 (August 1941), 79-87

The Ulster Literary Theatre.

1061 —. "Opera for the Country Theatre," *The Bell* (Dublin), II, No. 6 (September 1941), 76-82

Suggestions.

1062 —. "The Country Producer," *The Bell* (Dublin), III, No. 1 (October 1941), 71-76

A catalogue of plays and a summer course planned to help country producers.

1063 —. "Drama in Kerry," *The Bell* (Dublin), III, No. 2 (November 1941), 149-155

Survey of play productions.

1064 —. "Drama in Cork City," *The Bell* (Dublin), III, No. 3 (December 1941), 214-220

Survey of play productions.

1065 —. "The Country Theatre," *The Bell* (Dublin), III, No. 5 (February 1942), 386-391

Reflections on the state of the theatre.

1066 —. "Drama in Donegal," *The Bell* (Dublin), IX, No. 1 (October 1944), 66-73

Survey of play productions.

1067 —. "Drama in Kerry," *The Bell* (Dublin), IX, No. 4 (January 1945), 342-348

Survey of play productions.

1068 —. "The Theatre," *The Bell* (Dublin), IX, No. 5 (February 1945), 439-443; No. 6 (March 1945), 524-527; X, No. 1 (April 1945), 76-81; No. 2 (May 1945), 168-171

Survey of play productions.

1069 —. "Drama in Dundalk," *The Bell* (Dublin), X, No. 3 (June 1945), 258-264

Survey of play productions.

1070 —. "Theatre," *The Bell* (Dublin), X, No. 4 (July 1945), 354-359; No. 5 (August 1945), 442-446

Survey of play productions.

1071 —. "A Donegal Festival," *The Bell* (Dublin), X, No. 6 (September 1945), 526-530

Survey of play productions.

1072 —. "The Theatre," *The Bell* (Dublin), XI, No. 1 (October 1945), 630-634

Survey of play productions.

1073 —. "Drama in Kerry," *The Bell* (Dublin), XI, No. 2 (November 1945), 716-722

Survey of play productions.

1074 —. "The Theatre," *The Bell* (Dublin), XI, No. 3 (December 1945), 804-808; No. 4 (January 1946), 901-907

Survey of play productions.

1075 —. "The Theatre in 1945," *The Bell* (Dublin), XI, No. 5 (February 1946), 998-1003

Summary.

1076 —. "Drama Festivals in 1946," *The Bell* (Dublin), XI, No. 6 (March 1946), 1091-1096

Survey.

1077 —. "The Theatre," *The Bell* (Dublin), XII, No. 1 (April 1946), 66-71

Survey of play productions.

1078   —. "Drama Festivals in 1947," *The Bell* (Dublin), XIV,
        No. 1 (April 1947), 69-74

>   Survey.

1079   Faughnan, Leslie. "The Future of the Abbey Theatre; To-
        wards a New Dynamic," *Studies; An Irish Quarterly
        Review* (Dublin), LV (Autumn 1966), 236-246

>   Discusses all aspects of the new Abbey Theatre on the oc-
>   casion of its opening.

1080   Fay, Frank J. "The Irish Literary Theatre," *The United
        Irishman* (Dublin), V, No. 14 (4 May 1901), 6

>   "I would prefer to see a Theatre inaugurated here that would
>   abolish English completely, and conduct its operations outside
>   of the uncongenial atmosphere of an English commercial
>   theatre".

1081   —. "An Irish National Theatre," *The United Irishman* (Dub-
        lin), V, No. 115 (11 May 1901), 6; and No. 116
        (18 May 1901), 6

>   The Irish language should be used as a medium for the Irish
>   drama.

1082   —. *"Samhain,"* *The United Irishman* (Dublin), VI, No. 139
        (26 October 1901), 2

>   Discusses material in The Irish Literary Theatre's journal.

1083   —. "The Irish Literary Theatre," *The United Irishman* (Dub-
        lin), VI, No. 140 (2 November 1901), 2

>   Argues against English actors performing Irish plays.

1084   —. "The Irish Literary Theatre," *The United Irishman* (Dub-
        lin), VI, No. 143 (23 November 1901), 3

"The Irish Literary Theatre has been conducted on too large a scale and . . . its performances were too far apart to have the rousing effect they should have on the public mind".

1085 —. "The Irish Players," *The Saturday Review* (London), CXII (1 July 1911), 17

Letter to the Editor on the Abbey Theatre's first American tour.

1085a F[ay] G[erard]. "The Abbey Theatre's Growth: Irish Players for Irish Plays," *Manchester Guardian Weekly*, XXXIX (12 August 1938), 139

1086 —. "The Abbey Theatre and the One-Act Play," *One Act Play Magazine* (Boston), II, No. 4 (August-September 1938), 323-326.

1087 —. "At the Abbey," *The Spectator* (London), CXCIII (24 December 1954), 802, 804.

1088 —. "Ructions in the Abbey Theatre," *The Irish Digest* (Dublin), LIX, No. 2 (April 1957), 18-20

Recollections.

1089 —. "They Made Me an Abbey Theatre 'Rioter'," *The Irish Digest* (Dublin), LXXXII, No. 3 (January 1965), 13-15

During shooting an Irish film.

1090 —. "The Abbey Theatre," *Ireland of the Welcomes* (Dublin), XV, No. 2 (July-August 1966), 28-32

Recollections by the son of Frank Fay, the Abbey actor.

1091 —. "Theatre Built on Sand," *Hibernia* (Dublin), (August 1966), p. 8

Observations on the New Abbey Theatre.

1092   --. "My Hopes for the New Abbey," *The Irish Digest* (Dub-
        lin), LXXXVII, No. 3 (September 1966), 27-30

        The son of Frank Fay gives glimpses of some of the great
        figures associated with the National Theatre and looks forward
        to its becoming "an international theatrical showpiece".

1093   —. "The Abbey Theatre—Past, Present, and Future," *Hiber-
        nia* (Dublin), (March 1967), p. 11

        Reflections on the state of the Theatre.

1094   —. "The Irish Theatre,"*Drama* (London), No. 84 (Spring
        1967), 33-35

        "The regular professional theatre barely exists in the Republic
        of Ireland outside Dublin".

1095   —. "Festival at Large," *The Irish Times* (Dublin), (7 October
        1967), p. 10

        Observations on the Dublin Theatre Festival.

1096   Fay, S. "Ireland, Your Ireland," *The Spectator* (London),
        CCIX (12 October 1962), 559-560

        Review of the Dublin Theatre Festival.

1097   Fay, W. G. "How We Began the Abbey," *The Irish Digest*
        (Dublin), XXVIII, No. 4 (October 1947), 30-32

        "The original capital of our National Theatre was   £ 10!".

1098   Fay, William P. "Le Théâtre National Irlandais; ou, les
        Débuts de l'Abbey Theatre," *La Revue des Deux
        Mondes* (Paris), No. 17 (1 September 1959), 93-103

Reflections on the Abbey by the Irish Amabassador in Paris.

1099   "Features of New Theatre," *The Irish Press* (Dublin), (22 October 1958), p. 1

The new Abbey Theatre, which eventually opened in 1966.

1100   Feeney, William J. "The Rugged Path: A Modern View of Informers," *Eire-Ireland*, II, No. 1 (Spring 1967), 41-47

Explores changing dramatic attitudes toward informers.

1101   Fennell, Desmond. "The Theatre Festival," *Hibernia* (Dublin), (October 1961), p. 6

Survey of the Dublin International Theatre Festival.

1102   Ferrar, Harold. "Robert Emmet in Irish Drama," *Eire-Ireland*, I (Summer 1966), 19-28

Surveys the treatment of the Emmet legend from Dion Boucicault to Paul Vincent Carroll.

1103   "Film Being Made," *Evening Herald* (Dublin), (30 December 1958), p. 1

Documentary film on the Abbey Theatre.

1104   Finn, Seamus. "The Abbey Theatre," *The Irish Times* (Dublin), (29 July 1944), p. 3

Letter to the Editor on the condition of the Theatre.

1105   Finnian. "Gael-Linn Agus An Dramaiocht," *Iris Hibernia* (Fribourg, Switzerland), IV, No. 3 (1960), 58-62

On Gaelic drama.

1106 Fisher, Jonathan. "Another Dublin Theatre Festival?" *Hibernia* (Dublin), (May 1966), p. 10

Observations.

1107 Fitzgerald, Marion. "Arthur Shields Remembers the Abbey with Pride," *The Irish Digest* (Dublin), LXXXII, No. 2 (December 1964), 51-53

Recollections of the Abbey Theatre by an Irish actor.

1108 Fitzgerald, Maurice. "The Future of the Peasant Play," *Sinn Féin* (Dublin), New Series, IV, No. 163 (15 March 1913), 6-7

Mainly on J. M. Synge and Lady Gregory.

1109 Fitz-Simon, Christopher. "The Theatre in Dublin," *Modern Drama*, II, No. 3 (December 1959), 289-294

Discovers signs of vigour in recent productions.

1110 Flaccus, Kimball, "Irish Ambassadors of Culture," *Scholastic* (Pittsburgh), XXI, No. 6 (23 October 1937), 17-18

The Abbey Players at Broadway.

1111 Flannery, James W. "Action and Reaction at the Dublin Theatre Festival," *Educational Theatre Journal*, XIX (March 1967), 72-80

Survey of play productions.

1112 —. "W. B. Yeats and the Abbey Theatre Company," *Educational Theatre Journal*, XXVII (May 1975), 179-196.

1113 Florence, Jean. "Le théâtre irlandais," *Phalange* (Paris), X, No. 55 (20 January 1911), 52-61

On J. M. Synge and Lady Gregory.

1114 Ford, Mary K. "Is the Celtic Revival Distinctly Irish?" *North American Review* (New York), CLXXXIII, No. 601 (October 1906), 771-775.

1115 "Forty Years of Irish Drama: Yeats, Synge and Lady Gregory; From the Visionaries to the Realists," *The Times Literary Supplement* (London), (13 April 1940), pp. 182, 186

 Review article.

1116 "Foundation Stone of the Abbey Laid," *Evening Herald* (Dublin), (3 September 1963), p. 7

 The New Abbey Theatre, which eventually opened in 1966.

1117 "Four Reasons for Condemning the Irish Players," *The Irish World and American Industrial Liberator* (New York), (16 December 1911), p. 5

 On the Abbey Theatre's first American tour.

1118 Fox, R. M. "Realism in Irish Drama," *The Irish Statesman* (Dublin), X (23 June 1928), 310-312

 "The drama of low life is only now being written. Previously it was sentimentalised".

1119 —. "Modern Irish Drama," *Theatre Arts* (New York), XXIV (January 1940), 22-25

 Survey of play productions.

1120 —. "Adventures in Irish Drama," *The Millgate* (Manchester), XXXV (May 1940), 448-450

 On the Dublin art theatres.

1121 —. "Modern Irish Drama Surveyed," *The Irish Digest* (Dublin), VII, No. 1 (July 1940), 26-29

> Answers the question: Is Dublin the theatrical capital of the world?.

1122 —. "Drama De Profundis," *Drama* (London), No. 7 (July 1940), 4-6

> Survey of play productions at the Abbey and the Dublin Gate Theatres.

1123 —. "The Theatre Goes On in Ireland," *Theatre Arts* (New York), XXIV (November 1940), 783-790

> Reports that the War forced the Abbey to give up visits to England and America and to tour the Irish countryside with thrillers and farces.

1124 —. "Ups and Downs in the Irish Theatre," *Theatre Arts* (New York), XXV, No. 5 (May 1941), 353-358

> Survey of Irish drama during the War.

1125 —. "Irish Drama Today," *Drama* (London), No. 16 (January 1942), 1-3

> Survey of play productions.

1126 —. "What Next in Irish Drama?" *Theatre Arts* (New York), XXVI, No. 4 (April 1942), 245-249

> Answers the question: "What has Irish drama to say to the conflict in Europe and the world?".

1127 —. "The Theatre in Ireland," *Drama* (London), No. 22 (January 1943), 6

> Survey of play productions.

1128 —. "Wild Riders of Irish Drama," *Theatre Arts* (New York), XXVIII, No. 5 (May 1944), 301-304

Survey of the year's play productions.

1129 —. "Irish Theatre," *Theatre Arts* (New York), XXIX, No. 5 (May 1945), 286-293

"When we look at the past year there is nothing very original to record".

1130 —. "Irish Drama in War and Peace," *Theatre Arts* (New York), XXX, No. 4 (April 1946), 231-235

"Luckily the Irish theatre was not submerged in the chaos of world conflict as happened elsewhere in Europe".

1131 —. "Twilight over Irish Drama," *Theatre Arts* (New York), XXX, No. 12 (December 1946), 706-708

The theatre in Ireland "has been fighting desperately to retain its finest actors against the coaxings of the film companies".

1132 —. "The Theatre in Eire," *Theatre Arts* (New York), XXXI, No. 11 (November 1947), 30

Survey of play productions.

1133 —. "Maureen Delany Takes a Bow," *The Irish Digest* (Dublin), XXIX, No. 2 (December 1947), 21-23

Includes recollections of the Abbey Theatre.

1134 —. "Profile of Lady Longford," *The Irish Digest* (Dublin), XXIX, No. 4 (February 1948), 71-72

Longford Productions at the Dublin Gate Theatre.

1135 —. "Irish Drama Knocks at the Door," *Life and Letters*

(London), LXI, No. 140 (April 1949), 16-21

> The Irish theatre is beginning to express the complexity of modern life and thought in Ireland though the traditional approach still hampers this and imposes a time-lag".

1136 —. "Same Program, Fifty Years Later," *The American Mercury* (New York), LXXXI (July 1955), 43-44

> The Abbey Theatre on the occasion of its Golden Jubilee.

1137 —. "Foundations of the Abbey," *Aryan Path* (Bombay), XXXV (January 1964), 14-16

> "Since these formative years there have been many good plays but none which cast a beam like a searchlight on Ireland's past and future".

1138 Frank, André. "Georges Pitoëff et le baptême parisien du théâtre d'irlande," *Cahiers de la Compagnie Madeleine-Jean-Louis Barrault* (Paris), No. 37 (1962), 102-106

> Productions of plays by J. M. Synge, Lady Gregory, and Bernard Shaw.

1139 Friel, Brian. "Plays Pleasant and Unpleasant," *The Times Literary Supplement* (London), (17 March 1972), pp. 305-306

> On the subjects of Irish drama then and now.

1140 "The Future of the Abbey Theatre," *The Times* (London), (17 September 1963), p. 16.

1141 Gad, Carl. "Moderne irsk theater," *Ugens tilskuer* (Copenhagen), VI, No. 299 (23 June 1916), 313-315; No. 301 (7 July 1916), 329-331; No. 309 (1 September 1916), 391-394

Survey.

1142 Gallagher, J. F. "The Carrion Crows of Stageland," *The Irish World and American Industrial Liberator* (New York), (14 October 1911), p. 7

On the Abbey Theatre's first American tour.

1143 Gascoigne, Bamber. "Shem, Ham, and Siobhan," *The Spectator* (London), CCVII (29 September 1961), 425+

Review of the Dublin Theatre Festival.

1144 Gassner, John. "The Theatre Arts," *The Forum* (Philadelphia), CIX (April 1948), 212-214

On the Dublin Gate Theatre's 1948 tour of Canada and New York.

1145 —. "The Trifurcation of Drama and Theatre in English," *Quarterly Journal of Speech* (Chicago), XXXIX (1953), 323-334

On the advantages and disadvantages of having distinctive theatre in England, Ireland, and America.

1146 "Gate Crisis," *Hibernia* (Dublin), (23 January 1970), p. 4

The Dublin Gate Theatre is to receive a subsidy.

1147 Gaynor, Arthur, "Ireland & the Theatre," *Banba* (Dublin), III, No. 2 (June 1922), 106-112

Observations.

1148 Gebler, Ernest. "Irish Character on the English Stage," *Envoy* (Dublin), I, No. 1 (December 1949), 56-58

"The English theatre producer apparently at once associates

anything Irish with an absolute necessity to be funny at all costs".

1149   —. "A Theatre Festival," *Hibernia* (Dublin), (4 August 1972), p. 17

Observations on the Dublin International Theatre Festival.

1150   George, Michael. "Hilton Edwards Looks Ahead," *The Irish Digest* (Dublin), LXXIII, No. 3 (January 1962), 9-11

Drama on Irish Television.

1151   Gill, Michael J. "Neo-Paganism and the Stage," *The New Ireland Review* (Dublin), XXVII (May 1907), 179-187

Claims that the Irish plays are vulgar and brutal.

1152   Gossen, John. "The New Abbey," *Focus; A Monthly Review* (Belfast), IX (September 1966), 206-207

Observations.

1153   Gray, Ken. "T. E. on the Abbey," *The Irish Times* (Dublin), (21 July 1966), p. 8

Telefis Eireann's film on the Abbey Theatre.

1154   "Great Days at the Abbey," *The Irish Digest* (Dublin), LXXVII, No. 2 (April 1963), 71-74

Recollections of the Abbey Theatre by the actors J. M. Kerrigan and Arthur Shields.

1155   Gregory, Lady [Isabella Augusta] . "The Coming of the Irish Players," *Collier's Magazine* (Springfield, Ohio), XLVIII (21 October 1911), 15, 24

Abbey Theatre's first American tour.

1156 —. "A Repertory Theatre," *Herald Tribune* (New York), (26 November 1911), Part V, pp. 6-7

Gives information on the Abbey Theatre.

1157 —. "The Irish Theatre and the People," *Yale Review* (New Haven, Connecticut), I, No. 2 (January 1912), 188-191

How the Irish Theatre came into being.

1158 Grey, W. R. "Northern Theatre," *Focus; A Monthly Review* (Belfast), VIII (November 1965), 247-249

Survey of dramatic activities in Northern Ireland.

1159 [Griffith, Arthur]. "The Origins of the Abbey Theatre," *Sinn Féin* (Dublin), V (14 February 1914), 1

Yeats did not build the National Theatre; he ruined it.

1160 Grzebieniowski, Tadeusz. "Teatr i dramat w Irlandii jako czynniki odradzajacej sei kultury narodowej," *Kultura i spoleczénstwo* (Warsaw), II, No. 4 (1958), 190-200

Irish drama as an element of revival of Ireland's national culture.

1161 Gunnell, Doris. "Le Nouveau Théâtre Irlandais," *La Revue* (Paris), XCIV, No. 1 (1 January 1912), 91-106

On the plays of W. B. Yeats, J. M. Synge and Lady Gregory.

1162 Gunning, G. Hamilton. "The Decline of Abbey Theatre Drama," *The Irish Review* (Dublin), I, No. 12 (February 1912), 606-609

Claims that the dramatists who heralded and developed the decline of the Abbey Theatre are Lennox Robinson, T. C. Murray, and St. John Ervine.

1163   Guthrie, Tyrone. "Closeup of Ireland's Basic Problem," *New York Times Magazine* (19 January 1964), 22, 24, 28

       Includes background to the Irish drama.

1164   —. "Irish Theatre," *Hibernia* (Dublin), (22 January 1971), p. 16

       Observations on the state of the Irish drama.

1165   Gwynn, Aubrey, S. J. "The Origins of the Anglo-Irish Theatre," *Studies; An Irish Quarterly Review* (Dublin), XXVIII (June 1939), 260-274

       The absence of dramatic literature in the native Irish literary tradition.

1166   Gwynn, Stephen. "The Irish Literary Theatre and Its Affinities," *Fortnightly Review* (London), LXXVI, New Series LXX (December 1901), 1050-1062

       Survey.

1167   —. "An Uncommercial Theatre," *Fortnightly Review* (London), LXXII, New Series (September 1902), 1044-1054

       "What Mr. Yeats and his friends have done is to kindle in Ireland the desire for an art which is an art of ideas".

1168   —. "Poetry and the Stage," *Fortnightly Review* (London and New York), LXXXV, New Series (February 1909), 337-351

       Includes discussions of W. B. Yeats and Bernard Shaw.

1169   Habart, Michel. "Le théâtre irlandais," *Théâtre Populaire* (Paris), No. 9 (September-October 1954), 24-43

On W. B. Yeats, J. M. Synge, Lady Gregory, and Sean O'Casey.

1170 Halton, Thomas. "200 Rejected Plays," *Hibernia* (Dublin), (5 February 1960), p. 9

Observations on the state of the Irish drama.

1172 Hamilton, Clayton. "The Irish National Theatre," *The Bookman* (New York), XXXIV, No. 5 (January 1912), 508-516. Reprinted in *Studies in Stagecraft* (London: Grant Richards; New York: Henry Holt, 1914), pp. 123-144

Discusses the aims and achievements of the Irish National Theatre Society.

1173 —. "The Players," *Everybody's Magazine* (New York), XXVIII (May 1913), 678-680

Survey of the 1912-1913 American season.

1174 Hammond, Percy. "Cause of the Irish Riots," *The Chicago Sunday Tribune*, (4 February 1912), Part 2, p. 1

Abbey Theatre's first American tour.

1175 Hannay, J. O. "The Stage Irishman: His Origin and Development," *The Irish Times* (Dublin), (8 February 1912), p. 7

Lecture at the Theatre of the Royal Dublin Society.

1176 Hardie, Margaret. "Contemporary British Dramatists," *Cizé jazyky ve škole*, X (1967), 97-104, 145-153

Includes discussions on Sean O'Casey, Samuel Beckett, and Brendan Behan.

1177   Harmon, Maurice. "The Era of Inhibitions: Irish Literature 1920-60," *Emory University Quarterly* (Atlanta, Georgia), XXII (Spring 1966), 18-28

Includes references to J. M. Synge, Sean O'Casey, and Brendan Behan.

1178   —. "By Memory Inspired: Themes and Forces in Recent Irish Writing," *Eire-Ireland* (St. Paul, Minnesota), VIII, No. 2 (1973), 3-19

Background to the Irish drama of the 1950s.

1179   Hayes, J. J. "The Little Theatre Movement in Ireland," *The Drama Magazine* (Chicago), XVI (April 1926), 261-262

Reports a resurgence of amateur productions.

1180   —. "Who Will Go to Ireland for Aonach Tailteann?" *Theatre Arts Monthly* (New York), XV, No. 1 (January 1931), 78-80

Drama in the ancient Gaelic celebration inaugurated some 3,000 years ago in memory of Queen Tailte.

1181   —. "The Irish Scene," *Theatre Arts Monthly* (New York), XVI, No. 11 (November 1932), 922-926

Survey of play productions.

1182   —. "Theatre in Ireland," *Christian Science Monitor Magazine* (Boston), (15 March 1947), 19

Regrets the poor quality of the Abbey productions.

1183 "Helping Hands for Abbey Theatre," *The Times* (London), (18 February 1965), p. 16

> Names of the new shareholders.

1184 Henderson, Gordon. "An Interview with Denis Johnston," *Journal of Irish Literature* (Newark, Delaware), II (May-September 1973), 30-44

> On Irish drama.

1185 —. "An Interview with Hilton Edwards and Micheál Mac Liammóir," *Journal of Irish Literature* (Newark, Delaware), II (May-September 1973), 79-97

> On the Dublin Gate Theatre.

1186 Henderson, W. A. "The Irish Theatre Movement," *Sunday Independent* (Dublin), XVII, No. 38 (17 September 1922), 6

> Survey.

1187 Henn, T. R. "A Note on the Irish Theatre," *The Cambridge Review*, LVIII (12 February 1937), 250-251; (19 February 1937), 269-270

> Reflections on some Irish plays.

1188 Hewes, Henry. "Dublin," *The Saturday Review* (New York), XL (18 May 1957), 34-35

> Survey of the first Dublin Theatre Festival.

1189 —. "The September Rising," *The Saturday Review* (New York), XLIII (10 September 1960), 33, 36

> Survey of the Dublin Theatre Festival.

1190   "A History of the Abbey," *Sunday Independent* (Dublin),
       XLIV, No. 4 (23 January 1949), 3

       To be written by Lennox Robinson.

1191   Hoare, John Edward. "Ireland's National Drama," *North
       American Review* (New York), CXCIV (October
       1911), 566-575

       Mainly on the plays of J. M. Synge and Lady Gregory.

1192   Hobson, Harold. "Irish Theatre," *Hibernia* (Dublin), (26
       June 1970), p. 16

       Observations.

1193   Hogan, Robert. "The Year in Review: 1967. Theatre,"
       University Review (Dublin), V (1968), 103-112

       Survey.

1194   —. "Dublin: The Summer Season and the Theatre Festival,
       1967," *Drama Survey* (Minneapolis), VI (Spring 1968),
       315-323

       Survey of play productions.

1195   —. "An Interview with Michael Conniffe," *The Journal of
       Irish Literature* (Newark, Delaware), VI, No. 3 (Sep-
       tember 1977), 80-88

       Recollections of the Abbey Theatre.

1196   Hogan, Thomas. "Dublin Theatre," *The Bell* (Dublin), XIII,
       No. 1 (October 1946), 59-63

       Survey of play productions.

1197   —. "Theatre," *Envoy* (Dublin), I, No. 2 (January 1950),

64-70; No. 3 (February 1950), 63-68; No. 4 (March 1950), 78-82; No. 5 (April 1950), 72-77; No. 6 (May 1950), 80-84; II, No. 7 (June 1950), 91-93; III, No. 8 (July 1950), 82-85

Survey of play productions.

1198 "Hollywood's Abbey Veterans," *The Irish Times* (Dublin), (19 March 1963), p. 8

Recollections of Arthur Shields and F. J. McCormick.

1199 Homan, Sidney. "When the Theatre Turns to Itself," *New Literary History* (Charlottesville, Virginia), II (1971), 407-417

Includes brief discussions of Bernard Shaw and Samuel Beckett.

1200 Horniman, A. E. F. "Miss Horniman's Offer of Theatre and the Society's Acceptance," *Samhain* (Dublin & London), No. 4 (December 1904), 53-54

Two letters.

1201 —. "The Manchester Players," *Poet Lore* (Philadelphia), XXV, No. 2 (Spring 1914), 210-214

Includes some remarks on the Abbey Theatre.

1202 —. "The Origin of the Abbey Theatre," *John O'London's Weekly*, XXVII (20 August 1932), 741.

1203 Hoult, Norah. "The Abbey Theatre," *Life and Letters Today* (London), XIV (Spring 1936), 40-47

Survey.

1204 "How We Spoiled the Irish Actors," *The Literary Digest* (New York), XLV, No. 2 (13 July 1912), 63

Excerpts from English papers on the Abbey Theatre's first American tour.

1205 Howarth, William L. "Some Principles of Autobiography," *New Literary History*, V, No. 2 (Winter 1974), 363-381

Includes brief discussions on Sean O'Casey and W. B. Yeats.

1206 Hueffer [later Ford], Ford Madox. "The Irish Theatre," *Daily News* (London), (20 June 1910), p. 10

Letter to the Editor supporting Lady Gregory and W. B. Yeats's appeal on behalf of the Irish National Theatre.

1207 Hughes, Catharine. "Theatre in Dublin," *The Nation* (New York), CCIX, No. 18 (24 November 1969), 579-581

Survey of the Dublin Theatre Festival.

1208 Hughes, Glenn. "Concerning a Theatre of the People," *The Drama* (Chicago), XI (1920), 45-46

On W. B. Yeats' lecture "A Theatre of the People".

1209 Hunt, Hugh. "The Abbey," *Hibernia* (Dublin), (15 May 1970), p. 20

The policy of the Artistic Director of the Abbey Theatre.

1210 Hutchinson, Pearse. "Theatre," *The Bell* (Dublin), XIX, No. 8 (July 1954), 60-63

Survey of play productions.

1211 " 'I Will Not Attack the Abbey Theatre'," *The Irish Times* (Dublin), (21 February 1963), p. 1

Report on a lecture on "The Abbey Theatre Today", by Micheál MacLiamóir.

1212 "The Importance of Playwright's Vision," *The Irish Times* (Dublin), (7 October 1967), p. 10

> Report on the International Theatre Seminar at the Abbey Theatre.

1213 Innes, C. L. "Language in Black and Irish Nationalist Literature," *The Massachusetts Review*, XVI (1975), 77-91

> Includes several references to Irish plays.

1214 Ireland, Denis. "Belfast's Revolving Stage," *Hibernia* (Dublin), (12 May 1972), p. 19

> Review article on the theatre in Northern Ireland.

1215 "Ireland's Most Famous Theatre Reopens," *The Times* (London), (19 July 1966), p. 14.

1216 Iremonger, Valentin. "The Abbey's Great Ones," *Drama* (London), No. 61 (Summer 1961), 44-45

> Review article.

1217 Irial. "Has the Irish Literary Theatre Failed?" *The United Irishman* (Dublin), VI, No. 141 (9 November 1901), 3

> "To produce a play or two every twelve months . . . does not seem really the proper method of founding a school of native Irish drama".

1218 "The Irish Actors," *Public Ledger* (Philadelphia), (24 January 1912), p. 10

> Abbey Theatre's first American tour.

1219 "Irish Arts Theatre," *Performing Arts in Canada*, VIII (Winter 1971), 6

In Toronto

1220   "Irish Arts Theatre," *Performing Arts in Canada*, IX (Winter 1972), 4

       Plans of the Toronto Irish Arts Theatre.

1221   "The Irish Literary Theatre in New York," *The Gael* (New York), XIX (June 1900), 189-190

       Review of play productions.

1222   "The Irish National Literary Theatre," *The Observer* (London), (1 January 1905), p. 4.

       Survey.

1223   "The Irish National Theatre," *Samhain* (Dublin), No. 3 (October 1903), 34-36

       The Irish National Theatre's productions in London.

1224   "Irish National Theatre," *The Gael* (New York), XXIII (April 1904), 139

       Survey of play productions.

1225   "The Irish National Theatre," *The Irish Times* (Dublin), (7 October 1903), p. 7

       A preview.

1226   "The Irish Play of Today," *The Outlook* (New York), IC (4 November 1911), 561-563

       Reflections on Irish drama.

1227   "The Irish Players," *Boston Evening Transcript*, (14 September-24 October 1911)

Abbey Theatre's first American tour.

1228 "The Irish Players," *Theatre Magazine* (New York), XIV (October 1911), xvi

Abbey Theatre's first American tour.

1229 "The Irish Players," *The Nation* (New York), XCIII (30 November 1911), 528-529

Abbey Theatre's first American tour.

1230 "The Irish Players," *Everybody's Magazine* (New York), XXVI (February 1912), 231-240

Abbey Theatre's first American tour.

1231 "The Irish Players and Their Audiences," *The Sun* (New York), (26 November 1911), p. 8

Editorial on the Abbey Theatre's first American tour.

1232 "Irish Players Coming," *The Literary Digest* (New York), XLIII (23 September 1911), 489-490

Abbey Theatre's first American tour.

1233 "Irish Players Fear No Riot," *The New York Times*, (26 November 1911), p. 15

Abbey Theatre's first American tour.

1234 "The Irish Players in America," *World Today* (Chicago), XXI (November 1911), 1381

Abbey Theatre's first American tour.

1235 "The Irish Players in New York," *The Outlook* (New York), IC (2 December 1911), 801

Abbey Theatre's first American tour.

1236 "Irish Plays," *The Irish-American* (New York), (14 October 1911), p. 4

Editorial on the Abbey Theatre's first American tour.

1237 "Irish Plays and Players," *The Outlook* (New York), IIC (29 July 1911), 704

Abbey Theatre's first American tour.

1238 "Irish Plays Are Insult to Race," *The Washington Times*, (12 November 1911), pp. 1, 8

Abbey Theatre's first American tour.

1239 "The Irish Theatre as an Exponent of the Irish People," *The American Review of Reviews* (New York), XLV (March 1912), 356-357

Excerpts from reviews of the Abbey Theatre's first American tour.

1240 "The Irish Theatre," *The Literary World* (London), LXXIX (5 June 1913), 182-183

Review article.

1241 "The Irish Theatre," *The Living Age* (Boston), CCC (11 January 1919), 119-121

Review article.

1242 "The Irish Theatre: Sick or Sound?" *Aquarius* (Benburb, County Tyrone), No. 4 (1971), 17-25

Symposium contributed by Micheál Mac Liammóir, Tyrone Guthrie, and Eugene McCabe, with John D. Stewart.

1243 "Irish Writing Today," *The Times Literary Supplement* (London), (17 March 1972), pp. 289-317

> Includes Máire Cruise O'Brien, "The Living Gaelic"; Denis Donoghue, "The Problems of Being Irish"; Brian Friel, "Plays Peasant and Unpeasant"; Thomas Kilroy, "Tellers of Tales"; Liam Miller, "The Heirs of Saint Columba"; and John Montague, "Order in Donnybrook Fair".

1244 Jay, John. "Dublin Theatre Symposium," *The Dubliner*, I, No. 6 (January-February 1963), 53-60

> Discussion held after the fifth Dublin Theatre Festival.

1245 Johns, Eric. "Irish Export Boom," *Theatre World* (London), LIX (April 1963), 8-9

> The number of Irish plays recently produced successfully in London "should shatter once and for all the age-old fallacy that Irish plays acquire a jinx as they cross the Irish Sea".

1246 Johnston, Denis. "The Theatre in Ireland," *One-Act Play Magazine* (New York), I (October 1937), 557-559

> "The quality of the work turned out by the Dublin theatres varies enormously".

1247 —. "Plays of the Quarter," *The Bell* (Dublin), II, No. 1 (April 1941), 89-92

> Survey of play productions.

1248 —. "Plays of the Month," *The Bell* (Dublin), II, No. 2 (May 1941), 86-91

> Survey of play productions.

1249 —. "The Theatre," *The Bell* (Dublin), II, No. 4 (July 1941), 77-81; No. 5 (August 1941), 88-90

Survey of play productions.

1250   —. "The Dublin Theatre," *The Bell* (Dublin), III, No. 2 (November 1941), 157-161; No. 5 (February 1942), 357-360

Survey of play productions.

1251   —. "My First Play at the Gate," *The Irish Digest* (Dublin), LI, No. 1 (July 1954), 51-53

Recollections of the Dublin Gate Theatre.

1252   —. "Sunday Night at the Abbey," *The Irish Digest* (Dublin), LI, No. 4 (October 1954), 26-28

On the Dublin Drama League.

1253   —. "What Has Happened to the Irish?" *Theatre Arts* (New York), XLIII (July 1959), 11-12, 72

"Today there are probably as many good Irish authors as ever, but the atmosphere of the country is centrifugal rather than the reverse".

1254   —. "That's Show Business," *Theatre Arts* (New York), XLIV (February 1960), 82-83, 95

Reflections by an Irish playwright on the production of plays.

1255   —. "Humor—Hibernian Style," *The New York Times*, (5 February 1961), Drama Section, p. 3

Observations on humour in Irish writing.

1256   —. "Policy in Theatre," *Hibernia* (Dublin), (29 May 1970), p. 16

Observations on the policy of the Abbey Theatre.

1257　Jordan, John. "Dublin Theatre Festival," *Hibernia* (Dublin), (25 September 1959), p. 8

On the curious selection for the second Dublin International Theatre Festival.

1258　—. "Much Ado About the Abbey," *Hibernia* (Dublin), (5 August 1960), p. 6

The present Abbey is bad on all counts.

1259　—. "Report on the Festival," *Hibernia* (Dublin), (October 1961), pp. 20-21; (November 1961), p. 18

Dublin International Theatre Festival.

1260　—. "The Dublin Theatre Festival," *Hibernia* (Dublin), (November 1962), p. 14

Survey of play productions.

1261　—. "Dublin Theatre Festival," *Hibernia* (Dublin), (October 1965), p. 17; (November 1965), p. 17

Survey of play productions.

1262　—. "Dublin Theatre Diary," *Hibernia* (Dublin), (March 1966), p. 17

Survey of amateur play productions.

1263　—. "Together Again," *Hibernia* (Dublin), (5 March 1971), p. 15

Dublin Gate Theatre.

1264　Joy, Maurice. "The Irish Literary Revival; Some Limitations and Possibilities," *New Ireland Review* (Dublin), XXIII, No. 5 (July 1905), 257-266

The Irish National Theatre "is, at present, obnoxious to all but a handful of the Irish people."

1265   Kain, Richard M. "Genius Loci: The Spirit of Place in Irish Literature," *The Dublin Magazine*, X, No. 2 (1973), 33-41

Makes references to W. B. Yeats, J. M. Synge, and James Joyce.

1266   [Kavanagh, Patrick]. "Abbey Theatre," *Kavanagh's Weekly* (Dublin), I, No. 8 (31 May 1952), 2

"The Abbey is far more a Pre-Raphaelite creation than have been allowed to die its natural death."

1267   Kavanagh, Peter. "The Celtic Attitude Towards the Theater," *Hopkins Review* (Baltimore: John Hopkins University), V, No. 3 (1952), 64-66

Explains why the Abbey Theatre succeeded so well although the Celts did not make serious efforts at the drama.

1268   Kelleher, John V. "Irish Literature Today," *Atlantic Monthly* (Boston), CLXXV (March 1945), 70-76

Blames the pedestrian tone in Irish plays on the "diminished reality" of post-civil war life and the unestablished nature of Irish society.

1269   Kelleher, Terry. "Stagnation at the Abbey," *Hibernia* (Dublin), (25 June 1971), p. 10

On the administration of the Abbey Theatre.

1270   Keller, T. G. "The Irish Theatre Movement: Some Early Memories," *Sunday Independent* (Dublin), (6 January 1929), p. 7.

1271   Kelly, John C. "Festival Samplings," *Hibernia* (Dublin),

(18 October-1 November 1968), p. 23; (1 November-
14 November 1968), p. 21

Survey of play productions at the Dublin International Theatre
Festival.

1272 Kelly, Seamus. "Dublin," *Holiday* (Philadelphia), XIX,
No. 1 (January 1956), 38-43

Includes background to the Irish drama.

1273 —. "Where Motley is Worn," *The Spectator* (London),
CXCVI (20 April 1956), 538, 540

"While there is no dearth of acting or writing talent in the
Dublin theatre today, there is equally no very adequate economic encouragement for either".

1274 —. "My Plan to Revive the National Theatre," *The Irish
Digest* (Dublin), LVII, No. 1 (July 1956), 68-70

"There is no dearth of acting or play-writing talent, but they
need adequate economic encouragement".

1275 —. "The Early Days," *The Irish Times* (Dublin), (22 November 1958), p. 6

Review article on the Abbey Theatre.

1276 —. "Bridgehead Revisited," *The Spectator* (London), CCIV
(29 April 1960), 626-628

Survey of drama in Ireland, attacking Ernest Blythe's policies
at the Abbey Theatre and Ritchie McKee's at the Ulster Group
Theatre.

1277 Kennedy, David. "The Ulster Region and the Theatre,"
Lagan (Belfast), II, No. 1 (1946), 51-56. Reprinted as
"Ulster Theatre" in *Irish Bookman* (Dublin), I (1947),

33-39

Survey.

1278   —. "The Theatre in Ulster, 1944-53," *Rann; An Ulster Quarterly* (Belfast), No. 20 (1953), 39-42

Survey of play productions.

1279   Kennedy, Maurice. "Shining in Its Infancy," *Sunday Press* (Dublin), (10 June 1951), p. 9. Continued as "Those Early Days: Guilding the Prom," *ibid.*, (17 June 1951), p. 9

The Abbey Theatre.

1280   Kenny, M. "The Plays of the 'Irish' Players," *America* (New York), VI, No. 4 (4 November 1911), 78-79

Productions of Irish plays denounced during Abbey Theatre's first American tour.

1281   Keohler, Thomas. "The Irish National Theatre," *Dana* (Dublin), I, No. 10 (February 1905), 319-320; No. 11 (March 1905), 351-352

On the opening performances of the Irish National Theatre Society at the Abbey Theatre.

1282   Kiernan, T. J. "And So Began the Irish Literary Theatre," *The Irish Digest* (Dublin), LXVII, No. 1 (November 1959), 49-53

Survey.

1283   Kilroy, Thomas. "Groundwork for an Irish Theatre," *Studies; An Irish Quarterly Review* (Dublin), XLVIII, No. 190 (Summer 1959), 192-198

Suggests that the new Abbey Theatre should try to create a workshop atmosphere where aspiring playwrights would receive an apprenticeship in modern stagecraft and learn by practical experience the requirements of a particular body of actors.

1284 —. "Slings and Arrows," *Hibernia* (Dublin), (26 September 1969), p. 20

The Dublin Gate Theatre.

1285 Kirwan, H. N. "Irish Theatre," *Inisfail* (Dublin), I, No. 1 (March 1933), 35-37

Observations.

1286 Klauber, Adolph. "Acting of the Irish Players," *The New York Times*, (26 November 1911), Section VII, p. 2

Abbey Theatre's first American tour.

1287 Kornelius, Joachim. "Authorspecific and Groupspecific Variation of Style-Markers in 'Irish Renaissance' Drama," *Fu Jen Studies* (Taipei), No. 8 (1975), 33-46.

1288 Kovalev, I. "Irlandskii teatr: èkho krizisa i tragedii [The Irish Theatre: the Echo of Crisis and of Tragedy]," *Teatr* (Moscow), (1972), 162-168.

1289 Krajewska, Wanda. "Irlandskosc Eugene'a O'Neill," *Przeglad Humanistyczny* (Warsaw), X, No. 4 (1966), 51-66

The influence of the Irish theatre—especially W. B. Yeats, J. M. Synge, and Sean O'Casey—on O'Neill.

1290 Krause, David. "The Barbarous Sympathies of Antic Irish Comedy," *Malahat Review*, XXII (April 1972), 99-117

Examines J. M. Synge, Sean O'Casey, George Fitzmaurice, and W. B. Yeats.

1291 L., L. "Current Drama," *The Bell* (Dublin), I, No. 1 (October 1940), 82

Survey of play productions.

1292 La Barre, H. "Great Theatres of the World—Abbey: Dublin," *Cosmopolitan* (New York), (November 1959), 68-69

Describes the Abbey as "Ireland's National Theatre showcase for Irish playwrights".

1293 "Lady Gregory's Inane Talk," *The Gaelic American* (New York), (27 January 1912), p. 4

Editorial on the Abbey Theatre's first American tour.

1294 Lalec. "The Scandaleers: A Gilbertian Opera, Dedicated Respectfully to the Directors of the Abbey Theatre," *T. C. D.* (Dublin), XLV (18 May 1939), 159-161

Dramatis personae: Robinson, Starkie, Blythe, O'Connor, and O'Faolain.

1295 Lambert, J. W. "The London Theatre," *International Theatre Annual*, II (1956-7), 11-38

Includes discussions on plays by Brendan Behan and Samuel Beckett.

1296 L[awrence], W. J. "The First Subsidised Playhouse in Our Islands," *The Tatler* (London), XV (8 February 1905), 224

The Abbey Theatre.

1297 —. "Dublin As a Play-Producing Centre," *The Weekly Free-*

man (Dublin), XCI (14 December 1907), 25

> The last part of the article evaluates the eight years' record of the Irish National Theatre Society.

1298 —. "The Abbey Theatre: Its History and Mystery," *The Weekly Freeman* (Dublin), XCVI (7 December 1912), 11-12

> Survey.

1299 —. "Dramatic Mirroring of Irish Life and Character," *The Dublin Magazine*, XII, No. 2 (April-June 1937), 39-47

> The stage Irishman.

1300 —. [Lawrence's notebooks and correspondence containing much information on the history of the Theatre in Ireland are preserved in the Holloway Collection, National Library of Ireland.]

1301 "League Discovers the Irish Players," *The New York Press*, (4 November 1911), p. 10

> Abbey Theatre's first American tour.

1302 "League Not With Players," *The New York Press*, (4 December 1911), p. 10

> The Gaelic League has no connection with the Abbey Theatre's first American tour.

1303 Leclercq, R. "La situation du théâtre en Irlande," *Comoedia* (Paris), XXIII (27 August 1929), 5

> Observations.

1304 Lemon, Warren. "Yeats, Synge, Realism, and "The Tragic

Theatre'," *Southern Review* (Baton Rouge, Louisiai-
ana), XI (January 1975), 129-138.

1305   Leonard, Hugh. "Coming Home," *Hibernia* (Dublin), (11
           September 1970), p. 14

           Observations on the state of the Irish theatre.

1306   "Let Us Elevate the Stage," *The World* (New York), (29
           November 1911), p. 10

           Abbey Theatre's first American tour.

1307   Letts, Winifred. "The Fays at the Abbey Theatre," *The
           Fortnightly* (London), No. 978, New Series (June
           1948), 420-423

           Reflections by an Irish dramatist.

1308   —. "Early Days at the Abbey," *The Irish Digest* (Dublin),
           XXXI, No. 3 (September 1948), 8-11

           Recollections of the Abbey Theatre.

1309   —. "Young Days at the Abbey Theatre," *Irish Writing* (Cork),
           No. 16 (September 1951), 43-46

           Recollections.

1310   —. "When the Abbey Was Young," *Ireland of the Welcomes*
           (Dublin), I, No. 2 (July-August 1952), 9-11

           Recollections.

1311   —. "My First Abbey Play," *The Irish Digest* (Dublin), XLIII,
           No. 4 (December 1952), 25-27

           Recollections of the Abbey Theatre.

1312   Leventhal, A. J. "Dramtic Commentary," *The Dublin Maga-zine*, XVIII, No. 4 (October-December 1943), 52-55; XIX, No. 1 (January-March 1944), 39-42; No. 2 (April-June 1944), 48-51; No. 3 (July-September 1944), 47-50; No. 4 (October-December 1944), 49-52; XX, No. 2 (April-June 1945), 43-46; No. 3 (July-September 1945), 42-44; No. 4 (October-December 1945), 39-41; XXI, No. 1 (January-March 1946), 47-50; No. 2 (April-June 1946), 47-50; No. 3 (July-September 1946), 38-40; No. 4 (October-December 1946), 42-44; XXII, No. 1 (January-March 1947), 42-43; No. 2 (April-June 1947), 44-46; No. 3 (July-September 1947), 53-56; No. 4 (October-December 1947), 44-46; XXIII, No. 1 (January-March 1948), 40-42; No. 2 (April-June 1948), 43-45; No. 3 (July-September 1948), 44-46; No. 4 (October-December 1948), 48-51; XXIV, No. 1 (January 1949), 38-41; No. 2 (April-June 1949), 35-37; No. 3 (July-September 1949), 48-51; No. 4 (October-December 1949), 33-35; XXV, No. 1 (January-March 1950), 45-47; No. 2 (April- June 1950), 36-38; No. 3 (July-September 1950), 46-48; No. 4 (October-December 1950), 37-40; XXVI, No. 1 (January-March 1951), 49-51; No. 2 (April-June 1951), 42-44; No. 3 (July-September 1951), 51-53; No. 4 (October-December 1951), 47-49; XXVII, No. 1 (January-March 1952), 39-41; No. 2 (April-June 1952), 32-35; No. 3 (July-September 1952), 42-45; No. 4 (October-December 1952), 39-42; XXVIII, No. 1 (January-March 1953), 36-39; No. 2 (April-June 1953), 45-48; No. 3 (July-September 1953), 32-34; XXIX, No. 4 (October-December 1953), 39-41; XXX, No. 1 (January-March 1954), 40-42; No. 2 (April-June 1954), 34-36; No. 3 (July-September 1954), 51-53; No. 4 (October-December 1954), 50-52; XXI, No. 1 (January-March 1955), 47-49; No. 2 (April-June 1955), 28-32; No. 3 (July-September 1955), 51-54; No. 4 (October-December 1955), 32-34; XXXI, No. 1 (January-March 1956), 52-54; No. 2 (April-June 1956), 23-26; No. 3 (July-September 1956), 46-48; No. 4 (October-December

1956), 44-46; XXXII, No. 1 (January-March 1957),
41-43; No. 2 (April-June 1957), 23-26; No. 3 (July-
September 1957), 52-54; No. 4 (October-December
1957), 42-45; XXXIII, No. 1 (January-March 1958),
32-34; No. 2 (April-June 1958), 32-34

Survey of play productions and of dramatic books.

1313   —. "The Abbey Theatre and After," *The Dublin Magazine,*
XXVI, No. 4 (October-December 1951), 47-49

Reflections on the Abbey after it was destroyed by fire.

1314   Lewis, Saunders. "Recent Anglo-Celtic Drama," *Welsh Outlook* (Cardiff), (March 1922), 63-65

Includes discussions of W. B. Yeats and Daniel Corkery.

1315   Lewis, Theophilus. "The Play's the Thing on the Stage or in
the Page," *America* (New York), LIX (13 August
1938), 442-443

The Abbey Theatre reviewed.

See correspondence in the issues of 17 and 24 September.

1316   Lewis-Crosby, J. E. C. "CEMA and the Professional Theatre,"
Threshold (Belfast), III, No. 2 (Summer 1959), 21-23

Explains the rationale behind the 1958 government subsidies
given to the Belfast Arts Theatre and the Ulster Group Theatre.

1317   Little, Patrick. "Festival Preview," *Hibernia* (Dublin), (September 1963), pp. 10, 13

Dublin International Theatre Festival.

1318   "A Lively Discussion Over the 'Irish Plays'," *Boston Sunday
Post,* (8 October 1911), p. 37

Statements by W. B. Yeats, Lady Gregory and others on the

controversy over the production of Irish plays in America during the Abbey Theatre's first American tour.

1319   Livia, Anna. "Hilton Edwards and Micheál Mac Liammóir," *Ireland of the Welcomes* (Dublin), XXI, No. 6 (March-April 1973), 31-32

The founders of the Dublin Gate Theatre.

1320   Longford, Christine. "The Dublin Gate Theatre," *The Irish Review* (Albany), I (April 1934), 13-15

A short history.

1321   Longford, Lord. "A Dramatic Tour of Ireland," *Ireland Today* (Dublin), II, No. 3 (March 1937), 70-71

By Longford Productions.

1322   —. "A Strolling Player Goes Places," *The Irish Digest* (Dublin), VII, No. 2 (August 1940), 32-34

The manager of a theatrical company describes an Irish tour.

1323   Loudan, Jack. "Ulster and a Subsidised Theatre," *Lagan* (Belfast), II, No. 1 (1946), 57-62

Argues for a subsidy to free Northern playwrights from the need to write the innocuous comedies playgoers demanded.

1324   Loxton, A. S. G. "In Ulster Now," *Drama* (London), No. 3 (Winter 1946), 44-45; No. 6 (Autumn 1947), 28-29; No. 9 (Summer 1948), 26-27

Survey of dramatic activities in Ulster.

1325   "Loyalists Welcome the Playboys," *The Gaelic American* (New York), (13 April 1912), p. 4

Editorial on the Abbey Theatre's first American tour.

1326   L[ynd], R[obert] W[ilson]. "The Inspiration of Dublin,"
       Today (London), XLV (4 January 1905), 275-276

Mainly on the Abbey Theatre.

1327   Lyons, F. S. L. "Before the Storm," *The Times Literary
       Supplement* (London), (22 October 1976), p. 1334

The Abbey Theatre, 1902-1904.

1328   Lyons, J. B. "Play-Going in the 'Forties," *The Dublin Maga-
       zine*, IX, No. 4 (1972), 80-86

It was "the golden age of Dublin Theatre".

1329   M., M. "Belfast's Group Theatre Under Stree," *Hibernia*
       (Dublin), (13 November 1959), p. 12

As a result of the resignation of some leading actors.

1330   Macalernon, Don. "Trouble in the Theatre," *Focus; A
       Monthly Review* (Belfast), II (June 1959), 32

The theatre in Belfast.

1331   Mac An Aili, Rae. "The Missing Men: Priest-Critics?" *Hibern-
       ia* (Dublin), (30 October 1959), p. 8

The need for the presence of the priest in the Irish theatre.

1332   MacAnna, Tomas. "Ernest Blythe and the Abbey," *Thres-
       hold* (Belfast), No. 26 (1975), 100-125.

1333   Macardle, Dorothy. "Experiment in Ireland," *Theatre Arts
       Monthly* (New York), XVIII, No. 2 (February 1934),
       124-132

The Dublin Gate Theatre.

1334 McAuley, James J. "Dublin Theatre Festival," *The Kilkenny Magazine*, No. 10 (Autumn-Winter 1963), 93-99

Survey of play productions.

1335 MacBride, Maud Gonne. "A National Theatre," *The United Irishman* (Dublin), X (24 October 1903), 2-3

In Ireland a National Theatre "must draw its vitality from that hidden spring from which the seven fountains of Gaelic inspiration flow".

1336 McBrien, Peter. "Dramatic Ideals of Today," *Studies; An Irish Quarterly Review* (Dublin), XI, No. 42 (June 1922), 235-242

Calls for a return to the theatre of J. M. Synge, Padraic Colum, and T. C. Murray.

1337 —. "The Actor and the Dramatist," *Studies; An Irish Quarterly Review* (Dublin), XII, No. 48 (December 1923), 639-647

Includes illustrations from J. M. Synge and T. C. Murray.

1338 McCaffrey, Lawrence J. "Trends in Post-Revolutionary Irish Literature," *College English* (Chicago), XVIII (1956), 26-30

Includes discussion on Irish dramatists.

1339 McCormick, Jane L. "Drive That Man Away: The Theme of the Artist in Society in Celtic Drama, 1890-1950," *Susquehanna University Studies* (Selingrove, Pennsylvania), XIII (1969), 213-229

Discusses the relationship of the artist to society as an important theme in certain plays by W. B. Yeats, J. M. Synge, and
Sean O'Casey.

1340   McDermott, Hubert. "The Background to Anglo-Irish
Drama," *Topic* (Washington, Pennsylvania), XII, No.
24 (Fall 1972), 69-76

In the 1890s.

1341   MacDonagh, Donagh. "The Death-Watch Beetle," *Drama*
(London), No. 12 (February 1949), 4-7

"The Abbey was Yeats. When he lived it lived, too, and when he
died it died with him".

1342   MacDonagh, John. "Acting in Dublin," *The Commonweal*
(New York), X (19 June 1929), 185-186

Recollections of the players and directors of the Abbey Theatre.

1343   MacEntee, Patrick. "A Preview of the Festival," *Hibernia*
(Dublin), (9 September 1960), p. 7

Dublin International Theatre Festival.

1344   McFadden, Roy. "Belfast Theatre Controversy," *Threshold* (Belfast), III, No. 2 (Summer 1959), 25-27

Discusses the possible connection between the government subsidies and the Ulster Group Theatre's productions.

1345   McHugh, Roger. "Dublin Theatre," *The Bell* (Dublin), XII,
No. 2 (May 1946), 162-166; No. 3 (June 1946), 251-
256; No. 4 (July 1946), 336-340; No. 6 (September
1946), 520-524; XIII, No. 2 (November 1946), 145-
148; No. 3 (December 1946), 58-62

Survey of play productions.

1346   McHugh, Roger. "The Abbey Theatre Controversy," *Irish Library Bulletin* (Dublin), IX (January 1948), 9-13.

1347   —. "I Challenge the Abbey," *The Irish Digest* (Dublin), XXX, No. 2 (April 1948), 12-14

        "Has it lost the integrity that brought it fame?".

1348   —. "The Abbey and the Future," *The Irish Digest* (Dublin), XXXIV, No. 4 (October 1949), 38-40

        The Abbey Theatre "promises hope of a dramatic renascence in Ireland".

1349   —. "Towards a National Theatre," *Irish Library Bulletin* (Dublin), XII (September-October 1951), 131-134

        Observations.

1350   —. "Tradition and the Future of Irish Drama," *Studies: An Irish Quarterly Review* (Dublin), XL, No. 160 (December 1951), 467-474

        "Whatever may become of the Abbey Theatre, the tradition which it created is no longer the preserve of any one theatre but belongs to our nation".

1351   —. "What Can We Do about the Abbey?" *The Irish Digest* (Dublin), XLI, No. 2 (December 1951), 8-10

        Suggestions after the Abbey Theatre was destroyed by a fire.

1352   —. "Yeats, Synge and the Abbey Theatre," *Studies; An Irish Quarterly Review* (Dublin), XLI, Nos. 163-164 (September-December 1952), 333-340

        Review article.

1353   —. "Literary Treatment of the Deirdre Legend," *Threshold*

Belfast), I, No. 1 (Februry 1957), 36-49

In George Russell, W. B. Yeats, J. M. Synge, and James Stephens.

1354   —. "Drama in Ireland Today," *Iris Hibernia* (Fribourg, Switzerland), IV, No. 3 (1960), 40-42

Appraises the small playhouses and the Belfast theatre.

1355   —. "Frank O'Connor and the Irish Theatre," *Éire-Ireland* (St. Paul, Minnesota), IV, No. 2 (Summer 1969), 52-63

Frank O'Connor's efforts to revive the Abbey Theatre.

1356   MacIntyre, Tom. "First Night in Dublin," *Ireland of the Welcomes* (Dublin), XXIII, No. 5 (September-October 1974), 31-32

Reflections by an Irish playwright.

1357   Macken, Walter. "The New Abbey Theatre," *The Irish Digest* (Dublin), LXXXVI, No. 3 (May 1966), 85-87

Interview with the Artistic Adviser of the Abbey Theatre.

1358   McKenna, T. P. "A View on the Irish Theatre," *Labour Monthly* (London), IL, No. 4 (April 1967), 185-187

The decline of the Irish theatre is due to the tension between the Anglo-Irish and the Gaelic cultures.

1359   Mac Liammóir, Micheál. "And So Began the Gate Theatre," *The Irish Digest* (Dublin), XIV, No. 4 (February 1943), 24-26

Recollections of the Dublin Gate Theatre, which opened in 1928.

1360 —. "Yeats, Lady Gregory, Denis Johnston," *The Bell* (Dublin), VI, No. 1 (April 1943), 33-42

Recollections.

1361 —. "Theatre Building," *The Bell* (Dublin), VI, No. 3 (June 1943), 193-203

Recollections.

1362 —. "More Memoirs," *The Bell* (Dublin), VII, No. 4 (January 1944), 292-303.

1363 —. "Theatre Nights," *The Bell* (Dublin), VII, No. 6 (March 1944), 487-495

Recollections.

1364 MacManus, Francis. "The Abbey Theatre," *The Bell* (Dublin), XVII, No. 5 (August 1951), 5-6

Suggests a tour by the Abbey Theatre as an immediate means of maintaining the institution after the fire in 1951.

1365 McNeill, Janet. "Belfast Theatre Controversy," *Threshold* (Belfast), III, No. 2 (Summer 1959), 22-25

Discusses the possible connection between the government subsidies and the Ulster Group Theatre's decision not to produce Sam Thompson's *Over the Bridge*.

1366 —. "Belfast Theatre Controversy," *Threshold* (Belfast), III, No. 2 (Summer 1959), 24-25

On censorship.

1367 MacNulty, Edward. "The Adoration of the Peasant," *The New Age* (London), IX, No. 18 (31 August 1911), 416

Includes background to the Irish drama.

1368 MacR., S. "Theatre," *The Bell* (Dublin), XVI, No. 3 (December 1950), 67-70; No. 5 (February 1951), 62-66; No. 6 (March 1951), 64-72; XVII, No. 1 (April 1951), 67-72

Survey of play productions.

1369 McVeigh, Hugh. "When the Abbey Theatre Did Battle with the Castle," *The Irish Digest* (Dublin), LXXXI, No. 4 (October 1964), 50-52

Dublin Castle's attempts to stop production of Bernard Shaw's play.

1370 MacWilliam, Bourke. "Dublin," *Plays and Players* (London), II, No. 6 (March 1955), 26; II, No. 7 (April 1955), 26; II, No. 8 (May 1955), 26; II, No. 9 (June 1955), 23; II, No. 10 (July 1955), 23; II, No. 11 (August 1955), 23; III, No. 1 (October 1955), 28; III, No. 2 (November 1955), 23

Survey.

1371 —. "Ireland," *Plays and Players* (London), III, No. 3 (December 1955), 26; III, No. 5 (February 1956), 17; III, No. 7 (April 1956), 16; III, No. 11 (August 1956), 32

Survey.

1372 "Mahon, Christopher". "Ochone Agus Ochone!" *National Observer* (Dublin), I, No. 10 (April 1959), 4-5

On the current Abbey malaise.

1373 Malone, Andrew E. "The Decline of the Irish Drama," *The Nineteenth Century and After* (London), XCVII,

No. 578 (April 1925), 578-588

"Of the host of playwrights whose work has been produced at the Abbey Theatre in recent years very few give promise of important work in the future".

1374 —. "The Abbey Theatre, Dublin: Its Plays, Playwrights, and Players," *Millgate Monthly* (Manchester), XXI (July 1926), 522-525.

1375 —. "Late Development of Irish Drama," *Edinburgh Review*, CCXLV (April 1927), 364-374. Reprinted in *The Dublin Magazine*, III (July-September 1928), 16-30; and as "The Tardy Irish Drama," *English Journal*, XVII (June 1928), 469-480

Survey.

1376 —. "The Coming of Age of the Irish Drama," *The Dublin Review*, CLXXXI, No. 362 (July 1927), 101-114. Partially reprinted in *The Catholic World* (New York), CXXVI (October 1927), 109-110

The Abbey Theatre celebrated its 21st birthday on 27 December 1925.

1377 —. "The Abbey Theatre Season," *The Dublin Magazine*, II, No. 3 (July-September 1927), 30-38

Survey of play productions.

1378 —. "The Abbey Theatre Season," *The Dublin Magazine*, II, No. 4 (October-December 1927), 30-38

Survey of play productions.

1379 —. "The Late Development of Irish Drama," *The Dublin Magazine*, III, No. 3 (July-September 1928), 16-30

Survey.

1380 —. "Ireland," *The Drama Magazine* (Chicago), XXI (November 1930), 14, 34

On the Dublin Gate Theatre productions.

1381 —. "Ireland," *The Drama Magazine* (Chicago), XXI (December 1930), 19, 24

Survey of play productions.

1382 —. "Ireland," *The Drama Magazine* (Chicago), XXI (Janaury 1931), 18

Survey of play productions.

1383 —. "Ireland," *The Drama Magazine* (Chicago), XXI (February 1931), 16-17, 40

Survey of play productions.

1384 —. "Ireland," *The Drama Magazine* (Chicago), XXI (March 1931), 16-17

Survey of play productions.

1385 —. "Ireland," *The Drama Magazine* (Chicago), XXI (April 1931), 17-18, 24

Survey of play productions.

1386 —. "The Irish Theatre in 1930," *The Dublin Magazine*, VI, No. 2 (April-June 1931), 1-11

Survey.

1387 —. "Ireland," *The Drama Magazine* (Chicago), XXI, (May 1931), 14

Survey of play productions.

1388 —. "Ireland," *The Drama Magazine* (Chicago), XXI (June 1931), 11

Survey of play productions.

1389 —. "The Future of the Theatre," *The Dublin Magazine*, VII, No. 1 (January-March 1932), 31-41

Reflections.

1390 —. "The Irish Theatre Year," *The Dublin Magazine*, VIII, No. 3 (July-September 1933), 36-46

Survey of play productions.

1391 —. "The Irish Theatre in 1933," *The Dublin Magazine*, IX, No. 3 (July-September 1934), 45-54

Mainly on the Dublin Gate Theatre productions.

1392 —. "Some Recent Plays," *The Dublin Magazine*, X, No. 1 (January-March 1935), 49-60

Survey of play productions.

1393 —. "The Theatre in 1935," *The Dublin Magazine*, XI, No. 1 (January-March 1936), 48-59

Survey of play productions.

1394 "Malvolio". "Those Whom the 'Gods' Love," *Outlook* (Cork), I, No. 5 (18 November 1911), 10-11; No. 6 (25 November 1911), 2-3

A diatribe against the Abbey Olympians, particularly J. M. Synge and W. B. Yeats.

1395 Mannin, Ethel. "Irish Authors of Our Time," *The Irish Digest* (Dublin), XXV, No. 3 (September 1946),

32-35

"The most interesting writing in English today is coming from Ireland".

1396   Manning, Mary. "In Dublin Today," *The Saturday Review of Literature* (New York), VI (17 May 1930), 1048-1050

Survey of the theatrical season.

1397   —. "The Abbey Goes East," *Hibernia* (Dublin), (8 June 1973), p. 18

Report on the Abbey Theatre European tour.

1398   —. "The Abbey Theatre Tour," *The Arts in Ireland* (Dublin), II, No. 1 (Autumn 1973), 47-53

To Helsinki to perform at the Finnish National Theatre.

1399   —, ed. *Motley; The Dublin Gate Theatre Magazine*, I, No. 1 (March 1932)—III, No. 4 (May 1934).

1400   Marcus, Phillip L. "Old Irish Myth and Modern Irish Literature," *Irish University Review*, I, No. 1 (Autumn 1970), 67-85

Includes discussion on W. B. Yeats and Lady Gregory.

1401   Marowitz, Charles. "New Wave in a Dead Sea," *X: A Quarterly Review* (London), I (1960), 270-277

Includes discussion on Samuel Beckett and Brendan Behan.

1402   —. "In Dublin's Square City," *Encore* (London), VII, No. 6 (November-December 1960), 26-30

Survey of the Dublin International Theatre Festival.

1403   Martin, Augustine. "Inherited Dissent: The Dilemma of the Irish Writer," *Studies; An Irish Quarterly Review* (Dublin), LIV (Spring 1965), 1-20

Explains why the relations between the Irish writer and his society have been strained in the 20th century, including references to some Irish dramatists.

1404   Martyn, Edward. "A Comparison between Irish and English Theatrical Audiences," *Beltaine* (London), No. 2 (February 1900), 11-13

"Dublin audiences have awakened to the insipidity of the modern Enlgish theatre".

1405   —. "A Plea for a National Theatre in Ireland," *Samhain* (Dublin), No. 1 (October 1901), 14-15

The strolling English companies contribute to "Anglicising and corrupting the taste of the Irish people".

1406   —. "A Plea for the Revival of the Irish Literary Theatre," *The Irish Review* (Dublin), IV, No. 38 (April 1914), 79-84

Stresses the importance of producing "native Irish drama other than the peasant species".

1407   [Masefield, John]. The Irish National Theatre," *The Manchester Guardian* (2 January 1905), p. 3

Survey of play productions.

1408   "Match-Making at the Abbey," *Hibernia* (Dublin), (25 September 1959), p. 9

Survey of play productions at the second Dublin International Theatre Festival.

1409   Matthews, Brander. "Irish Plays and Irish Playwrights,"

Scribner's Magazine, LXI (January 1917), 85-90.
Reprinted in *The Principles of Playmaking and Other Discussions of the Drama* (New York: Scribner's 1919), pp. 196-213

Survey.

1410   Matthews, Harold. "1962 Dublin [International Theatre] Festival," *Theatre World* (London), LVIII (November 1962), 45-48

Survey of play productions.

1411   —. "1963 Dublin [International Theatre] Festival," *Theatre World* (London), LIX (November 1963), 16-18

Survey of play productions.

1412   —. "Dublin [International Theatre] Festival," *Theatre World* (London), LX (November 1964), 4-7, 12

Survey of play productions.

1413   —. "Dublin Festival 1965," *Theatre World* (London), LXI (November 1965), 17-19, 23

Survey of play productions.

1414   Maxwell, D. E. S. "Imagining the North: Violence and the Writers," *Éire-Ireland* (St. Paul, Minnesota), VIII, No. 2 (Summer 1973), 91-107

Looks mainly at the Irish drama.

1415   Mayne, Rutherford. "The Theatre," *The Bell* (Dublin), IV, No. 1 (April 1942), 47-54

Survey of play productions.

1416 —. "The Ulster Literary Theatre," *The Dublin Magazine*, XXXI (April-June 1955), 15-21

> This theatre, which celebrated its Golden Jubilee in 1954, has a tradition of fine actors and unique plays, with 1904-1909 being a particularly rich period in its history.

1417 "The Mayor and the 'Play Boy'," *The Chicago Record-Herald*, (31 January 1912), p. 14

> Editorial on the Abbey Theatre's first American tour.

1418 Mennloch, Walter. "Dramatic Values," *The Irish Review* (Dublin), I, No. 7 (September 1911), 325-329

> The Abbey Theatre has become a fixture.

1419 Mercier, Vivian. "The Dublin Tradition," *The New Republic* (New York), CXXXV, No. 6 (6 August 1956), 21-22

> Argues that in Dublin "a healthy theatre is living off its traditions."

1420 Miller, Liam. "Across the River," *Hibernia* (Dublin), (July 1966), p. 3

> The New Abbey Theatre will provide chance to improve Irish drama.

See reply by Gerard Fay, *ibid.*, (August 1966), p. 8.

1421 —. "Eden and After: The Irish Theatre 1945-1966," *Studies; An Irish Quarterly Review* (Dublin), LX (Autumn 1966), 231-235

> Surveys the Irish Theatre since the end of World War II and concludes that "however one looks at the situation today, it is on the National Theatre that our hopes for the future of the theatre in Ireland must be based".

1422   —. "Dublin Theatre 1966-1967," *Ireland of the Welcomes*
        (Dublin), XVI, No. 2 (July-August 1967), 23-26

>   Highlights of the season.

1423   Milligan, Alice. "Literary Theatre Week in Dublin," *The Gael*
        (New York), (December 1901), 363-364

>   Survey of play productions.

1424   M[itchell], S[usan]. "Dramatic Rivalry," *Sinn Fein* (Dublin),
        IV (8 May 1909), 1

>   Berates W. B. Yeats for letting go Maire Nic Shiubhlaigh.

1425   Montague, John. "The Theatre," *The Bell* (Dublin), XVII,
        No. 10 (January 1952), 55-58; No. 11 (Februry 1952),
        55-57; No. 12 (March 1952), 114-116; XVIII, No. 1
        (April 1952), 50-54; No. 2 (May 1952), 111-114

>   Survey of play productions.

1426   —. "Order in Donnybrook Fair," *Quarryman*, (1973), 6-8

>   A critical review of contemporary Irish writing; revised version
>   of article previously published in *The Times Literary Supple-
>   ment*, 17 March 1972.

1427   Montgomery, K. L. "Some Writers of the Celtic Renais-
        sance," *Fortnightly Review* (London and New York),
        XC, New Series (September 1911), 545-561

>   "Perhaps the most original achievement of this Celtic Renais-
>   sance has been the organisation of the National Literary The-
>   atre".

1428   Moore, George. "The Irish Literary Theatre," *Samhain*
        (Dublin), No. 1 (October 1901), 11-13

"Our three years have shown that an endowed theatre may be of more intellectual service to a community than a university or a public library".

1429 —. "The Irish Theatre," *Boston Evening Transcript*, (23 September 1911), Part 3, p. 8

Recollections of the Abbey Theatre.

1430 Morin, Jean-Henry. "La Lutte de l'Irlande pour l'Indépendence," *Liberté* (Paris), LVI (2 September 1921), 2

The Abbey Theatre.

1431 Moroney, Helen. "The Most Exciting Day of My Life," *The Irish Statesman* (Dublin), IV, No. 2 (21 March 1925), 42-43

A visit to the Abbey Theatre.

1432 Morrow, Gerald. "The Belfast Theatre," *The Bell* (Dublin), III, No. 5 (February 1942), 361-362; No. 6 (March 1942), 481; IV, No. 1 (April 1942), 55-56; No. 4 (July 1942), 301-302; V, No. 3 (December 1942), 238-241

Survey of play productions.

1433 —. "An Ulster Arts Theatre," *Lagan* (Belfast), No. 2 (1944), 100-101

On the aims of the proposed new theatre.

1434 Morrow, H. L. "Have the Irish a Sense of Humour?" *Ireland of the Welcomes* (Dublin), VIII, No. 5 (January-February 1960), 25-28

Includes illustrations from Irish dramatists.

1435   Mortished, R. J. P. "What Is Wrong with the Abbey The-
       atre?" *The Irish Statesman* (Dublin), II, No. 1 (15
       March 1924), 13

       Argues for a municipal subsidy, more foreign plays, more pit
       seats, and a substitute for "the atrocious gong".

1436   Moseley, Virginia. "A Week in Dublin," *Modern Drama*,
       IV, No. 2 (September 1961), 164-171

       Survey of play productions and an account of a drama sympo-
       sium, whose participants included Brendan Behan, John B.
       Keane, and Rae MacAnally.

1437   Moses, Montrose J. "W. B. Yeats and the Irish Players,"
       The Metropolitan Magazine (New York), XXV, No.
       3 (January 1912), 23-25, 61-62

       Survey of the Irish dramatic movement on the occasion of the
       Abbey Theatre's first American tour.

1438   —. "Dramatists Without a Country," *The Book-News Month-
       ly* (Philadelphia), XXX (February 1912), 408-409

       Abbey Theatre's first American tour.

1439   "Mr. Roosevelt as a Critic," *The Literary Digest* (New York),
       XLIV, No. 8 (24 February 1912), 375-376

       Of the Abbey Theatre's first American tour.

1440   Mulkerns, Val. "Theatre," *The Bell* (Dublin), XVIII, No. 5
       (October 1952)—XIX, No. 7 (June 1954)

       Survey of play productions.

1441   Murphy, Daniel J. "Yeats and Lady Gregory: A Unique
       Dramatic Collaboration," *Modern Drama*, VII, No.
       3 (December 1964), 322-328.

1442 Murphy, Martin. "Memoirs of a Dublin Stage-Hand," *The Irish Digest* (Dublin), IX, No. 1 (March 1941), 101-103

Recollections of some stage productions.

1443 Murphy, Sheila Ann. "A Political History of the Abbey Theatre," *Literature and Ideology* (Montreal), XVI (1973), 53-60

Survey.

1444 Murray, Thomas C. "Two Abbey Dramatists," *Ireland-American Review* (New York), I, No. 2 (n. d.), 172-187

George Shiels and Brinsley Macnamara.

1445 Musek, Karel. "Irské literární divadlo," *Divadelní list máje* (Praha), III, No. 2 (2 November 1906), 17-19

The Irish Literary Theatre.

1446 Musgrave, Donal. "Writers' Week in Listowel," *Ireland of the Welcomes*, XXI, No. 6 (1972), 6-9

Includes background to the Irish drama.

1447 Nathan, George Jean. "Erin Go Blah," *Newsweek* (Dayton, Ohio), (27 December 1937), 24

Reviews an Abbey American tour.

1448 —. "Lament for Irish Playwrights," *The American Mercury* (New York). LII, No. 208 (April 1941), 483-489

"Except for O'Casey . . . the quondam rich vein appears to have run dry".

1449   "National Theatre," *The Bell* (Dublin), XV, No. 6 (March 1948), 1-2

>   Editorial on the state of the Irish Theatre.

1450   Nelick, Frank C. "Yeats, Bullen, and the Irish Drama," *Modern Drama*, I (December 1958), 196-202

>   Survey of the Yeats collection of the late P. S. O'Hegarty recently purchased by the University of Kansas, including *The Abbey Theatre Series* and 171 Abbey Theatre programmes from 1904-1922.

1451   "New Abbey Theatre by End of 1960," *The Irish Times* (Dublin) (22 October 1958), pp. 1, 7

>   Plans for the building of the new Abbey Theatre.

1452   "New Abbey Theatre, Dublin," *Architect & Building News* (London), CCXXX (31 August 1966), 371-374.

1453   "New Directors for Abbey Theatre," *The Times* (London), (14 January 1965), p. 5.

1454   "New Irish Plays Produced," *The Gael* (New York), XXI (May 1902), 166-167

>   Review of play productions.

1455   "New Plays at the Dublin Theatre Festival," *Focus; A Monthly Review* (Belfast), III (October 1960), 17-21

>   Survey of play productions.

1456   "A New Thing in the Theater: Some Impressions of the Much-discussed 'Irish Players'," *Harper's Weekly* (New York), IV (9 December 1911), 19

>   Abbey Theatre's first American tour.

1457 O'Carroll, Michael. "Drama in the New Age," *Iris Hibernia* (Fribourg, Switzerland), IV, No. 3 (1960), 15-19

General discussion on the drama.

1458 O'Connor, Frank. "The Future of Irish Literature," *Horizon* (London), V, No. 25 (January 1942), 55-63

Regrets that recent plays do not grapple with real problems.

1459 —. "The Theatre," *The Bell* (Dublin), IV, No. 2 (May 1942), 146-148

Survey of play productions.

1460 —. "The Art of the Theatre," *The Bell* (Dublin), IX, No. 6 (March 1945), 487-501; X, No. 1 (April 1945), 49-63; No. 2 (May 1945), 131-139; No. 3 (June 1945), 240-245

Discusses the audience, the writer, and the actor.

1461 —. "Myself and the Abbey Theatre," *The Irish Digest* (Dublin), XXXIX, No. 3 (May 1951), 16-19

Recollections.

1462 —. "The New Abbey Will Be a Vested Interest When It Should Be Free," *Sunday Independent* (Dublin), (8 September 1963), p. 10.

1463 —. "All the Olympians," *The Saturday Review* (New York), XLIX, No. 50 (10 December 1966), 30-32, 99. Reprinted in *The Backward Look; A Survey of Irish Literature* (London: Macmillan, 1967), pp. 183-193

On J. M. Synge, W. B. Yeats, and Lady Gregory.

1464 O'Connor, Ulick. "Dublin's Dilemma," *Theatre Arts* (New

York), XL, No. 7 (July 1956), 64-65, 96

Comparison between   the Irish theatre now and "the golden
years of the Abbey".

1465   —. "Theatre in Ireland," *The Dubliner*, III, No. 4 (Winter
       1964), 78-79

Review article.

1466   —. "Abbey Memories," *Everyman* (Benburb, County Ty-
       rone), No. 2 (1969), 46-47

Recollections of actors Arthur Shields and J. M. Kerrigan.

1467   O'D., D. "The Irish National Theatre Company," *The United
       Irishman* (Dublin), XI (9 April 1904), p. 6

Survey of play productions.

See reply by James Connolly, "Some Plays and a
Critic," (7 May 1904), p. 6.

1468   "O'Donnell, Donat" [Conor Cruise O'Brien] . "The Abbey:
       Pheonix Infrequent," *The Commonweal* (New York),
       LVII (30 January 1953), 423-424

Social calm, literary indolence and dialect conventions are
some of the reasons "why the flame of the Abbey burns low
just now".

1469   O'Donnell, Frank J. Hugh. "The Irish Theatre: Its Inception
       and Progress," *Red Hand Magazine* (Glasgow), I, No.
       2 (October 1920), 51-54.

1470   O'Donovan, Fred, "Aim of Irish Players to Reproduce on
       Stage True Effect of Nature," *The World* (New York),
       (26 November 1911), p. 6

Interview during the Abbey Theatre's first American tour.

1471 O'Faoláin, Seán. "The Abbey Festival," *The New States-man and Nation* (London), XVI, (20 August 1938), 281-282

>   Detects a deterioration in acting and production.

1472 —. "Drama in Wexford," *The Bell* (Dublin), V, No. 5 (February 1943), 390-396

>   Survey of play productions.

1473 —. "Our New National Theatre," *The Irish Digest* (Dublin), XXVII, No. 2 (April 1947), 6-8

>   Building plan to house the National Theatre Society.

1474 —. "I Like the Stage Irishman!" *The Irish Digest* (Dublin), XXIX, No. 2 (December 1947), 10-12

>   "Is he merely an exaggeration of reality?"

1475 —. "The Dilemma of Irish Letters," *Month* (London), II, New Series, No. 6 (December 1949), 366-379

>   Includes discussion on some Irish dramatists.

1476 —. "Ireland after Yeats," *Books Abroad* (Norman, Oklahoma), XXVI, No. 4 (Autumn 1952), 325-333. Reprinted in *The Bell* (Dublin), XVIII, No. 11 (Summer 1953), 37-48

>   Considers the reasons for the decline of the theatre in the 1930s and the 1940s.

1477 O'Farrell, Mairin. "A Discussion on the Theatre in Ireland," *Hibernia* (Dublin), (October 1964), p. 17

>   Interview with Alpho O'Reilly.

1478 Ó hAodha, Micheál. "Ireland's Amateur Drama Festivals,"

Ireland of the Welcomes (Dublin), VI, No. 3 (September-October 1957), 12-14

Survey during the past 25 years.

1479   —. "Theatre in Dublin," *The Irish Press* (Dublin), (24 November 1962), p. 4

Review article.

1480   O'Hegarty, P. S. "About Drama," *Inis Fáil* (London), No. 46 (August 1908), 5-6

The Iish Dramatic Movement is not progressing.

1481   —. "Art and the Nation," *Irish Freedom* (Dublin), No. 16 (February 1912), 8; No. 17 (March 1912), 2; No. 18 (April 1912), 7; No. 19 (May 1912), 2

A defense of the Abbey Theatre.

1482   —. "The Abbey Theatre," *The Irish Times* (Dublin), (6 September 1944), p. 3

Letter to the Editor on the general condition of the Theatre.

1483   O'Laoghaire, Liam. "Producing at the Abbey," *The Bell* (Dublin), XV, No. 4 (January 1948), 27-39

Describes his work as a Gaelic producer at the Abbey Theatre.

1484   —. "Theatre and Films," *The Bell* (Dublin), XV, No. 5 (February 1948), 52-57; No. 6 (March 1948), 57-60

Survey of play productions.

1485   O'Mahony, T. P. "Theatre in Ireland," *Eire-Ireland* (St. Paul, Minnesota), IV (Summer 1969), 93-100

Discusses the role of the Abbey Theatre in Irish society from the time of Yeats to the end of the 1960s.

1486 O'Malley, Mary. "Belfast Theatre Controversy," *Threshold* (Belfast), III, No. 2 (Summer 1959), 27-28

Discusses the possible connection between the government subsidies and the Ulster Group Theatre's productions.

1487 —. "Theatre in Belfast," *Iris Hibernia* (Fribourg, Switzerland), IV, No. 3 (1960), 55-57

Survey of Theatrical activities in Belfast past and present.

1488 —. "Irish Theater Letter," *Massachusetts Review* (Amherst), VI (Autumn 1964), 181-186

Survey of drama in Ulster from 1902.

1489 O'Mangain, H. C. "The National Drama," *Evening Telegraph* (Dublin), (4 February 1907), p. 4

Discusses W. B. Yeats, J. M. Synge, William Boyle, and Lady Gregory.

1490 O'Meadhra, Séan. "Theatre," *Ireland Today* (Dublin), I, No. 1 (June 1936), 64-66; No. 2 (July 1936), 62-65; No. 3 (August 1936), 62-64; No. 4 (September 1936), 62-63; No. 5 (October 1936), 55-60; No. 6 (November 1936), 69-72; No. 7 (December 1936), 64-67, II, No. 1 (January 1937), 69-73; No. 2 (February 1937), 66-68; No. 3 (March 1937), 67-69; No. 4 (April 1937), 65-68; No. 5 (May 1937), 67-71; No. 6 (June 1937), 71-77; No. 7 (July 1937), 61-66; No. 8 (August 1937), 67-72; No. 9 (September 1937), 64-68; No. 10 (October 1937), 67-70; No. 11 (November 1937), 70-75; No. 12 (December 1937), 67-68; III, No. 1 (January 1938), 63-65; No. 2 (February 1938), 162-165; No. 3 (March

1938), 249-252; No. 3 (March 1938), 249-252

Survey of play productions.

1491   —. "Sack of the Abbey," *Ireland Today* (Dublin), II, No. 2 (February 1937), 25-32

Defends the Abbey from the attacks made by John Dowling and Mervyn Wall in the January issue of this periodical.

1492   O'Neill, George. "The Inauguration of the Irish Literary Theatre," *The New Ireland Review* (Dublin), XI (June 1899), 246-252

Survey.

1493   —. "Recent Irish Drama and Its Critics," *The New Ireland Review* (Dublin), XXV (March 1906), 29-36

On the controversy over the prevalence "of certain unpleasant types of the Irish peasant in various plays produced during the last few years by writers hailed as representative and eminent Irish dramatists".

1494   —. "Some Aspects of Our Anglo-Irish Poets: The Irish Literary Theatre; Foreign Inspiration of Alleged Irish Plays," *The Irish Catholic* (Dublin), XXIV, No. 51 (23 December 1911), 5

Text of a lecture delivered before the Students' National Literary Society in Dublin.

1495   —. "Irish Drama and Irish Views," *American Catholic Quarterly Review* (Philadelphia), XXXVII, No. 146 (April 1912), 322-332. Reprinted in *The Irish Catholic* (Dublin), XXV, No. 33 (31 August 1912), 6; and XXV, No. 34 (7 September 1912), 6

Irish plays as a picture of Irish life.

1496 O'Ryan, Agnes. "The Drama of the Abbey Theatre," *The Irish Educational Review* (Dublin), VI, No. 3 (December 1912), 154-163

On the plays of W. B. Yeats, J. M. Synge, Padraic Colum, Lady Gregory, Lennox Robinson, and William Boyle.

1497 O'Sullivan, Seumas. "How Our Theatre Began," *The Irish Digest* (Dublin), XXVII, No. 4 (June 1947), 5-7

Recollections of the beginning of the Irish Dramatic Movement.

1498 P., E. J., and St. John Ervine, "After the Abbey?" *New Ireland* (Dublin), II, No. 42 (4 March 1916), 276-278.

1499 P., H. T. "Irish Plays and Irish Acting," *Boston Evening Transcript*, (19 September 1911), p. 14

Impressions of the Abbey Theatre's play productions in London, 1909.

1500 P., T. "The Old Abbey," *Irish Independent* (Dublin), (8 November 1958), p. 8

Review article on the Abbey Theatre.

1501 Page, Sean. "The Abbey Theatre," *The Dublin Magazine*, V, Nos. 3-4 (Autumn-Winter 1966), 6-14

Examines the Abbey as a national theatre.

1502 Palmer, John. "The Success of the Irish Players," *The Saturday Review* (London), CXIV (13 July 1912), 42-43

Abbey Theatre's first American tour.

1503 Parsons, Chauncey L. "Lady Gregory: Guiding Genius of the Irish Players," *The New York Dramatic Mirror*, (27

December 1911), p. 5

Interview during the Abbey Theatre's first American tour.

1504   Passeur, Stève. "Le théâtre irlandais," *Oeuvre; Revue International des Arts du Theatre* (Paris), No. 75 (Spring-Summer 1925), 81-85

Survey.

1505   Paul-Dubois, Louis. "Le théâtre irlandais," *Revue des Deux Mondes* (Paris), XXVII, No. 3 (1 June 1935), 631-657

Mainly on J. M. Synge and Sean O'Casey.

1506   Payne, Basil. "Two Hard Men," *The Irish Times* (Dublin), (8 December 1962), p. 10

Review article on Samuel Beckett and Brendan Behan.

1507   Pettet, Edwin Burr. "Report on the Irish Theatre," *Educational Theatre Journal*, VIII (May 1956), 109-114

Survey of play productions.

1508   Phillipson, Wulstan. "An Irish Occasion," *The Month* (London), XXVI, No. 6 (December 1961), 356-362

At the opening of Duras House as a youth hostel, a plaque was unveiled with the following inscription: "It was in this house ... that Augusta, Lady Gregory of Coole Park, in the summer of 1898, met William Butler Yeats at the request of her neighbour, Edward Martyn, and there began between them the conversation which led to the founding of the Abbey Theatre".

1509   Pierrot. "Of Playwrights and Players," *The Dublin Magazine*, I, No. 6 (January 1924), 543-546; No. 7 (February 1924), 577-579; No. 8 (March 1924), 759-763; No. 9 (April 1924), 803-806

Survey of play productions.

1510 "Plan Group to Oppose the Abbey," *Irish Independent* (Dublin), (21 September 1963), p. 8

> A group of actors to form a separate national theatre company in opposition to the Abbey Theatre, which "was dead as a national theatre".

1511 "The Players," *Everybody's Magazine* (New York), XXVI (February 1912), 231-240

> "The monotony of the current theatre season in America was emphatically interrupted by the advent of the Irish Players from the Abbey Theatre, Dublin".

1512 "Plays and Controversies," *The Dubliner*, I, No. 3 (May-June 1962), 46-50; No. 4 (July-August 1962), 55-59

> Survey of play productions.

1513 "The Playwright in Ireland," *The Irish Times* (Dublin), (18 May 1976), p. 8; (19 May 1976), p. 10; (20 May 1976), p. 8; and (21 May 1976), p. 10

> Discussions by David Hayes, James Douglas, Michael Judge, Liam MacUistin, and John O'Donovan.

1514 Plunkett, Joseph. "The Irish Theatre," *The Irish Review* (Dublin), IV, No. 41 (September-November 1914), 337-338

> The productions of "The Irish Theatre," the new project by Edward Martyn.

1515 Pollock, C. "The Irish Players," *Green Book Magazine* (Chicago), VII (February 1912), 349-350

> Abbey Theatre's first American tour.

1516   "A Poor Way to Treat Poor Plays," *The Brooklyn Daily Eagle* (New York), (28 November 1911), p. 4

   Editorial on the Abbey Theatre's first American tour.

1517   P[orter], C[harlotte]. "The Irish Players in Philadelphia," *Poet Lore* (Boston), XXIII (March-April 1912), 159-160

   Abbey Theatre's first American tour.

1518   Post, Julester Shrady. "The Dear Old Morgue," *Capuchin Annual* (Dublin), XXI (1964), 376-379

   The Abbey Theatre.

1519   Powell, York. "A Fragment of Irish Literary History: Irish Influence on English Literature," *The Freeman's Journal* (Dublin), CXXX, (8 April 1902), 6

   Lecture delivered before the National Literary Society, Dublin.

1520   "President [de Valera] Lays Abbey Foundation Stone," *The Irish Times* (Dublin), (4 September 1963), p. 1. See also de Valera's recollections, p. 8.

1521   "The Priest, the Drama, and Mr. Fallon," *Hibernia* (Dublin), (June 1963), p. 10

   The controversy over the participation by priests in Irish theatrical activities.

1522   "Problems That Confront the New Abbey Theatre," *The Irish Digest* (Dublin), LXXVIII, No. 4 (October 1963), 79-82

   On the occasion of laying the foundation-stone of the new Abbey Theatre.

1523 Quinn, Hugh. "Playwright in the Back Yard," *The Irish Digest* (Dublin), IX, No. 4 (June 1941), 16-20

Recollections of a play production in Belfast.

1524 Quinn, John. "Lady Gregory and the Abbey Theater," *The Outlook* (New York), XCIX (16 December 1911), 916-919

Deals also with W. B. Yeats and J. M. Synge.

1525 R., L. "Dublin Drama Notes," *The Dublin Magazine*, XVI, No. 2 (April-June 1941), 58-59

Survey of play productions.

1526 Rafroidi, Patrick. "La Scène Littéraire Irlandaise Contemporaine," *Les Langues Modernes* (Paris), II (March 1967), 84-89

Survey.

1527 Ray, Moira L. "Birth of Ireland's National Drama," *Theatre Magazine* (New York), III, No. 29 (July 1903), 167-168

The Irish Literary Theatre.

1528 "Rebuilding the Abbey Theatre in Dublin," *Architects' Journal* (London), CXXIX (19 February 1959), 305-308

1528a Rees, Leslie. "Irish Drama," *New English Weekly* (London), II, No. 17 (9 February 1933), 397-398

Survey.

1529 Reid, Alec. "Dublin's Abbey Theatre Today," *Drama Survey* (Minneapolis), III, No. 4 (Fall 1964), 507-519

A brief history of the Abbey Theatre plus some observations on its organisation today and its plans for the future.

1530   Rhodes, Raymond Crompton. "The Irish National Theatre,"
        T. P.'s Weekly (London), XXI, No. 545 (18 April
        1913), 504

        Letter to the Editor.

1531   "Riotous Criticism," *Public Ledger* (Philadelphia), (18 Jan-
        uary 1912), p. 10

        Abbey Theatre's first American tour.

1532   "Riots in Theatres," *The Philadelphia Inquirer,* (18 January
        1912), p. 8

        Editorial on the Abbey Theatre's first American tour.

1533   Rivoallan, A[natole]. "Dublin au Théâtre," *Mercure de
        France* (Paris), CCLXXV (15 April 1937), 299-307

        Survey of play productions.

1534   Roberts, Peter. "Dublin Festival," *Plays and Players* (Lon-
        don), X, No. 2 (November 1962), 61-63

        Survey of play productions.

1535   —. "Mixed Blessings," *Plays and Players* (London), XII, No.
        2 (November 1964), 8-9

        Survey of the 1964 Dublin Theatre Festival.

1536   —. "Dublin 1965," *Plays and Players* (London), XIII, No.
        3 (December 1965), 19-22

        Survey of Dublin Theatre Festival.

1537   —. "Dublin Theatre Festival,"*Plays and Players* (London),

XIV, No. 2 (November 1966), 56-59, 67

Survey.

1538   --. "Operation Survival," *Plays and Players* (London), XV, No. 3 (December 1967), 46-47, 50

Survey of the 1966 Dublin Theatre Festival.

1539   —. "Dublin," *Plays and Players* (London), XVI, No. 3 (December 1968), 64-66

Survey of the 1968 Dublin Theatre Festival.

1540   —. "Dublin," *Plays and Players* (London), XVIII, No. 8 (May 1971), 53-55

Survey of the 1971 Dublin Theatre Festival.

1541   Robinson, Lennox. "To Help the Abbey Theatre," *The Nation* (London), XXIX, (23 April 1921), 128-129

A plea, in the form of a Letter to the Editor, to pay the Theatre's debt.

1542   —. "Recipe for a National Theatre," *The Realist* (London), (June 1929), 130-141

"Our recipe for a National Theatre could only have been cooked over an Irish fire".

1543   —. "The Birth of a Nation's Theater," *The Emerson Quarterly* (Boston), XIII, No. 2 (January 1933), 3-4, 16-18, 20

Background piece on the Abbey Theatre, written to prepare American audiences for the 1933 tour.

1544   —. "The Irish National Theatre," *The Irish Digest* (Dublin),

I, No. 3 (September 1938), 40-43

> Condensed from *The Abbey Theatre Dramatic Festival Sou-*
> *venir*, August 1938.

1545   —. "Them Were the Days," *Ireland of the Welcomes* (Dublin),
       III, No. 4 (November-December 1954), 13-14, 30

> Recollections of the Abbey Theatre by the Irish dramatist.

1546   —. "My Early Days with the Abbey," *The Irish Digest* (Dub-
       lin), LXII, No. 3 (May 1958), 83-86

> Recollections of the Abbey Theatre.

1547   Rocke, William. "May Craig Recalls That Abbey Uproar,"
       The Irish Digest (Dublin), LXXX, No. 1 (March 1964),
       71-73

> Recollections of the Abbey Theatre productions.

1548   Rodway, Norman. "Drama Critics as I See Them," *The Irish*
       Digest (Dublin), LXXX, No. 1 (March 1964), 22-24

> Observations by an Irish actor.

1549   Rollins, Ronald G. "Portraits of Four Irishmen as Artists:
       Verisimilitude and Vision," *Irish University Review*
       (Dublin), I (Spring 1971), 189-197

> James Joyce, W. B. Yeats, Sean O'Casey, and J. M. Synge.

1550   Roosevelt, Theodore. "The Irish Theatre," *The Outlook*
       (New York), (16 December 1911), 915-916

> Abbey Theatre's first American tour.

1551   "Roosevelt As a Critic," *The Literary Digest* (New York),
       XLIV (24 February 1912), 375-376

Abbey Theatre's first American tour.

1552 Rosenfield, Judith. "Belfast's New Theatre," *Theatre World* (London), LVII (June 1961), 50

The Arts Theatre, which opened in April 1961.

1553 —. "Theatre in the North," *Hibernia* (Dublin), (February 1968), p. 21

Survey of play productions in Ulster.

1554 —. "Belfast," *Plays and Players* (London), XVI, No. 6 (March 1969), 62-63

Survey.

1555 Rosenfield, Ray. "Belfast," *Plays and Players* (London), I, No. 12 (september 1954), 26; II, No. 1 (October 1954), 26; II, No. 3 (December 1954), 26; II, No. 4 (January 1955), 26; II, No. 8 (May 1955), 26; II, No. 9 (June 1955), 23; III, No. 4 (January 1956), 30; III, No. 8 (May 1956), 33; III, No. 11 (August 1956), 33; III, No. 12 (September 1956), 33; IV, No. 1 (October 1956), 33; IV, No. 2 (November 1956), 32; IV, No. 4 (January 1957), 30; IV, No. 5 (February 1957), 33; IV, No. 6 (March 1957), 32; IV, No. 9 (June 1957), 32; IV, No. 10 (July 1957), 32; V, No. 2 (November 1957), 32; V, No. 4 (January 1958), 32; V, No. 6 (March 1958), 33; V, No. 9 (June 1958), 32; V, No. 12 (September 1958), 32; VI, No. 1 (October 1958), 33; VI, No. 2 (November 1958), 32; VI, No. 3 (December 1958), 32; VI, No. 5 (February 1959), 32; VI, No. 6 (March 1959), 33; VI, No. 7 (April 1959), 32; VI, No. 9 (June 1959), 32; VI, No. 10 (July 1959), 33; VI, No. 11 (August 1959), 32; VII, No. 1 (October 1959), 33; VII, No. 3 (December 1959), 31-32; VII, No. 5 (February 1960), 33; VII, No. 6 (March 1960), 32; VII, No. 7 (April

1960), 31; VII, No. 11 (August 1960), 33; VII, No. 12 (September 1960), 31-32; VIII, No. 2 (November 1960), 31; VIII, No. 5 (February 1961), 33; VIII, No. 6 (March 1961), 33; VIII, No. 7 (April 1961), 32; VIII No. 9 (June 1961), 36; VIII, No. 10 (July 1961), 37; VIII, No. 11 (August 1961), 34; VIII, No. 12 (September 1961), 34-35; IX, No. 3 (December 1961), 35; IX, No. 4 (January 1961), 28

Survey.

1556   —. "Theatre in Belfast: Achievement of a Decade," *Threshold* (Belfast), II, No. 1 (1958), 66-67

Survey.

1557   Ross, Arthur. "In Ulster Now," *Drama* (London), No. 24 (May 1943), 4-6

Survey of dramatic activities in Ulster.

1558   Rouleau, Suzanna. "Irish Arts Theatre," *Performing Arts in Canada*, VIII, No. 4 (Winter 1971), 6

Plans of the new Theatre in Toronto outlined.

1559   Roy, James A. "J. M. Synge and the Irish Literary Movement," *Anglia* (Halle), XXXVII, New Series XXV (1913), 129-145

Emphasizes the poetic origins and Celtic tone of the Irish theatre.

1560   Rushe, Desmond. "Theatre," *Eire-Ireland* (St. Paul, Minnesota), V, No. 4 (Winter 1970) to the present

Survey of Irish theatre activities and of play productions.

1561   —. "The Abbey's New Policies," *Eire-Ireland* (St. Paul,

Minnesota), VII, No. 4 (Winter 1972), 32-47

1562 Russell, George W. "The Coming of Age of the Abbey," *The Irish Statesman* (Dublin), V, No. 17 (2 January 1926), 517-519

> "Frankly we wish, for the sake of the Abbey itself, that it shall continue to live in that exasperating atmosphere in which it grew up."

1563 Ruttledge, Paul [George Moore]. "Stage Management in the Irish National Theatre," *Dana* (Dublin), No. 5 (September 1904), 150-152

> A cutting article. "Paul Ruttledge" has been identified as George Moore.

1564 Ryan, George E. " 'Stage Irishmen' in America," *Ireland of the Welcomes* (Dublin), VIII, No. 2 (July-August 1959), 22-24

> Survey since 1865.

> Also in *Hibernia* (Dublin), (December 1958), p. 3.

1565 —. "The Stage Irishman—Yesterday and Today," *The Irish Digest* (Dublin), LXVI, No. 3 (September 1959), 53-55

> Survey.

1566 Ryan, Stephen P. "Theatre in Dublin," *America* (New York), XCII (30 October 1954), 128-129

> Survey of play productions.

1567 —. "Crisis in Irish Letters; Literary Life in Dublin," *The Commonweal* (New York), LXXI, No. 12 (18 December 1959), 347-349

"The present crop of dramatists includes men of more than average talent . . . but simply not endowed with the touch of genius necessary for enduring fame in the theater".

1568 —. "Ireland and Its Writers," *The Catholic World* (New York), XCII (December 1960), 149-155

Complaint against the influence of the Church and the sterility of Irish society.

1569 S. W. T. "The Past and Future of Our Drama," *Academy* (London), LXVII (3 September 1904), 168-169

The Irish National Theatre Society.

1570 "Salvaging the Remains of Ireland's Most Famous Theatre," *The Illustrated London News*, CCIX (28 July 1951), 153

Photographs of the Abbey Theatre which burnt out on 18 July 1951.

1571 Sampson, Martin W. "The Irish Literary Theatre," *The Nation* (New York), LXXIII (21 November 1901), 395-396

Survey of play productions.

1572 "Scathing Denunciation Accorded 'Irish' Players by an Appointed Committee," *The Irish World and American Industrial Liberator* (New York), (28 October 1911), p. 7

On the Abbey Theatre's first American tour.

1573 Schull, Rebecca. "The Preparation of King Oedipus," *The Arts in Ireland* (Dublin), II, No. 1 (Autumn 1973), 15-21

The Abbey Theatre's staging of Sophocles.

1574 Scott, Michael, and Pierre Sonrel. "The New Abbey Theatre. Dublin," *The Builder* (London), CVC (21 November 1958), 856-859.

1575 Scudder, Vida D. "The Irish Literary Drama," *Poet Lore* (Philadelphia), XVI (Spring 1905), 40-53

Survey, with a list of Irish plays.

1576 Sears, William P., Jr. "New Dublin Players' Group Challenges Abbey Theater," *The Literary Digest* (New York), CXVII, No. 23 (9 June 1934), 26

The Dublin Gate Theatre.

1577 Shaw, Bernard. "The Irish Players," *The Evening Sun* (New York), (9 December 1911), pp. 4-5

An "interview" written entirely by Shaw during the Abbey Theatre's first American tour.

1578 "Sheilah Richards: Great Lady of the Irish Theatre," *The Irish Digest* (Dublin), LXXXVII, No. 4 (October 1966), 12-14

Includes recollections of the Abbey Theatre.

1579 Sheridan, John D. "Irish Writing Today," *Studies: An Irish Quarterly Review* (Dublin), XLIV (Spring 1955), 81-85

Includes discussion of some Irish dramatists.

1580 Shorter, Eric. "Dublin," *Drama* (London), No. 95 (Winter 1969), 34-36

Survey of play productions.

1581   Sigerson, George. "The Irish Peasantry and the Stage,"
         United Irishman (Dublin), (17 February 1906), 2-3.

1582   Silke, Elizabeth. "Drama in Belfast," *The Bell* (Dublin), XV,
         No. 4 (January 1948), 65-67

         Admits that Belfast had no first class theatre but sees potential
         in The Group Theatre Company.

1583   Simpson, Alan. "Paddy in Shaftesbury Avenue," *The Spec-
         tator* (London), (21 December 1962), 963-964

         Comparison between Englih and Irish theatrical tastes by an
         Irishman living in London.

1584   Skeffington, F. Sheehy. "The Irish National Theatre,"
         T. P.'s Weekly (London), XXI, No. 547 (2 May 1913),
         566

         Letter to the Editor.

1585   Skelton, Robin. "Twentieth-Century Irish Literature and the
         Private Press Tradition: Dun Emer, Cuala, and Dol-
         men Presses, 1902-1963," *Massachusetts Review*
         (Amherst), V (1964), 368-377.

1586   Smalley, George W. "The Irish Players," *The Literary Digest*
         (New York), XLIV (24 February 1912), 375-376

         Abbey Theatre's first Ameican tour.

1587   Smith, Brendan. "The Dublin Theatre Festival," *Hibernia*
         (Dublin), (25 August 1972), p. 16

         Observations.

1588   Smith, Hester Travers. "Drama in Ireland, 1919-1920,"
         Drama Magazine (Chicago), X (June 1920), 308-309

         Survey.

1589 Smith, Hugh. "Twilight of the Abbey?" *The New York Times*, (31 March 1935), Section XI, p. 2

Notes a decline in the quality of the Abbey plays and attacks its new policy of bringing in outside advisers and staging Continental plays.

1590 Smith, Paul. "Dublin's Lusty Theater," *Holiday* (Philadelphia), XXXIII (April 1963), 119+

Reflections on the Irish theatre then and now.

1591 Snoddy, Oliver. "Yeats and Irish in the Theatre," *Éire-Ireland* (St. Paul, Minnesota), IV, No. 1 (Spring 1969), 39-45

Outlines the progress of Gaelic drama from Douglas Hyde to Ernest Blythe.

1592 Speers, Neill. "Drama and Theatre in Time of Conflict and Violence," *Aquarius* (Benburb, County Tyrone), VII (1974), 58-62

"During the past three years in Belfast professional and amateur productions . . . have pointed to the many changes in public and private life brought about by violent and social conditions".

1593 "Stage Topics of the Moment," *The Philadelphia Record*, (21 January 1912), Part 4, p. 6

Abbey Theatre's first American tour.

1594 "Stage Workshop," *The Times Literary Supplement* (London), (28 August 1959), p. 495

Editorial on the Abbey Theatre's need to create a workshop atmosphere.

1595 Stahl, Ernest Leopold. "Von dem modernen irischen

Drama," *Masken* (Düsseldorf), VI, No. 11 (14 November 1919), 165-166

Survey.

1596   Stamm, Rudolf. "die neu-irische Theaterbewegung und wir," *Schweizer Annalen* (Aarau), I, No. 3 (May 1944), 156-166

What the Swiss theater could learn from the Irish Dramatic Movement.

1597   —. "Von Theaterkrisen und ihrer Überwindung," *Jahrbuch der Gesellschaft fur Schweizerische Theaterkultur* (Einsiedeln), XVI (1946), 1-102

The Irish Dramatic Movement and the plays of W. B. Yeats and J. M. Synge.

1598   "Stamp Out the Atrocious Libel," *The Gaelic American* (New York), (14 October 1911), p. 4

Editorial on the Abbey Theatre's first American tour.

1599   Starkie, Walter. "Den irländska nationalteatern," translated from the author's MS. by A. L. W., *Ord Och Bild* (Stockholm), XXXVIII, No. 10 (October 1929), 529-548; No. 11 (November 1929), 593-608

On W. B. Yeats, J. M. Synge, Lady Gregory, Padraic Colum, T. C. Murray, Lennox Robinson, and Sean O'Casey.

1600   —. "Ireland To-day," *Quarterly Review* (London), CCLXXI (October 1938), 343-360

On the Abbey Theatre, *passim*.

1601   "A State Theatre," *The Irish Press* (Dublin), (22 May 1947), p. 4

Editorial on the need for a suitable building for the Abbey.

1602 Stephenson, P. J. "The Abbey Theatre," *Dublin Historical Record*, XIII, No. 1 (March-May 1952), 22-29

A history of the buildings in which the Irish Literary Theatre and its successors played.

1603 Stewart, Andrew J. "The Acting of the Abbey Theatre," *Theatre Arts Monthly* (New York), XVII, No. 3 (March 1933), 243-245

"An actor from the Abbey Theatre in Dublin is noted for sincerity, naturalness, and simplicity".

1604 Stewart, John D. "Theatre: Afterthoughts on *Danger, Men Working,*" *Rann; An Ulster Quarterly* (Belfast), No. 13 (1951), 16-20.

1605 "The Stormy Debut of the Irish Players," *Current Literature* (New York), LI (December 1911), 675-676

Abbey Theatre's first American tour.

1606 "The Story of the Irish Players," *The Sunday Record-Herald* (Chicago), (4 February 1912), Part 7, p. 1

As told by George Moore, Sara Allgood, T. W. Rolleston, Lady Gregory, and W. B. Yeats.

1607 Sutton, E. Graham. "The Irishman in the Theatre," *English Review* (London), XXXIV (May 1922), 442-446

Presenting modern Irish comedy to English audiences.

1608 Sweeney, Maxwell. "Presenting Micheál Mac Liammóir," *The Irish Digest* (Dublin), XXV, No. 3 (September 1946), 9-11

The Dublin Gate Theatre.

1609   —. "Dynamic Hilton Edwards," *The Irish Digest* (Dublin),
        XXV, No. 4 (October 1946), 12-14

        The Dublin Gate Theatre.

1610   —. "Dublin," *Plays and Players* (London), I, No. 2 (Novem-
        ber 1953), 24; I, No. 3 (December 1953), 23; I, No.
        5 (February 1954), 22; I, No. 6 (March 1954), 22

        Survey of play productions.

1611   Swift, Carolyn. "The Pike; Four Dubliners and an Idea,"
        Encore (London), III, No. 3 (Summer 1956), 11-12

        The story of the Pike Theatre, which opened in Dublin in 1953.

1612   Tennyson, Charles. "Irish Plays and Playwrights," *Quarterly
        Review* (London), CCXV, No. 428 (July 1911), 219-
        243

        Review article.

1613   —. "The Rise of the Irish Theatre," *The Contemporary
        Review* (London), C (August 1911), 240-247

        The story of the Abbey Theatre.

1614   "Theatre," *Hibernia* (Dublin), 1959 to the present.

        Surveys of play productions by various critics including Thomas
        Kilroy, John Jordan, John C. Kelly, Mary Manning, Pearse
        Hutchinson, Patrick Gallagher, Patrick MacEntee, Basil Payne,
        Tim Pat Coogan, and Gerald Colgan.

1615   "Theatre in Dublin," *The Dublin Magazine*, V, Nos. 3-4
        (Autumn-Winter 1966), 3-5

        Editorial. "There is no denying that Dublin is suffering from a
        famine as far as the theatre is concerned".

1616 "Theatregoer". "The Abbey Theatre," *The Irish Times* (Dublin), (25 July 1944), p. 3. See correspondence on the Abbey crisis in the following issues.

1617 Tobin, Michael. "The Ponderings of a Playgoer," *Iris Hibernia* (Fribourg, Switzerland), IV, No. 3 (1960), 27-39

Remarks about the Irish theatre past and present.

1618 Tobin, Richard L. "The Paycock and the Playboy," *Saturday Review* (New York), LI (10 Februry 1968), 51

Review of recorded plays by Sean O'Casey and J. M. Synge.

1619 Tomelty, Joseph. "The Theatre in Northern Ireland," *Drama* (London), No. 28 (Spring 1953), 15-18

Survey of dramatic activities in Ulster.

1620 "Tonson, Jacob" [Arnold Bennett]. "Books and Persons," *The New Age* (London), IX, No. 16 (17 August 1911), 374-375

On the Abbey Theatre Company.

See Letters to the Editor by an Irish Playgoer, "The Abbey Theatre," (13 August 1911), 431; and by Sidheog Ní Annaín, "The Abbey Theatre," (7 September 1911), 454.

1621 Townshend, George. "The Irish Drama," *Drama Magazine* (Chicago), No. 3 (August 1911), 93-104

Survey.

1622 Treanor, Ann. "Behind the Abbey Scenes," *The Irish Digest* (Dublin), II, No. 2 (December 1938), 113-114

Recollections of the Abbey Theatre stage.

1623   Trilling, Ossia. "From the Emerald Isle," *Theatre World*
       (London), LV (November 1959), 21-23, 26

       Survey of the second Dublin International Theatre Festival.

1624   ―. "Report from Dublin," *Theatre World* (London), LVI
       (November 1960), 31-34, 48

       Survey of the 1960 Dublin International Theatre Festival.

1625   ―. "The Fourth Dublin Theatre Festival," *Theatre World*
       (London), LVII (November 1961), 31-34

       Survey of play productions.

1626   ―. "Dublin Discovers Arthur Johansson," *Encore* (London),
       X, No. 6 (November-December 1963), 44-47

       The Dublin International Theatre Festival.

1627   "Two Actors Relive Great Days at the Abbey Theatre,"
       The Times (Lodnon), (28 January 1963), p. 5

       Recollections by Arthur Shields and J. M. Kerrigan.

1628   Ua Fuaráin, Eoghan. "The Anglo-Irish Dramatic Movement,"
       Irisleabhar Muighe Nuadhad (Maynooth), I, No. 4
       (An Chaisg [Easter] 1910), 6-16

       Survey.

1629   "Ulster Books and Authors 1900-1953," *Rann; An Ulster
       Quarterly* (Belfast), No. 20 (1953), 55-73

       Includes brief biographies of fourteen Ulster playwrights.

1630   "Unusual Dramatic Happenings of the Past Month," *New
       England Magazine* (Boston), XLV (October 1911),
       226-228

The Abbey Theatre's first American tour.

1631 "The Vagabonds," *The Irish-American* (New York), (2 December 1911), p. 4

Editorial on the Abbey Theatre's first American tour.

1632 Valois, Ninette de. "Talk about the Abbey Theatre and W. B. Yeats," *Trinity News* (Dublin), XI, No. 10 (13 February 1964), 5.

1633 Van Hamel, A. G. "An Anglo-Irish Syntax," *Englische Studien* (Leipzig), XLV (1912), 272-292

Draws examples from the plays of W. B. Yeats and J. M. Synge.

1634 "Vital Drama," *The Times Literary Supplement* (London), (13 April 1940), p. 183

Editorial on Irish drama.

1635 W., J. "The Ulster Literary Theatre," *Ulad: A Literary and Critical Magazine* (Belfast), I, No. 2 (February 1905), 4-8

Survey of the Theatre's productions.

1636 —. "The Theatre and the People," *Ulad: A Literary and Critical Magazine* (Belfast), I, No. 3 (May 1905), 13-14

On the Ulster Literary Theatre.

1637 Walbrook, H. M. "Irish Dramatists and Their Countrymen," *The Fortnightly Review*, XCIV (November 1913), 957-961. Reprinted in *The Living Age* (Boston), CCLXXIX (27 December 1913), 789-793

Examines modern Irish drama as a picture of Irishmen.

1638   Wall, Mervyn. "Some Thoughts on the Abbey Theatre,"
        Ireland Today (Dublin), I, No. 4 (September 1936),
        59-62

        "The position of the Abbey Theatre is an insecure one".

1639   —. "The Abbey Theatre Attacked," *Ireland Today* (Dublin),
        II, No. 1 (January 1937), 43-47

        For its selection of plays, for the constitution of its Board of
        Directors, and for appointing an English producer.

1640   Walsh, Louis J. "The Defiance of 'The Abbey'," *Irish Rosary*
        (Dublin), XXXIX, No. 9 (September 1935), 650-
        654

        "Unless steps can be taken to ensure that the Theatre is not
        going to be allowed to trample all our ideas of morality and all
        our national ideals under foot, then it is the clear duty of the
        Government to withdraw its subsidy . . ."

1641   —. "A Catholic Theatre for Dublin," *Irish Rosary* (Dublin),
        XXXIX, No. 10 (October 1935), 749-754

        The Abbey Theatre is unsuited for a Catholic audience.

1642   Watkins, Ann. "The Irish Players in America: Their Purpose
        and Their Art," *Craftsman* (New York), XXI, No. 4
        (January 1912), 352-363

        Points out differences between productions of Irish plays and
        conventional Broadway ones and tells the story of the Irish
        Dramatic Movement on the occasion of the Abbey Theatre's
        first American tour.

1643   Webber, John E. "The Irish Players," *The Canadian Maga-
        zine* (Toronto), XXXVIII, No. 5 (March 1912), 471-
        481

        Abbey Theatre's first American tour.

1644 Weygandt, Cornelius. "The Irish Literary Revival," *Sewanee Review* (Sewanee, Tennessee), XII, No. 4 (October 1904), 420-431

> Part of the article deals with the Irish National Theatre.

1645 —. "The Art of the Irish Players and a Comment on Their Plays," *The Book News Monthly* (Philadelphia), XXX (February 1912), 379-381

> Abbey Theatre's first American tour.

1646 "What Ireland Now Offers Us," *The Literary Digest* (New York), XLIII (14 October 1911), 632-633

> Abbey Theatre's first American tour.

1647 "What's Wrong With the Abbey?" *Plays and Players* (London), X, No. 5 (February 1963), 22-24

> Views of director Hilton Edwards; dramatist Hugh Leonard; manager Phyllis Ryan; and critic Maurice Kennedy.

1648 Wheeler, Ethel Rolt. "Ideals in Irish Poetry and Drama," *Irish Book Lover* (Dublin and London), II, No. 5 (December 1910), 79

> Synopsis of lecture delivered on 5 November 1910 before the Irish Literary Society, Dublin.

1649 Wilmot, Seamus. "The Gaelic Theatre," *Éire-Ireland* (St. Paul, Minnesota), III (Summer 1968), 63-71

> Survey of the drama in the Irish language.

1650 Wittig, Kurt. "Die Nachkriegsliteratur Irlands," *Archiv* (Braunschweig) CLXXVI, Nos. 1-4 (November 1939), 12-28

> A survey of Anglo-Irish prose drama and fiction after 1918.

1651 Wood, J. Bertram. "The Irish Drama," *Humberside* (Manchester), VI, No. 2 (October 1938), 99-116

>   Concentrates on W. B. Yeats, Lady Gregory, J. M. Synge, and Sean O'Casey.

1652 Woodbridge, Homer E. "A Group of Irish Plays," *The Dial* (Chicago), LXI (30 November 1916), 462-463

>   Review article on Padraic Colum and St. John Ervine.

1653 "The World and the Theatre," *Theatre Arts* (New York), XIX, No. 12 (December 1935), 886

>   Survey of productions at the Abbey and the Dublin Gate Theatres.

1654 Yeats, W. B. "The Irish Literary Theatre," *The Freeman's Journal* (Dublin), (12 January 1899), p. 5

>   Letter to the Editor.

1655 —. "Important Announcement—The Irish Literary Theatre," *The Daily Express* (Dublin), (12 January 1899), p. 5

>   Letter to the Editor.

1656 —. "The Irish Literary Theatre," *The Daily Express* (Dublin), (14 January 1899), p. 3

>   Most of this article was printed in a revised form as "Plans and Methods," *Beltaine* (London), I (May 1899), 6-9.

1657 —. "Mr. Moore, Mr. Archer, and the Literary Theatre," *The Daily Chronicle* (London), (30 January 1899), p. 3

>   Letter to the Editor.

1658 —. "The Theatre," *The Dome* (London), III (April 1899),

48-52. Reprinted in *Beltaine* (London), I, No. 1 (May 1899), 20-23.

1659 —. "The Irish Literary Theatre," *Literature* (London), No. 81 (6 May 1899), 474.

1660 —. "Irish Literary Theatre," *The Irish Literary Society Gazette* (London), I, No. 4 (June 1899), 5-7

Lecture delivered on 23 April 1899.

1661 —. "The Irish Literary Theatre," *The Irish Literary Society Gazette* (London), (January 1900), 17

Letter to the Editor.

1662 —. "The Irish Literary Theatre, 1900," *The Dome* (London), V (January 1900), 234-236. Reprinted in *Beltaine* (London), I, No. 2 (February 1900), 22-24

"Because Ireland's moral nature has been aroused by political sacrifices, and her imagination by a political preoccupation with her own destiny, she is ready to be moved by profound thoughts that are a part of the unfolding of herself".

1663 —. "*The Last Feast of the Fiana, Maive,* and *The Bending of the Bough* in Dublin," *Beltaine* (London), I, No. 3 (April 1900), 4-6.

1664 —. "The Acting at St. Teresa's Hall," *The United Irishman* (Dublin), VII, No. 163 (12 April 1902), 3; No. 165 (26 April 1902), 3.

1665 —. "Notes," *Samhain* (Dublin and London), No. 2 (October 1902), 3-10.

1666 —. "The Freedom of the Theatre," *The United Irishman* (Dublin), VIII, No. 192 (1 November 1902), special supplement, 5.

1667   —. "Irish Plays and Players," *The Academy and Literature* (London), (16 May 1903), 495.

1668   —. "The Theatre, the Pulpit, and the Newspapers," *The United Irishman* (Dublin), X, No. 242 (17 October 1903), 2

    Reply to an attack on the Irish National Theatre.

1669   —. "The Irish National Theatre and Three Sorts of Ignorance," *The United Irishman* (Dublin), X, No. 243 (24 October 1903), 2

    Letter to the Editor and the Editor's reply.

1670   —. "Notes," *Samhain* (Dublin and London), No. 3 (October 1903), 3-8.

1671   —. "The Reform of the Theatre," *Samhain* (Dublin and London), No. 3 (October 1903), 9-12.

1672   —. "The Irish National Theatre," *The Gael* (New York), (June 1904), 234.

1673   —. "The Dramatic Movement," *Samhain* (Dublin and London), No. 4 (December 1904), 3-33.

1674   —. "Notes and Opinions," *Samhain* (Dublin and London), No. 5 (November 1905), 3-14.

1675   —. "Notes," *Samhain* (Dublin and London), No. 6 (December 1906), 3.

1676   —. "Abbey Theatre Scene," *Evening Telegraph* (Dublin), (29 January 1907), pp. 3-4

    Interview.

1677   —. " 'Abbey' Scenes Sequel: Prosecution in Police Court,"

Evening Herald (Dublin), (30 January 1907), pp. 1-2

Interview.

1678 —. "The Poet Is Pleased," *Evening Herald* (Dublin), (1 February 1907), p. 5

Interview.

1679 —. "The Abbey Theatre: Audience Overawed by Police," *Freeman's Journal* (Dublin), (4 February 1907), p. 4

Interview.

1680 —. "The Controversy over the Playboy," *The Arrow* (Dublin), I, No. 3 (23 February 1907), 1-2.

1681 —. "The Abbey Theatre: Resignation of Two Actors," *The Dublin Evening Mail*, (14 January 1908), p. 6

Frank and William G. Fay.

1682 —. "The Abbey Theatre," *The Dublin Evening Mail* (16 January 1908), p. 3.

1683 —. "A Correction," *The Dublin Evening Mail*, (17 January 1908), p. 3

Letter to the Editor.

1684 —. "The Abbey Theatre," *The Dublin Evening Mail*, (18 January 1908), p. 5

Letter to the Editor.

1685 —. "Mr. W. Fay and the Abbey Theatre," *The Dublin Evening Mail*, (21 May 1908), p. 5.

1686 —. "Events," *Samhain* (Dublin and London), No. 7

(November 1908), 1-5.

1687 —. *"The Shewing-Up of Blanco Posnet;* Statement by the Directors," *The Arrow* (Dublin), I, No. 5 (25 August 1909), 1-2.

1688 —. "The Irish Theatre," *Daily News* (London), (6 June 1910), p. 4

Interview by Robert Lynd.

1689 —. "The Irish National Theatre," *The Times* (London), (16 June 1910), p. 12.

1690 —. "The Irish Theatre," *The Nation* (London), (18 June 1910), 425

Letter to the Editor.

1691 —. "The Art of the Theatre," *The New Age* (London), (16 June 1910), 162-163.

1692 —. "The Tragic Theatre," *The Mask* (Florence), III (October 1910), 77-81.

1693 —. "Abbey Theatre: New System of Scenery," *The Evening Telegraph* (Dublin), (9 January 1911), p. 3.

1694 —. "Plymouth Theatre," *Boston Evening Record*, (26 September 1911), p. 6

Interview during Abbey Theatre's first American tour.

1695 —. "Yeats Replies to His Critics," *Boston Post*, (5 October 1911), p. 8

During Abbey Theatre's first American tour.

1696 —. "A Lively Discussion over the 'Irish Plays'," *Sunday Post*

(Boston), (8 October 1911), p. 37

Interview.

1697 —. "Yeats Defends 'The Playboy'," *Boston Herald*, (12 October 1911), p. 8

During Abbey Theatre's first American tour.

1698 —. "Mr. Yeats Explains," *Boston Evening Transcript*, (13 October 1911), p. 14

Interview.

1699 —. "Abbey Theatre: Pupils' Performance," *Evening Telegraph* (Dublin), (17 November 1911), p. 5

Address during Abbey Theatre's first American tour.

1700 —. "Aims of the Irish Theatre," *The Sun* (New York), (18 November 1911), p. 12

Talks of it in its educational aspect during Abbey Theatre's first American tour.

1701 —. "The Irish Drama," *Twentieth Century Magazine* (Boston), V (November 1911), 12-15

An address before the Drama League of Boston during the Abbey Theatre's first American tour.

1702 —. "On Those Who Dislike the Playboy," *The Irish Review* (Dublin), I, No. 10 (December 1911), 476. Reprinted as "On Those That Hated 'The Playboy of the Western World', 1907" in *Responsibilities* (1914)

A poem.

1703 —. *The Playboy*: Another American Surprise; Players Arrested," *Evening Telegraph* (Dublin), (19 January 1912),

p. 3

Interview during Abbey Theatre's first American tour.

1704 —. *"The Playboy:* A Stay in the Court Proceedings," *Irish Independent* (Dublin), (20 January 1912), p. 5

Interview during Abbey Theatre's first American tour.

1705 —. "The Story of the Irish Players: What We Try to Do," *The Sunday Record-Herald* (Chicago), (4 February 1912), part 7, p. 1

Discussion during Abbey Theatre's first American tour.

1706 —. "A People's Theatre; A Letter to Lady Gregory," *The Irish Statesman* (Dublin), (29 November 1919), 547-549; (6 December 1919), 572-573. Reprinted in *The Dial* (Chicago), LXVIII, No. 4 (April 1920), 458-468

"I did not know until very lately that there are certain things, dear to both our hearts, which no 'People's Theatre' can accomplish".

1707 —. *"The Plough and the Stars;* Mr. Sean O'Casey's New Play," *The Irish Times* (Dublin), (12 January 1926), p. 9

Interview.

1708 —. "A Defence of the Abbey Theatre," *The Dublin Magazine*, I, No. 2 (April-June 1926), 8-12

A speech delivered at a meeting of the Dublin Literary Society, on 23 February 1926.

1709 —. "Abbey Theatre and the Free State: A Misunderstanding Corrected," *The Sunday Times* (London), (7 October

1934), p. 27

Letter to the Editor.

1710 —. "W. B. Yeats Looks Back; Ireland in the Early Days of Abbey Theatre," *Irish Press* (Dublin), (14 October 1935), p. 9

Interview.

1711 —, ed. *Beltaine; The Organ of the Irish Literary Theatre* (London), (May 1899-April 1900). Reprinted and ed. B. C. Bloomfield (London: Frank Cass, 1970).

1712 —. ed. *Samhain* (Dublin and London), (October 1901-November 1908). Reprinted and ed. B. C. Bloomfield (London: Frank Cass, 1970)

The successor to *Beltaine.*

1713 "Yeats Slanders American Irish," *The Gaelic American* (New York), (30 March 1912), p. 4

Editorial on the Abbey Theatre's first American tour.

1714 "Yeats's Anti-Irish Campaign," *The Gaelic American* (New York), (18 November 1911), p. 4

Editorial on the Abbey Theatre's first American tour.

1715 "Yeats Upon Irish Drama," *Boston Evening Transcript*, (29 September 1911), p. 14.

Report on a lecture by W. B. Yeats at the Plymouth Theatre.

V

Dissertations

1716 Abood, Edward F. "The Reception of the Abbey Theatre in America, 1911-14," Ph. D., University of Chicago, 1963.

1717 Allt, G. D. P. "The Anglo-Irish Literary Movement in Relation to Its Antecedents," Ph. D., Cambridge University, 1952.

1718 Bergholz, Harry. "Die Neugestaltung Des Modernen Englischen Theaterwesens und Ihre Bedeutung Fur Den Spielplan," Ph. D., Berlin University, 1933.

1719 Bernardbehan, Brother Merrill. "Anglo-Irish Literature," M. A., University of Montreal, 1939.

1720 Berrow, J. H. "A Study of the Background Treatment and Presentation of Irish Character in British Plays from the Late 19th Century to the Present Day," M. A., University of Wales, Swansea, 1966.

1721 Butler, Henry J. "A Thesis on the Abbey Theatre and the Principal Writers Connected Therewith," Ph. D., the National University of Ireland, Dublin, 1952.

1722 Byars, John Arthur. "The Heroic in the Irish Legendary Dramas of W. B. Yeats, Lady Gregory, and J. M. Synge, 1903-1910," Ph. D., University of North Carolina, Chapel Hill, 1963.

1723 Carlson, Avis Duncan. "Realism in the New Irish Drama," M. A., University of Illinois, 1922.

1724 Cleveland, Louis O. "Trials in the Soundscape: Achievements of the Experimental British Radio Play," Ph. D., University of Wisconsin, Madison, 1974

Includes discussions of Samuel Beckett and Louis MacNeice.

1725 Cole, Alan Sargent. "Stagecraft in the Modern Dublin Theatre," Ph. D., Trinity College Dublin, 1952.

1726 Coleman, Sr. Anne G. "Social and Political Satire in Irish Drama," Ph. D., Fordham University, 1954.

1727 Cooper, Mabel. "The Irish Theatre: Its History and Its Dramatists," M. A., University of Manitoba, 1931.

1728 Cotter, Eileen Mary. "The Deirdre Theme in Anglo-Irish Literature," Ph. D., University of California, Los Angeles, 1967.

1729 Flannery, James W. "W. B. Yeats and the Idea of a Theatre: The Early Abbey Theatre in Theory and Practice," Ph. D., Trinity College Dublin, 1970.

1730 Harvey, J. L. "The Development of Irish Drama," M. A., University of Melbourne, 1947.

1731 Higgins, Paul Vincent. "Religious Themes in the Irish Drama of the Twentieth Century," M. A., New York University, 1948.

1732 Holzapfel, R. P. "A Survey of Irish Literary Periodicals from 1900 to the Present Day," M. Litt., Trinity College Dublin, 1963.

1733 Hussey, Mary E. "The Peasant in Modern Irish Drama," M. A., Columbia University, 1926.

1734 Keeler, Chester W. "The Abbey Theatre and the Brothers Fay: An Examination and Assessment of the Influence of the Theatrical Practice of the Irish National Theatre Society and the National Theatre Society, Limited, upon the Irish Dramatic Movement, 1902-1908," Ph. D., University of California, Santa Barbara, 1974.

1735 Kelson, John Hofstad. "Nationalism in the Theater: The Ole Bull Theater in Norway and the Abbey Theater in Ireland: A Comparative Study," Ph. D., University of Kansas, 1964.

1736 Kent, Constance Kember. "Stasis and Silence: A Study of Certain Symbolist Tendencies in the Modern Drama," Ph. D., Columbia University, 1973

Includes W. B. Yeats and Samuel Beckett.

1737 Krochalis, Jeanne Brown. "The Development of the Irish National Theatre Movement," M. A., Wesleyan University, Middletown, Connecticut, 1946.

1738 Lyman, Kenneth C. "Critical Reaction to Irish Drama on the New York Stage, 1900-1958," Ph. D., University of Wisconsin, 1960.

1739 Mc Guire, James Brady. "Realism in Irish Drama," Ph. D., Trinity College Dublin, 1954.

1740 Mc Henry, Margaret. "The Ulster Theatre in Ireland," Ph. D., University of Pennsylvania, 1931.

1741 McIntosh, Decourcy Eyre. "The Abbey Theatre, 1898-1912: The National Theme," Honors thesis, Harvard University, 1965.

1742 Madden, Regina D. "The Literary Criticism of the Irish Renaissance," Ph. D., University of Boston, 1938.

1743 Marcus, Philip Leduc. "The Beginnings of the Irish Literary Renaissance 1885-1899," Ph. D., Harvard University, 1968.

1744   Marshall, K. L. "Modern Irish Poets and Dramatists and the
       Fenian Cycle," Ph. D., Trinity College Dublin, 1974

       Includes W. B. Yeats, Austin Clarke, George Moore, Lady
       Gregory, and Padraic Fallon.

1745   Miller, Marcia S. K. "The Deirdre Legend in English Lit-
       erature," Ph. D., University of Pennsylvania, 1950.

1746   Nardin, Frances Louise. "A Study of Tragic Situation and
       Character in English Drama, 1900-1912," Ph. D.,
       University of Missouri, 1914

       Includes a section on "Dramas Using Themes from Irish Leg-
       ends".

1747   O'Neill, Michael J. "The Diaries of a Dublin Playgoer as a
       Mirror of the Irish Literary Revival." Ph. D., National
       University, Dublin, 1952.

1748   Oppren, Genevieve L. "The Irish Players in America," M. A.,
       University of Washington, 1943.

1749   Peake, Donald James. "The Influence of the Abbey Theatre
       on Irish Political Opinion, 1899-1924," M. A., South-
       ern Illinois University, 1964.

1750   Peteler, Patricia M. "The Social and Symbolic Drama of the
       English-Language Theatre, 1929-1949," Ph. D., Uni-
       versity of Utah, 1961.

1751   Randall, Ethel Claire. "The Celtic Movement; The Awaken-
       ing of the Fire," M. A., University of Chicago, 1906.

1752   Russell, Brenda Lee. "The Influence of the Saga Tradition
       on the Irish Drama: 1900-1920," Ph. D., University
       of Oregon, 1971.

1753   Saddlemyer, E. Ann. "A Study of the Dramatic Theory

Developed by the Founders of the Irish Literary Theatre and the Attempt to Apply This Theory in the Abbey Theatre, with Particular Reference to the Achievement of the Major Figures during the First Two Decades of the Movement," Ph. D., Bedford College, University of London, 1961.

1754 Schmitz-Mayr-Harting, Elisabeth. "The Irish National Theatre, from Edward Martyn to Sean O'Casey," Dr. Phil., University of Wien, 1956.

1755 Scrimgeour, James Richard. " 'The Ougly Shake': Despair in British and American Drama," Ph. D., University of Massachusetts, 1972

Includes J. M. Synge and Sean O'Casey.

1756 Smyth, Dorothy Pearl. "The Playwrights of the Irish Literary Renaissance," M. A., Acadia University, 1936.

1757 Stalder, Hansjörg. "Land and Emigration in Anglo-Irish Peasant Drama," Ph. D., University of Basel, 1977.

1758 Stewart, Andrew James. "Irish Plays and Players in America," Ph. D., University of Pennsylvania, 1932.

1759 Stokes, J. A. A. "The Non-Commercial Theatres in London and Paris in the Late Nineteenth Century and the Origins of the Irish Literary Theatre and Its Successors," Ph. D., University of Reading, 1968.

1760 Sullivan, James T. "*A Gay Goodnight*: A Study of Irish Tragedy," Ph. D., Brandeis University, 1974

Focuses on W. B. Yeats, J. M. Synge, James Joyce, and Sean O'Casey.

1761 Suss, Irving David. "The Decline and Fall of Irish Drama," Ph. D., Columbia University, 1951.

1762 Thompson, William I. "Easter 1916: A Study of Literature and Revolution," Ph. D., Cornell University, 1966.

1763 Wickstrom, Gordon Minton. "The Deirdre Plays of AE, Yeats, and Synge: Patterns of Irish Exile," Ph. D., Stanford University, 1968.

1764 Wieczorek, Hubert. "Irische Lebenshaltung Im Neuen Irischen Drama," Ph. D., Breslau University, 1937

Irish attitudes toward life in modern Irish drama.

1765 Wintergeist, Marianne. "Die Selbstdarstellung der Iren. Eine Untersuchung zum modernen Anglo-Irischen Drama," Ph. D., München University, 1973

Self-Representation of the Irish: An Essay on Modern Anglo-Irish Drama.

1766 Worth, Katharine J. "Symbolism in Modern English Drama," Ph. D., Bedford College, University of London, 1953.

Collections in Libraries

1767 Allgood, Sara. "Memories".

    Typescript.

    In the Berg Collection, New York Public Library.

1768 "The DeLury Collection of Anglo-Irish Literature."

    Emphasis on W. B. Yeats, James Joyce, Sean O'Casey, J. M. Synge, Lady Gregory, St. John Ervine, George Moore, and Lord Dunsany. There are also over 50 programmes for the Abbey Theatre (1903-1925) and a selection of Irish literary journals.

    In the University of Toronto Library.

1769 "The Fay Papers".

    Letters, programmes and various papers of William G. Fay, director of the Abbey Theatre in its early days, and relative to the careers of W. G. Fay and of his brother, Frank, both at the Abbey and elsewhere.

    In the National Library of Ireland, Dublin.

1770 Henderson, W. A. "The Irish National Theatre Movement"

    Eight large scrap-books of press cuttings, portraits, letters, programmes, etc. concerning the Movement between 1879-1911.

    In the National Library of Ireland, Dublin.

1771 Holloway, Joseph. "Impressions of a Dublin Playgoer".

    Two-hundred and twenty-one volumes of his journal treating

literary and theatrical subjects between 1895-1940; and re-
porting public response, newspaper articles, overheard comments, conversations in which he participated, and glimpses
of public gatherings and of dramatists at the theatre.

In the National Library of Ireland, Dublin.

1772   Horniman, A. E. F., ed. "Abbey Theatre".

A collection of 10-volume extracts from periodicals, 1903-
1917, relating to the Abbey Theatre.

In the John Rylands Library, Manchester, England.

1773   Lawrence, W. J. "The W. J. Lawrence Papers".

Comprise 22 volumes of notes and correspondence, containing
much information on the history of the theatre in Ireland,
collected by W. J. Lawrence, the theatre historian.

In the National Library of Ireland, Dublin.

1774   O'Hegarty, P. S. "The P. S. O'Hegarty Collection".

Playbills of the Abbey Theatre, 1904-1941.

In the University of Kansas Library.

1775   Roberts, George. "The Roberts Papers".

Comprise the letters, notebooks, etc., of George Roberts, who
was connected with the leading personalities and organisations
of the Irish National Theatre.

In the National Library of Ireland, Dublin.

Index of Subjects